P O R T A B L E

Acapulco, Ixtapa & Zihuatanejo

2nd Edition

by Lynne Bairstow

IDG Books Worldwide, Inc.
An International Data Group Company
Foster City, CA • Chicago, IL • Indianapolis, IN • New York, NY

ABOUT THE AUTHOR

Lynne Bairstow is a writer specializing in travel and the Internet, who has lived in Puerto Vallarta, Mexico, at least part-time for the past 9 years. She now lives there year-round, and was assisted in her research for this book by Claudia Velo. In a previous professional life, Lynne was a vice president for Merrill Lynch in Chicago and New York.

She is also the author of Frommer's *Portable Los Cabos and Baja* and the co-author of *Frommer's Mexico, Frommer's Cancún, Cozumel & the Yucatán,* and *Frommer's Portable Puerto Vallarta, Manzanillo & Guadalajara,* which won Mexico's Pluma de Plata (Silver Quill) award for excellence in foreign travel writing about Mexico.

IDG BOOKS WORLDWIDE, INC.

909 Third Avenue
New York, NY 10022

Find us online at **www.frommers.com**

Copyright © 2001 by IDG Books Worldwide, Inc.
Maps copyright © 2001 by IDG Books Worldwide, Inc.

FROMMER'S is a registered trademark of Arthur Frommer. Used under license.

ISBN: 0-02-863872-7
ISSN: 1042-8399

Editor: Kelly Regan
Production Editor: Tammy Ahrens
Photo Editor: Richard Fox
Design by Michele Laseau
Cartographer: John Decamillis
Production by IDG Books Indianapolis Production Department

SPECIAL SALES

For general information on IDG Books Worldwide's books in the U.S., please call our Consumer Customer Service department at 1-800-762-2974. For reseller information, including discounts, bulk sales, customized editions, and premium sales, please call our Reseller Customer Service department at 1-800-434-3422.

Manufactured in the United States of America

5   4   3   2   1

Contents

1   **Planning a Trip to Southern Pacific Mexico   1**

   1   The Region at a Glance   1

   2   Visitor Information, Entry Requirements & Money   5

   3   When to Go   11

      Mexico Calendar of Events   12

   4   Active Vacations in Pacific Coast Mexico   16

   5   Health, Safety & Insurance   17

      What to Do If You Get Sick   18

   6   Tips for Travelers with Special Needs   21

   7   Getting There   24

   8   The Pros & Cons of Package Tours   26

   9   Getting Around   29

      Fast Facts: Mexico   32

2   **Acapulco   38**

   1   Essentials   39

      Fast Facts: Acapulco   44

   2   Where to Stay   46

   3   Where to Dine   55

   4   Activities on & off the Beach   61

      A Masterpiece of a House   62

      Death-Defying Divers   67

   5   Shopping   67

   6   Acapulco After Dark   68

3   **Northward to Zihuatanejo & Ixtapa   73**

   1   Essentials   73

      Fast Facts: Zihuatanejo & Ixtapa   78

   2   Where to Stay   78

   3   Where to Dine   88

   4   Activities on & off the Beach   93

5 Shopping 98

6 Ixtapa & Zihuatanejo After Dark 100

4 **The Oaxaca Coast: From Puerto Escondido to Huatulco 102**

1 Puerto Escondido 102

Fast Facts: Puerto Escondido 107

Ecotours & Other Adventurous Explorations 110

2 Puerto Ángel: Backpacking Beach Haven 120

3 Bahías de Huatulco 124

Fast Facts: Bahías de Huatulco 128

5 **Inland to Old Mexico: Taxco & Cuernavaca 138**

1 Taxco: Cobblestones & Silver 138

Fast Facts: Taxco 141

2 Cuernavaca: Land of Eternal Spring 151

Take a Luxury Bus Direct from the Mexico City Airport 154

Fast Facts: Cuernavaca 155

Appendix: Useful Terms & Phrases 169

1 Telephones & Mail 169

2 Basic Vocabulary 170

Index 175

General Index 175

Accommodations Index 180

Restaurant Index 181

List of Maps

Mexico   2
Acapulco Bay Area   40
Zihuatanejo & Ixtapa
   Area   75

Downtown Zihuatanejo   81
Puerto Escondido   103
Taxco   139
Cuernavaca   153

An Invitation to the Reader

In researching this book, we discovered many wonderful places—resorts, inns, restaurants, shops, and more. We're sure you'll find others. Please tell us about them, so we can share the information with your fellow travelers in upcoming editions. If you were disappointed with a recommendation, we'd love to know that, too. Please write to:

Frommer's Portable Acapulco, Ixtapa & Zihuatanejo, 2nd Edition
IDG Books Worldwide, Inc.
909 Third Avenue
New York, NY 10022

An Additional Note

Please be advised that travel information is subject to change at any time—and this is especially true of prices. We therefore suggest that you write or call ahead for confirmation when making your travel plans. The authors, editors, and publisher cannot be held responsible for the experiences of readers while traveling. Your safety is important to us, however, so we encourage you to stay alert and be aware of your surroundings. Keep a close eye on cameras, purses, and wallets, all favorite targets of thieves and pickpockets.

A Few Words About Prices

The peso's value continues to fluctuate—as this book went to press it was slightly less than 10 pesos to the dollar. Prices in this book (which are always given in U.S. dollars) have been converted to U.S. dollars at 10 pesos to the dollar. Most hotels in Mexico—with the exception of places that receive little foreign tourism—quote prices in U.S. dollars. Thus, currency fluctuations are unlikely to affect the prices charged by most hotels.

Mexico has a **value-added tax** of 15% (*Impuesto de Valor Agregado*, or *IVA*, pronounced "*ee*-bah") on most everything, including restaurant meals, bus tickets, and souvenirs. (Exceptions are Cancún, Cozumel, and Los Cabos, where the IVA is 10%; as ports of entry, they receive a special 5% break on taxes.) Hotels charge the usual 15% IVA, plus a locally administered bed tax of 2% (in many but not all areas), for a total of 17%. In Cancún, Los Cabos, and Cozumel, hotels charge the 10% IVA plus the 2% room tax. IVA will not necessarily be included in the prices quoted by hotels and restaurants. You may find that upper-end properties (three stars and above) quote prices without IVA included, while lesser-price hotels include IVA in their quotes. Always ask to see a printed price sheet, and always ask if the tax is included.

What the Symbols Mean

✪ Frommer's Favorites

Our favorite places and experiences—outstanding for quality, value, or both.
The following abbreviations are used for credit cards:

AE	American Express	EC	Eurocard
CB	Carte Blanche	JCB	Japan Credit Bank
DC	Diners Club	MC	MasterCard
DISC	Discover	V	Visa
ER	enRoute		

Find Frommer's Online

www.frommers.com offers up-to-the-minute listings on almost 200 cities around the globe—including the latest bargains and candid, personal articles updated daily by Arthur Frommer himself. No other Web site offers such comprehensive and timely coverage of the world of travel.

Planning a Trip to Southern Pacific Mexico

A little advance planning can make the difference between a good trip and a great trip. When should you go? What's the best way to get there? How much should you plan on spending? What festivals or special events will be taking place during your visit? What safety or health precautions are advised? We'll answer these and other questions for you in this chapter.

1 The Region at a Glance

Though Pacific Mexico may be uniform in its exotic, tropical beaches and jungle scenery, the resorts along this coast couldn't be more varied in personality. From high-energy seaside cities to pristine, primitive coves, this is the Mexico that first lured vacationers around the globe.

Spanish conquistadors were attracted to this coast for its numerous sheltered coves and protected bays from which they set sail to the Far East. Years later, Mexico's first tourists found the same elements appealing, but for different reasons—they were seeking escape in the warm sunshine, and stretches of blue coves nicely complemented the heady tropical landscape of the adjacent coastal mountains.

Time at the beach is generally the top priority for most travelers to this part of Mexico. Each of the beach towns detailed in this book is capable of satisfying your sand-and-surf needs for a few days, or even a week or more. You could also combine several coastal resorts into a single trip, or mix the coastal with the colonial, say, with visits to both Puerto Escondido and Oaxaca City, or Acapulco and Taxco.

The resorts have distinct personalities, but you get the requisite beach wherever you go, whether you choose a city that offers virtually every luxury imaginable or a rustic town providing little more than basic (but charming) seaside relaxation.

Mexico

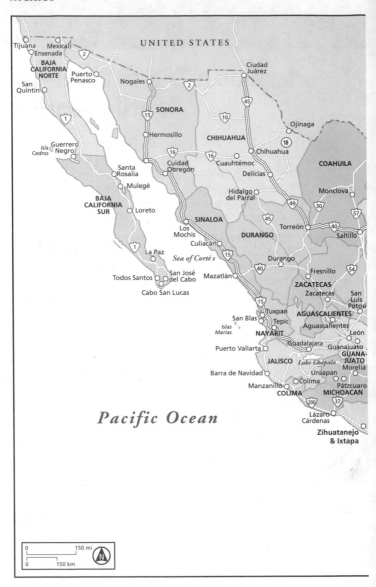

UNITED STATES

Gulf of Mexico

Piedras Negras

Nuevo Laredo

Monterrey
Matamoros

NUEVO
LEÓN

TAMAULIPAS

Ciudad Victoria

Ciudad Mante
Tampico

SAN LUIS
POTOSÍ

San Miguel
de Allende

QUERÉTARO
Tuxpan

HIDALGO
Poza Rica

Querétaro
Pachuca

Mexico City
Xalapa

Toluca
Tlaxcala
TLAXCALA

Cuernavaca
Puebla
Veracruz

MORELOS
PUEBLA
Orizaba

Taxco
Tehuacán
VERACRUZ
Catemaco

GUERRERO
Coatzacoalcos

Chilpancingo

Acapulco
Oaxaca

OAXACA

Salina
Cruz

Puerto Escondido
Huatulco

Puerto
Ángel
Gulf of
Tehuantepec

Tapachula

Bay of
Campeche

Campeche

CAMPECHE

Escárcega

TABASCO
Villahermosa

San Cristóbal
de las Casas

Tuxtla
Gutiérrez

CHIAPAS
Comitán

GUATEMALA

HONDURAS

EL
SALVADOR

BELIZE

Caribbean Sea

Chetumal

Bacalar

Majahual
Peninsula

QUINTANA
ROO

Punta
Allen

Mérida
Playa del
Carmen

YUCATÁN

Celestún

Progreso
Valladolid

Río Lagartos

Cancún

Cozumel

Isla
Mujeres

Over the years, a diverse selection of resorts has evolved in the area. Each is distinct, yet together they offer an ideal attraction for almost any type of traveler. The region encompasses the country's oldest, largest, and most decadent resort, **Acapulco,** one-time playground of Hollywood's biggest celebrities. Of all the resorts, Acapulco has the best airline connections, the broadest range of late-night entertainment, the most savory dining, and the widest range of accommodations—from hillside villas and luxury resort hotels to modest inns on the beach and in the city center.

The resort of **Ixtapa** and its neighboring seaside village, **Zihuatanejo,** offer beach-bound tourist attractions, but on a smaller, newer, and less hectic scale than Acapulco. They attract travelers for their complementary contrasts—sophisticated high-rise hotels in one, plus the local color and leisurely pace of the other. To get here, many people fly into Acapulco, then make the 4- to 5-hour trip north (by rental car or bus).

South of Acapulco, along the Oaxacan Coast, lie the small, laid-back beach towns of **Puerto Escondido** and **Puerto Ángel,** both on picturesque bays bordered by relaxed communities. The region's newest resort community, **Bahías de Huatulco,** couples an unspoiled, slow-paced nature with the kind of modern infra-structure and luxurious facilities you'd find in the country's crowded, overdeveloped megaresorts. Nine bays encompass 36 beaches—many are isolated stretches of pure white sand—and countless inlets and coves. Huatulco has become increasingly known for its ecotourism attractions; you won't find much in the way of shopping or nightlife, but for most visitors, the clear blue waters and quiet, restful beaches are reason enough to come.

From Acapulco a road leads inland to **Taxco,** a colonial city that clings to the side of a mountain and is famed for its hundreds of silver shops. And verdant **Cuernavaca,** known as the land of eternal spring, has gained a reputation for exceptional spa facilities, while also boasting a wealth of cultural and historic attractions.

The whole region is graced with a stunning coastline and trop-ical mountains. Outside the urban centers, however, paved roads are few, and these two states remain among Mexico's poorest, despite decades-long influx of U.S. tourist dollars (and many other currencies).

2 Visitor Information, Entry Requirements & Money

SOURCES OF INFORMATION

The **Mexico Hotline** (☎ 800/44-MEXICO) is an excellent source for general information; you can request brochures on the country and get answers to the most commonly asked questions. If you have a fax, Mexico's Ministry of Tourism also offers extensive written information on a variety of topics from general destination information to accommodations (the service lists 400 hotels), shopping, dining, sports, sightseeing, festivals, and nightlife. Call the same number above, and they can fax you a listing of what is available.

More information (15,000 pages worth, they say) about Mexico is available on the Mexico Ministry of Tourism's Web site: **mexico-travel.com**.

The **U.S. State Department** (☎ 202/647-5225 for travel information and Overseas Citizens Services) offers a **Consular Information Sheet** on Mexico, with a compilation of safety, medical, driving, and general travel information gleaned from reports by official U.S. State Department offices in Mexico. You can also request the Consular Information Sheet by fax (☎ 202/647-3000). The State Department is also on the Internet: check out **travel.state.gov/mexico.html** for the Consular Information Sheet on Mexico; **travel.state.gov/travel_warnings.html** for other Consular Information sheets and travel warnings; and **travel.state.gov/tips_mexico.html** for the State Department's *Tips for Travelers to Mexico*.

The **Centers for Disease Control Hotline** (☎ 800/311-3435 or 404/639-3534) is another source for medical information affecting travelers to Mexico and elsewhere. The center's Web site, **www.cdc.gov/**, provides lengthy information on health issues for specific countries. The Web page with health information for travelers to Mexico and Central America is **www.cdc.gov/travel/camerica.htm**. The U.S. State Department offers medical information for Americans traveling abroad at **travel.state.gov/medical.html**. This site provides general information and a list of air ambulance services and international travel insurance providers.

MEXICAN GOVERNMENT TOURIST OFFICES   Mexico has foreign tourist offices (MGTO) in the United States and Canada. They include the following:

United States: Chicago, IL (☎ **312/606-9252**); Houston, TX (☎ **713/772-2581**); Los Angeles, CA (☎ **213/351-2069;** fax 213/351-2074); Miami, FL (☎ **305/718-4091**); New York, NY (☎ **800/446-3942**); and the Mexican Embassy Tourism Delegate, 1911 Pennsylvania Ave., Washington, DC 20005 (☎ **202/728-1750**). The MGTO offices have been combined with Mexican Consulate offices in the same cities, providing one central source for official information on Mexico.

Canada: 1 Place Ville-Marie, Suite 1931, Montréal, Québec H3B 2C3 (☎ **514/871-1052**); 2 Bloor St. W., Suite 1502, Toronto, Ontario M4W 3E2 (☎ **416/925-2753**); and 999 W. Hastings, Suite 1110, Vancouver, British Columbia V6C 2W2 (☎ **604/669-2845**). The Embassy is located at 1500-45 O'Connor St., Ottawa, Ontario K1P 1A4 (☎ **613/233-8988;** fax 613/235-9123).

ENTRY REQUIREMENTS

DOCUMENTS   All travelers to Mexico are required to present **proof of citizenship,** such as an original birth certificate with a raised seal, a valid passport, or naturalization papers. Those using a birth certificate should also have a current photo identification such as a driver's license or official ID. Those whose last name on the birth certificate is different from their current name (a woman using a married name, for example) should also bring a photo identification card *and* legal proof of the name change such as the *original* marriage license or certificate. This proof of citizenship may also be requested when you want to reenter either the United States or Mexico. Note that photocopies are *not* acceptable. If you will be reentering the United States, you must prove both your citizenship and your identity, so always take a picture ID, such as a driver's license or valid passport with you.

You must also carry a **Mexican Tourist Permit (FMT),** which is issued free of charge by Mexican border officials after proof of citizenship is accepted. The tourist permit is more important than your passport in Mexico, so guard it carefully. If you lose it, you may not be permitted to leave the country until you can replace it—a bureaucratic hassle that can take anywhere from a few hours to a week. (If you do lose your tourist permit, get a police report from local authorities indicating that your documents were stolen; having one *might* lessen the hassle of exiting the country without all your identification.)

A tourist permit can be issued for up to 180 days, although your stay south of the border may be shorter than that. Sometimes officials don't ask—they just stamp a time limit, so be sure to say "6 months" (or at least twice as long as you intend to stay). If you should decide to extend your stay, you may request that additional time be added to your permit from an official immigration office in Mexico.

Note that children under age 18 traveling without parents or with only one parent must have a notarized letter from the absent parent or parents authorizing the travel.

Lost Documents   To replace a **lost passport,** contact your embassy or nearest consular agent (see "Fast Facts: Mexico," below). You must establish a record of your citizenship and also fill out a form requesting another Mexican Tourist Permit if it, too, was lost. Without the **tourist permit** you can't leave the country, and without an affidavit affirming your passport request and citizenship, you may have problems at Customs when you get home. So it's important to clear everything up *before* trying to leave. Mexican Customs may, however, accept the police report of the loss of the tourist permit and allow you to leave.

CUSTOMS ALLOWANCES   When you enter Mexico, Customs officials will be tolerant as long as you have no illegal drugs or firearms. You're allowed to bring in two cartons of cigarettes, or 50 cigars, plus a kilogram (2.2 lb.) of smoking tobacco; the liquor allowance is two 1-liter bottles of anything, wine or hard liquor; you are also allowed 12 rolls of film. A laptop computer, camera equipment, and sporting equipment (golf clubs, scuba gear, a bicycle) that could feasibly be used during your stay are also allowed. The underlying guideline is: don't bring anything that looks like it's meant to be resold in Mexico.

When you reenter the **United States,** federal law allows you to bring in up to $400 in purchases duty free every 30 days. The first $1,000 over the $400 allowance is taxed at 10%. You may bring in a carton (200) of cigarettes, 100 cigars, or 2 kilograms (4.4 lb.) of smoking tobacco, plus 1 liter of an alcoholic beverage (wine, beer, or spirits).

Canadian citizens are allowed $20 in purchases after a 24-hour absence from the country or $100 after a stay of 48 hours or more. In addition, Canadian citizens may bring 200 cigarettes or 50 cigars plus 1 kilo (2.2 lb.) of chewing tobacco, and 1.1 liter of hard liquor or wine.

British travelers returning from outside the European Union are allowed to bring in £145 worth of goods, in addition to the following: up to 200 cigarettes, 50 cigars, or 250 grams of tobacco; 2 liters of wine; 1 liter of liqueur greater than 22% alcohol by volume; and 60 cubic centimeters/milliliters of perfume. If any item worth more than the limit of £145 is brought in, payment must be made on the full value, not just on the amount above £145.

Citizens of **New Zealand** are allowed to return with a combined value of up to NZ$1,000 in goods, duty free.

GOING THROUGH CUSTOMS   Mexican Customs inspection has been streamlined. At most points of entry, tourists are requested to press a button in front of what looks like a traffic signal, which alternates on touch between red and green signals. Green light and you go through without inspection; red light and your luggage or car may be inspected briefly or thoroughly. If you have an unusual amount of luggage or an oversized piece, you may be subject to inspection despite the traffic signal routine.

MONEY

CASH/CURRENCY   The currency in Mexico is the Mexican **peso.** Paper currency comes in denominations of 20, 50, 100, 200, and 500 pesos. Coins come in denominations of 1, 2, 5, 10, and 20 pesos and 20 and 50 **centavos** (100 centavos equal 1 peso). The current exchange rate for the U.S. dollar is around 10 pesos; at that rate, an item that costs 10 pesos would be equivalent to U.S.$1.

Getting **change** continues to be a problem in Mexico. Small-denomination bills and coins are hard to come by, so start collecting them early in your trip and continue as you travel. Shopkeepers everywhere seem always to be out of change and small bills; that's doubly true in a market.

Many establishments that deal with tourists, especially in coastal resort areas, quote prices in dollars. To avoid confusion, they use the abbreviations "Dlls." for dollars and "M.N." (*moneda*

Money Matters

The **universal currency sign ($)** is used to indicate pesos in Mexico. The use of the symbol in this book, however, denotes U.S. currency.

nacional, or national currency) for pesos. All dollar equivalencies in this book were based on an exchange rate of 10 pesos per dollar.

EXCHANGING MONEY   The rate of exchange fluctuates a tiny bit daily, so you probably are better off not exchanging too much of your currency at once. Don't forget, however, to have enough pesos to carry you over a weekend or Mexican holiday, when banks are closed. In general, avoid carrying the U.S.$100 bill, the bill most commonly counterfeited in Mexico, and therefore the most difficult to exchange, especially in smaller towns. Since small bills and coins in pesos are hard to come by in Mexico, the U.S.$1 bill is very useful for tipping.

The bottom line on exchanging money of all kinds: It pays to ask first and shop around. Banks pay the top rates.

Exchange houses (*casas de cambio*) are generally more convenient than banks since they have more locations and longer hours; the rate of exchange may be the same as a bank or only slightly lower. *Note:* Before leaving a bank or exchange-house window, always count your change in front of the teller before the next client steps up.

Large airports have currency-exchange counters that often stay open whenever flights are arriving or departing. Though convenient, these generally do not offer the most favorable rates.

A hotel's exchange desk commonly pays less favorable rates than banks; however, when the currency is in a state of flux, higher-priced hotels are known to pay *higher* than bank rates, in their effort to attract dollars. The bottom line: It pays to shop around, but in almost all cases, you receive a better exchange by changing money first, then paying for goods or services, rather than by paying with dollars directly to an establishment.

BANKS & ATMs   Banks in Mexico are rapidly expanding and improving services. New hours tend to be from 9am until 5 or 6pm, with many open for at least a half day on Saturday, and some even offering limited hours on Sunday. The exchange of dollars, which used to be limited until noon, can now be accommodated anytime during business hours in the larger resorts and cities. Some, but not all, banks charge a service fee of about 1% to exchange traveler's checks. However, most purchases can be paid for directly with traveler's checks at the stated exchange rate of the establishment. Don't even bother with personal checks drawn on a U.S. bank—although theoretically they may be cashed, it's not without weeks of delay, and the bank will wait for your check to clear before giving you your money.

Travelers to Mexico can also easily access money from **automated teller machines (ATMs),** now available in most major cities and resort areas in Mexico. Universal bank cards (such as the Cirrus and PLUS systems) can be used, and this is a convenient way to withdraw money from your bank and avoid carrying too much with you at any time. There is often a service fee charged by your bank for each transaction, but the exchange rate is generally more favorable than one found at a currency house. Most machines offer Spanish/English menus and dispense pesos, but some offer the option of withdrawing dollars. Be sure to check the daily withdrawal limit before you depart, and ask your bank whether you need a new personal ID number. For Cirrus locations abroad, call ☎ **800/424-7787,** or check out MasterCard's Web site (**www.mastercard.com/atm/**). For PLUS usage abroad, call ☎ **800/843-7587,** or visit Visa's Web site (**www. visa.com/atms**).

TRAVELER'S CHECKS   Traveler's checks are readily accepted nearly everywhere, but they can be difficult to cash on a weekend or holiday or in an out-of-the-way place. Their best value is in replacement in case of theft. Frequently in Mexico, a bank or establishment will pay more for traveler's checks than for cash dollars.

CREDIT CARDS   You'll be able to charge most hotel, restaurant, and store purchases, as well as almost all airline tickets, on your credit card. You can get cash advances of several hundred dollars on your card, but there may be a wait of 20 minutes to 2 hours. You generally can't charge gasoline purchases in Mexico; however, with the new franchise system of Pemex stations taking hold, this may change as well. Visa ("Bancomer" in Mexico), MasterCard ("Carnet"), and American Express are the most accepted cards.

Credit-card charges will be billed in pesos, then converted into dollars by the bank issuing the credit card. Generally you receive the favorable bank rate when paying by credit card. However, be aware that some establishments add a 5 to 7% surcharge when you pay with a credit card.

THEFT   Almost every credit card company has an emergency toll-free number that you can call if your wallet or purse is stolen.

They may be able to wire you a cash advance off your credit card immediately, and in many places they can deliver an emergency credit card in a day or two. The issuing bank's toll-free number is usually on the back of the credit card—though of course that doesn't help you much if the card was stolen. The toll-free information directory will provide the number if you dial ☎ **800/555-1212.** Citicorp Visa's U.S. emergency number is ☎ **800/336-8472.** American Express cardholders and traveler's check holders should call ☎ **800/221-7282** for all money emergencies. MasterCard holders should call ☎ **800/307-7309.**

If you opt to carry traveler's checks, be sure to keep a record of their serial numbers, separately from the checks, of course, so you're ensured a refund in just such an emergency.

Odds are that if your wallet is gone, the police won't be able to recover it for you. However, after you realize that it's gone and you cancel your credit cards, it is still worth informing them. Your credit card company or insurer may require a police report number.

3 When to Go

SEASONS   Mexico has two principal travel seasons: high and low. **High season** begins around December 20 and continues to Easter, although in some places high season can begin as early as mid-November. **Low season** begins the day after Easter and continues to mid-December; during low season, prices may drop 20% to 50%. In beach destinations popular with Mexican travelers, such as Acapulco, the prices will revert back to high season during the months of July and August, the traditional national summer vacation period.

Mexico has two main climate seasons as well: **rainy** (May to mid-Oct) and **dry** (mid-Oct through Apr). The rainy season can be of little consequence in the dry, northern region of the country. The Pacific coastal region typically receives tropical showers, which begin around 4 or 5pm and last a few hours. Though these rains can come on suddenly and be quite strong, they usually end just as fast and cool off the air for the evening. **Hurricane season** particularly affects the southern Pacific coast, especially from June through October. However, if no hurricanes strike, the light, cooling winds, especially from September through November, can make it a perfect time to more comfortably explore the area. Most of coastal Mexico experiences temperatures in the 80s in the hottest months.

MEXICO CALENDAR OF EVENTS

January

- **New Year's Day (Año Nuevo).** National holiday. Parades, religious observances, parties, and fireworks welcome in the new year everywhere. In traditional indigenous communities, new tribal leaders are inaugurated with colorful ceremonies rooted in the pre-Hispanic past. January 1.
- **Three Kings Day (Día de Reyes),** nationwide. Commemorates the Three Kings' bringing of gifts to the Christ Child. On this day, children receive gifts, much like the traditional gift giving that accompanies Christmas in the United States. Friends and families gather to share the *Rosca de Reyes,* a special cake. Inside the cake there is a small doll representing the Christ Child; whoever receives the doll in his or her piece must host a tamales-and-*atole* party the next month. January 6.

February

- **Candlemass (Día de la Candelaria),** nationwide. Music, dances, processions, food, and other festivities lead up to a blessing of seed and candles in a tradition that mixes pre-Hispanic and European traditions marking the end of winter. All those who attended the Three Kings Celebration reunite to share *atole* and tamales at a party hosted by the recipient of the doll found in the Rosca. February 2.
- ✪ **Carnaval.** Carnaval takes place the 3 days preceding Ash Wednesday and the beginning of Lent. Transportation and hotels are packed, so it's best to make reservations 6 months in advance and arrive a couple of days ahead of the beginning of celebrations. In 2001, the dates are February 25 to 27.
- **Ash Wednesday.** The start of Lent and time of abstinence. It's a day of reverence nationwide, but some towns honor it with folk dancing and fairs. In 2001, the date is February 28.

March

- **Benito Juárez's Birthday.** National holiday. Small hometown celebrations countrywide, especially in Juárez's birthplace— Guelatao, Oaxaca. March 21.

April

- ✪ **Holy Week.** Celebrates the last week in the life of Christ from Palm Sunday through Easter Sunday with somber religious processions almost nightly, spoofing of Judas, and reenactments of specific biblical events, plus food and craft fairs.

Special celebrations are held in Taxco. Businesses close during this traditional week of Mexican national vacations.

If you plan on traveling to or around Mexico during Holy Week, make your reservations early. Airline seats on flights into and out of the country will be reserved months in advance. Buses to these towns or to almost anywhere in Mexico will be full, so try arriving on the Wednesday or Thursday before Good Friday. Easter Sunday is quiet. For 2001, April 8 to April 14 is Holy Week, Easter Sunday is April 15, and the week following is a traditional vacation period.

May

- **Labor Day,** nationwide. Workers parade countrywide and everything closes. May 1.
- **Holy Cross Day (Día de la Santa Cruz).** Workers place a cross on top of unfinished buildings and celebrate with food, bands, folk dancing, and fireworks around the work site. May 3.
- **Cinco de Mayo.** A national holiday that celebrates the defeat of the French at the Battle of Puebla. May 5.
- **Feast of San Isidro.** The patron saint of farmers is honored with a blessing of seeds and work animals. May 15.

June

- **Navy Day (Día de la Marina),** celebrated in all coastal towns with naval parades and fireworks. June 1.
- ✪ **Corpus Christi,** celebrated nationwide. Honors the Body of Christ (the Eucharist) with religious processions, masses, and food. Festivities include performances of *voladores* (flying pole dancers) beside the church and at the ruins of El Tajín. Dates vary.
- **Día de San Pedro (St. Peter and St. Paul's Day),** nationwide. Celebrated wherever St. Peter is the patron saint, and honors anyone named Pedro or Peter. June 29.

July

- **The Guelaguetza Dance Festival,** Oaxaca. One of Mexico's most popular events. Villagers from the seven regions around Oaxaca gather in the city's amphitheater. All dress in traditional costumes, and many wear colorful "dancing" masks. The celebration goes back to pre-Hispanic times when a similar celebration was held to honor the fertility goddess who would, in exchange, grant a plentiful corn harvest. Make advance reservations, as this festival gathers visitors from around the world in Oaxaca to witness the celebration. June 21 to 28.

August

✪ **Assumption of the Virgin Mary.** Celebrated throughout the country with special masses and in some places with processions. August 20 to 22.

September

• **Independence Day.** Celebrates Mexico's independence from Spain. A day of parades, picnics, and family reunions throughout the country. The schedule of events is the same in every village, town, and city across Mexico, following that of the capital: At 11pm on September 15, the president of Mexico gives the famous independence *grito* (shout) from the National Palace in Mexico City. People crowd into the central plaza to hear it and to watch the traditional fireworks display that follows. A parade follows the following morning. September 15 to 16.

October

• **Día de la Raza ("Ethnicity Day" or Columbus Day).** Commemorates the fusion of the Spanish and Mexican peoples. October 12.

November

✪ **Day of the Dead.** What's commonly called the Day of the Dead is actually 2 days: All Saints' Day—honoring saints and deceased children—and All Souls' Day, honoring deceased adults. Relatives gather at cemeteries countrywide, carrying candles and food, often spending the night beside graves of loved ones. Weeks before, bakers begin producing bread formed in the shape of mummies or round loaves decorated with bread "bones." Decorated sugar skulls emblazoned with glittery names are sold everywhere. Many days ahead, homes and churches erect special altars laden with Day of the Dead bread, fruit, flowers, candles, favorite foods, and photographs of saints and of the deceased. On the 2 nights, children dress in costumes and masks, often carrying mock coffins and pumpkin lanterns, into which they expect money will be dropped, through the streets. Cemeteries around Oaxaca are well known for their solemn vigils and some for their Carnaval-like atmosphere. November 1 to 2.

• **Revolution Day.** Commemorates the start of the Mexican Revolution in 1910 with parades, speeches, rodeos, and patriotic events. November 20.

- **National Silver Fair,** Taxco. A competition of Mexico's best silversmiths and some of the world's finest artisans. Features exhibits, concerts, dances, and fireworks. November 29 to December 6.

December

✪ **Feast of the Virgin of Guadalupe.** Throughout the country the patroness of Mexico is honored with religious processions, street fairs, dancing, fireworks, and masses. It is one of Mexico's most moving and beautiful displays of traditional culture. The Virgin of Guadalupe appeared to a young man, Juan Diego, in December 1531, on a hill near Mexico City. He convinced the bishop that he had seen the apparition by revealing his cloak, upon which the Virgin was emblazoned. It's customary for children to dress up as Juan Diego, wearing mustaches and red bandanas. Every village celebrates this day, often with processions of children carrying banners of the Virgin and with *charreadas* (rodeos), bicycle races, dancing, and fireworks. December 12.

- **Christmas Posadas.** On each of the 9 nights before Christmas, it's customary to reenact the Holy Family's search for an inn, with door-to-door candlelit processions in cities and villages nationwide. You may see them especially in Taxco. These are also hosted by most businesses and community organizations, taking the place of the northern tradition of a Christmas party. December 15 to 24.

- **Christmas.** Mexicans extend this celebration and leave their jobs often beginning 2 weeks before Christmas all the way through New Year's. Many businesses close, and resorts and hotels fill up. Significant celebrations take place on December 23. In Oaxaca it's the "Night of the Radishes," with displays of huge carved radishes, as well as elaborate figures made of corn husks and dried flowers. On the evening of December 24 in Oaxaca, processions culminate on the central plaza.

- **New Year's Eve.** As in the rest of the world, New Year's Eve in Mexico is celebrated with parties, fireworks, and plenty of noise. Special festivities take place at Tlacolula, near Oaxaca, with commemorative mock battles for good luck in the new year. December 31.

4 Active Vacations in Pacific Coast Mexico

Golf, tennis, waterskiing, surfing, bicycling, and **horseback riding** are all sports visitors can enjoy in Pacific coast Mexico. **Scuba diving** is excellent, as is snorkeling, all along this coast. **Mountain climbing** is a rugged sport where you'll meet like-minded folks from around the world. A popular spot for this is in the mountainous areas surrounding Huatulco.

PARKS   Most of the national parks and nature reserves are understaffed or unstaffed. In addition to the reliable Mexican companies offering adventure trips (such as the AMTAVE members; see below), many U.S.-based companies also offer this kind of travel, with trips led by specialists.

OUTDOORS ORGANIZATIONS & TOUR OPERATORS
There's a new association in Mexico of eco- and adventure-tour operators called **AMTAVE** (Asociación Mexicana de Turismo de Aventura y Ecoturismo, A.C.). They publish an annual catalog of participating firms and their offerings, all of which must meet certain criteria for security, quality, and training of the guides, as well as for sustainability of natural and cultural environments. For more information, contact them (in Mexico City) at ☎/fax **5/663-5381;** www.amtave.com.mx;e-mail:amtave@mexico.com; ask for Marlene Ehrenberg or Daniel Martínez.

The Archaeological Conservancy, 5301 Central Ave. NE, Suite 1218, Albuquerque, NM 87108-1517 (☎ **505/266-1540;** www.americanarchaeology.com; e-mail: archonn@nm.net) presents one trip to Mexico per year led by an expert, usually an archaeologist. The trips change from year to year and space is limited, so you must make reservations early in the year.

Culinary Adventures, 6023 Reid Dr. NW, Gig Harbor, WA 98335 (☎ **253/851-7676;** fax 253/851-9532), specializes in a short but special list of cooking tours in Mexico, featuring well-known cooks and traveling to particular regions known for excellent cuisine. The owner, Marilyn Tausend, is the co-author of *Mexico the Beautiful Cookbook* and *Cocinas de la Familia* (Family Kitchens).

Trek America, P.O. Box 189, Rockaway, NJ 07866 (☎ **800/ 221-0596** or 973/983-1144; fax 973/983-8551; www.trekamerica. com; e-mail: info@trekamerica.com), organizes lengthy, active trips that combine trekking, hiking, van transportation, and camping in the Yucatán, Chiapas, Oaxaca, the Copper Canyon, and Mexico's Pacific coast, and a trip that covers Mexico City, Teotihuacán, Taxco, Guadalajara, Puerto Vallarta, and Acapulco.

Oaxaca Reservations/Zapotec Tours, 4955 N. Claremont Ave., Suite B, Chicago, IL 60625 (☎ **800/44-OAXACA** outside Ill., or 773/506-2444; fax 773/506-2445; www.oaxacainfo.com; e-mail: ohg@oaxacainfo.com), offers a variety of tours to Oaxaca City and the Oaxaca coast (including Puerto Escondido and Huatulco), and several specialty trips, including Day of the Dead in Oaxaca and the Food of the Gods Tour of Oaxaca. Coastal trips emphasize nature. Oaxaca City tours focus on the immediate area with visits to weavers, potters, markets, and archaeological sites. They are also the U.S. contact for several hotels in Oaxaca City and for the Oaxaca State route of Aerocaribe (serving the Oaxaca coast and Oaxaca City). Call them for information, but all reservations must be made through a travel agent.

5 Health, Safety & Insurance

STAYING HEALTHY

COMMON AILMENTS   **Mosquitoes** and **gnats** are prevalent along the coast. Insect repellent (*repelente contra insectos*) is a must, and it's not always available in Mexico. If you'll be in these areas, bring a repellent along that contains the active ingredient DEET. Avon's Skin So Soft also works extremely well. If you're sensitive to bites, pick up some antihistamine cream from a drugstore at home.

Most readers won't ever see a scorpion (*alacrán*). But if you're stung by one, go immediately to a doctor.

MORE SERIOUS DISEASES   You shouldn't be overly concerned about tropical diseases if you stay on the normal tourist routes and don't eat street food. However, both dengue fever and cholera have appeared in Mexico in recent years. Talk to your doctor or a medical specialist in tropical diseases about any

Over-the-Counter Drugs in Mexico

Antibiotics and other drugs that you'd need a prescription to buy in the States are sold over the counter in Mexican pharmacies. Mexican pharmacies also have common over-the-counter cold, sinus, and allergy remedies, although not the broad selection we're accustomed to finding easily in the United States.

What to Do If You Get Sick

It's called "travelers' diarrhea" or *turista,* the Spanish word for "tourist": the persistent diarrhea, often accompanied by fever, nausea, and vomiting, that used to attack many travelers to Mexico. Some in the United States call this "Montezuma's revenge," but you won't hear it referred to this way in Mexico. Widespread improvements in infrastructure, sanitation, and education have practically eliminated this ailment, especially in well-developed resort areas. Most travelers make a habit of drinking only bottled water, which also helps to protect against unfamiliar bacteria. In resort areas, and generally throughout Mexico, only purified ice is used. Doctors say it's not caused by just one "bug," but by a combination of consuming different foods and water, upsetting your schedule, being overtired, and experiencing the stresses of travel. A good high-potency (or "therapeutic") vitamin supplement, and even extra vitamin C is a help; yogurt is good for healthy digestion. If you do happen to come down with this ailment, nothing beats Pepto Bismol, readily available in Mexico.

How to Prevent It: The U.S. Public Health Service recommends the following measures for preventing travelers' diarrhea:

* *Drink only purified water.* This means tea, coffee, and other beverages made with boiled water; canned or bottled carbonated beverages and water; or beer and wine. Most restaurants with a large tourist clientele use only purified water and ice.

* *Choose food carefully.* In general, avoid salads, uncooked vegetables, and unpasteurized milk or milk products (including cheese). However, salads in a first-class restaurant, or one serving a lot of tourists, are generally safe to eat. Choose food that is freshly cooked and still hot. Peelable fruit is ideal. Don't eat undercooked meat, fish, or shellfish.

In addition, something as simple as clean hands can go a long way toward preventing turista.

Since **dehydration** can quickly become life threatening, the Public Health Service advises that you be especially careful to replace fluids and electrolytes (potassium, sodium, and the like) during a bout of diarrhea. Do this by drinking Pedialyte, a rehydration solution available at most Mexican pharmacies, or glasses of natural fruit juice (high in potassium) with a pinch of salt added. Or you can also try a glass of boiled pure water with a quarter teaspoon of sodium bicarbonate (baking soda) added.

precautions you should take. You can also get medical bulletins from the U.S. State Department and the Centers for Disease Control (see "Sources of Information," above). You can protect yourself by taking some simple precautions: Watch what you eat and drink; don't swim in stagnant water (ponds, slow-moving rivers, or wells); and avoid mosquito bites by covering up, using repellent, and sleeping under mosquito netting. The most dangerous areas seem to be on Mexico's west coast, away from the big resorts, which are relatively safe.

EMERGENCY EVACUATION   For extreme medical emergencies, there's a service from the United States that will fly people to American hospitals: **Air-Evac,** a 24-hour air ambulance (☎ **888/554-9729,** or call collect 510/293-5968). You can also contact the service in Guadalajara (☎ **01-800/305-9400** or 3/616-9616 or 3/615-2471). There is now an expanding list of companies that offer air evacuation services. For a good list of companies, refer to the U.S. State Department Web site at travel. state.gov/medical.html.

SAFETY

CRIME   I have lived and traveled in Mexico for almost a decade, have never had any serious trouble, and rarely feel suspicious of anyone or any situation. You will probably feel physically safer in most Mexican cities and villages than in any comparable place at home. However, crime in Mexico has received much attention in the North American press over the past 2 years. Many in Mexico feel this unfairly exaggerates the real dangers of traveling there, but it should be noted that crime is in fact on the rise, including taxi robberies, kidnappings, and highway carjackings. The most severe crime problems have been concentrated in Mexico City, where even longtime foreign residents will attest to the overall lack of security. Isolated incidents have also occurred in Ixtapa, and even the traditionally tranquil Puerto Escondido. See "Sources of Information" above for information on how to access the latest **U.S. State Department advisories.**

Precautions are necessary, but travelers should be realistic. When traveling anyplace in the world, common sense is essential. A good rule of thumb is that you can generally trust people whom you approach for help, assistance, or directions—but be wary of anyone who approaches you offering the same. The more insistent they are, the more cautious you should be. The crime rate is on the whole much lower in Mexico than in most parts of the United States, and the nature of crimes in general is less violent—most crime is motivated by robbery, or by jealousy. Random, violent, or serial crime is essentially unheard of in Mexico. You are much more likely to meet kind and helpful Mexicans than you are to encounter those set on thievery and deceit.

Although these general comments on crime are basically true throughout Mexico, the one notable exception is in **Mexico City,** where violent crime is seriously on the rise. Do not wear fine jewelry, expensive watches, or any other obvious displays of wealth. Muggings—day or night—are common. Avoid the use of the **green Volkswagen taxis,** as many of these have been involved in "pirate" robberies, muggings, and even kidnappings. Car theft and carjackings are also a common occurrence. Despite the rise in Mexico City's crime, you should be fine if you avoid ostentatious displays of wealth, follow commonsense precautions, and take taxis only dispatched from official sites (*sitios*).

BRIBES & SCAMS As is the case around the world, there are the occasional bribes and scams in Mexico, targeted at people believed to be naive in the ways of the place—such as obvious tourists. For years Mexico was known as a place where bribes— called *propinas* (tips) or *mordidas* (bites)—were expected; however, the country is rapidly changing. Frequently, offering a bribe today, especially to a police officer, is considered an insult, and it can land you in deeper trouble.

If you believe a **bribe** is being requested, here are a few tips on dealing with the situation. Even if you speak Spanish, don't utter a word of it to Mexican officials. That way you'll appear innocent, all the while understanding every word.

When you are crossing the border, should the person who inspects your car ask for a tip, you can ignore this request—but understand that the official may suddenly decide that a complete search of your belongings is in order. There's a number to **report irregularities with Customs officials** (☎ **01/800-001-4800** in Mexico). Your call will go to the office of the Comptroller and Administrative Development Secretariat (SECODAM); however, be forewarned that most personnel do not speak English. Be sure you have some basic information—such as the name of the person who requested a bribe or acted in a rude manner, as well as the place, time, and day of the event.

Whatever you do, **avoid impoliteness;** under no circumstances should you insult a Latin-American official. Mexico is ruled by extreme politeness, even in the face of adversity. In Mexico, *gringos* have a reputation for being loud and demanding. By adopting the local custom of excessive courtesy, you'll have greater success in negotiations of any kind. Stand your ground, but do it politely.

INSURANCE

HEALTH/ACCIDENT/LOSS   Even the most careful of us can still experience a traveler's nightmare: You discover you've lost your wallet, your passport, your airline ticket, or your tourist permit. Always keep a photocopy of these documents in your luggage—it makes replacing them easier. To be reimbursed for insured items once you return, you'll need to report the loss to the Mexican police and get a written report. If you don't speak Spanish, take along someone who does. If you lose official documents, you'll need to contact both Mexican and U.S. officials in Mexico before you leave the country.

Health Care Abroad, Wallach and Co., Inc., 107 W. Federal St. (P.O. Box 480), Middleburg, VA 22117 (☎ **800/237-6615** or 540/687-3166), offers medical and accident insurance as well as coverage for luggage loss and trip cancellation. Always read the fine print on the policy to be sure that you're getting the coverage you want.

Your homeowner's insurance should cover **stolen luggage.** The airlines are responsible for $2,500 on domestic flights if they lose your luggage; if you plan to carry anything more valuable than that, keep it in your carry-on bag.

6 Tips for Travelers with Special Needs

FOR FAMILIES   Children are considered the national treasure of Mexico, and Mexicans will warmly welcome and cater to your children. Where many parents were reluctant to bring young children into Mexico in the past, primarily due to health concerns, I can't think of a better place to introduce children to the exciting adventure of exploring a different culture. Some of the best destinations for children include Acapulco and Huatulco. Hotels can often arrange for a baby-sitter. Some hotels in the moderate-to-luxury range have small playgrounds and pools for children and hire caretakers with special activity programs during the day. Few budget hotels offer these amenities.

Before leaving, you should check with your doctor to get advice on medications to take along. Disposable diapers cost about the same in Mexico but are of poorer quality. You can get Huggies Supreme and Pampers, but you'll pay. Gerber's baby foods are sold in many stores. Dry cereals, powdered formulas, baby bottles, and purified water are all easily available in midsize and large cities or resorts.

Cribs, however, may present a problem; only the largest and most luxurious hotels provide them. However, rollaway beds to accommodate children staying in the room with parents are often available. Child seats or high chairs at restaurants are common, and most restaurants will go out of their way to accommodate the comfort of your child.

FOR GAY & LESBIAN TRAVELERS   Mexico is a conservative country, with deeply rooted Catholic religious traditions. Public displays of same-sex affection are rare and still considered shocking for men, especially outside of urban or resort areas. Women in Mexico frequently walk hand in hand, but anything more would cross the boundary of acceptability. However, gay and lesbian travelers are generally treated with respect and should not experience any harassment, assuming the appropriate regard is given to local culture and customs.

The International Gay & Lesbian Travel Association (IGLTA) (☎ **800/448-8550** or 954/776-2626; fax 954/776-3303; www.iglta.org), can provide helpful information and additional tips.

FOR TRAVELERS WITH DISABILITIES   Mexico may seem like one giant obstacle course to travelers in wheelchairs or on crutches. At airports, you may encounter steep stairs before finding a well-hidden elevator or escalator—if one exists. Airlines will often arrange wheelchair assistance to the baggage area for passengers. Porters are generally available to help with luggage at airports and large bus stations, once you've cleared baggage claim.

In addition, escalators (and there aren't many in the country) are often out of operation. Stairs without handrails abound. Few rest rooms are equipped for travelers with disabilities, or when one is available, access to it may be via a narrow passage that won't accommodate a wheelchair or a person on crutches. Many deluxe hotels (the most expensive) now have rooms with baths for people with disabilities. Those traveling on a budget should stick with one-story hotels or hotels with elevators. Even so, there will probably still be obstacles somewhere. Generally speaking, no matter where you are, someone will lend a hand, although you may have to ask for it.

Few airports offer the luxury of boarding an airplane from the waiting room. You either descend stairs to a bus that ferries you to the waiting plane that's boarded by climbing stairs, or you walk across the airport tarmac to your plane and ascend the stairs. Deplaning presents the same problem in reverse.

FOR SENIORS   Mexico is a popular country for retirees. For decades, North Americans have been living indefinitely in Mexico by returning to the border and recrossing with a new tourist permit every 6 months. Mexican immigration officials have caught on, and now limit the maximum time in the country to 6 months within any year. This is to encourage even partial residents to comply with the proper documentation.

Some of the most popular places for long-term stays are Cuernavaca, Morelos, and Oaxaca.

AIM, Apdo. Postal 31-70, 45050 Guadalajara, Jalisco, Mexico, is a well-written, candid, and very informative newsletter for prospective retirees. Recent issues evaluated retirement in Puerto Ángel, Puerto Escondido, Huatulco, Oaxaca, and Taxco. Subscriptions are $18 to the United States and $21 to Canada. Back issues are three for $5.

Sanborn Tours, 2015 South 10th St., P.O. Drawer 519, McAllen, TX 78505-0519 (☎ **800/395-8482**), offers a "Retire in Mexico" Guadalajara orientation tour.

FOR SINGLES   Mexico may be an old favorite for romantic honeymoons, but it's also a great place to travel on your own without really being or feeling alone. Although offering an identical room rate regardless of single or double occupancy is slowly becoming a trend in Mexico, many of the hotels mentioned in this book still offer singles at lower rates.

Mexicans are very friendly, and it's easy to meet other foreigners. But if you don't like the idea of traveling alone, then try **Travel Companion Exchange,** P.O. Box 833, Amityville, NY 11701 (☎ **800/392-1256** or 516/454-0880; fax 516/454-0170), which brings prospective travelers together. Members complete a profile, then place an anonymous listing of their travel interests in the newsletter. Prospective traveling companions then make contact through the exchange. Membership costs $99 for 6 months or $159 for a year. They also offer an excellent booklet on avoiding theft and scams while traveling abroad, for $3.95.

FOR WOMEN As a female traveling alone, I can tell you first-hand that I feel safer traveling in Mexico than in the United States. But I use the same commonsense precautions I use traveling anywhere else in the world and am alert to what's going on around me.

Mexicans in general, and men in particular, are nosy about single travelers, especially women. If taxi drivers or anyone else with whom you don't want to become friendly asks about your marital status, family, etc., my advice is to make up a set of answers (regardless of the truth): "I'm married, traveling with friends, and I have three children."

Saying you are single and traveling alone may send out the wrong message about availability. Movies and television shows exported from the United States have created an image of sexually aggressive North American women. If bothered by someone, don't try to be polite—just leave or head into a public place.

FOR STUDENTS Because higher education is still considered more of a luxury than a birthright in Mexico, there is no formal network of student discounts and programs. Also, most Mexican students travel with their families, rather than with other students, so student discount cards are not commonly recognized here.

For those wishing to study in Mexico, however, there are a number of university-affiliated and independent programs geared for intensive Spanish-language study. Frequently, these will also assist with accommodations, usually with a local family in their home. One such program is **KABAH Travel and Education Tourism,** based in Guadalajara, which offers study and travel programs throughout the country. You can receive information by faxing ☎ **800/596-4768,** or through e-mail at tursonri@ foreigner.class.udg.mx. More information is available at their Web site: **www.mexplaza.udg.mx/kabah/**.

7 Getting There

BY PLANE

The airline situation in Mexico is changing rapidly, with many new regional carriers offering scheduled service to areas previously not served. In addition to regularly scheduled service, charter service direct from U.S. cities to resorts is making Mexico more accessible.

CyberDeals for Net Surfers

A great way to find the cheapest fare is by using the Internet to do your searching for you. **Travelocity** (www.travelocity.com) is Frommer's online travel-planning and -booking partner. Travelocity uses the SABRE system to offer reservations and tickets for more than 400 airlines, plus reservations and purchase capabilities for more than 45,000 hotels and 50 car-rental companies. With its **Fare Watcher** e-mail feature, you can select up to five routes and receive e-mail notices when the fare changes by $25 or more. In addition, Travelocity's **Destination Guide** includes updated information on some 260 destinations worldwide—all supplied by Frommer's. Other well-respected booking sites are **Microsoft Expedia** (www.expedia.com), **Trip.com** (www.trip.com) and **Yahoo! Travel** (www.travel.yahoo.com).

THE MAJOR INTERNATIONAL AIRLINES The main airlines operating direct or nonstop flights from the United States to points in Mexico include **Aerocalifornia** (☎ 800/237-6225), **Aeromexico** (☎ 800/237-6639), **Air France** (☎ 800/235-9292), **American** (☎ 800/433-7300), **Continental** (☎ 800/231-0856), **Lacsa** (☎ 800/225-2272), **Mexicana** (☎ 800/531-7921), **Northwest** (☎ 800/225-2525), **United** (☎ 800/241-6522), and **US Airways** (☎ 800/428-4322). **Southwest Airlines** (☎ 800/435-9792) serves the U.S. border.

The main departure points in North America for international airlines are Atlanta, Chicago, Dallas/Fort Worth, Denver, Houston, Los Angeles, Miami, New Orleans, New York, Orlando, Philadelphia, Raleigh/Durham, San Antonio, San Francisco, Seattle, Toronto, Tucson, and Washington, D.C.

BY CAR

Driving is not the cheapest way to get to Mexico, but it is the best way to see the country. Even so, you may think twice about taking your own car south of the border once you've pondered the bureaucracy that affects foreign drivers here. One option is to rent a car, for touring around a specific region, once you arrive in Mexico. Rental cars in Mexico are now generally new, clean, and very well maintained. Although pricier than in the United States, discounts are often available for rentals of a week or longer, especially when arrangements are made in advance from the United States. (See "Car Rentals," below, for more details).

If, after reading the section that follows, you have any additional questions or you want to confirm the current rules, call your nearest Mexican consulate, or the Mexican Government Tourist Office. To check on road conditions or to get help with any travel emergency while in Mexico, call ☎ **01-800/903-9200,** or 5/250-0151 in Mexico City. Both numbers are staffed by English-speaking operators.

In addition, check with the **U.S. State Department** (see "Sources of Information," at the beginning of this chapter) for their warnings about dangerous driving areas.

BY SHIP

Numerous cruise lines serve Mexico. Possible trips might cruise from California down to ports of call on the Pacific Coast. Several cruise-tour specialists arrange substantial discounts on unsold cabins if you're willing to take off at the last minute. One such company is **The Cruise Line,** 150 NW 168 St., North Miami Beach, Miami, FL 33169 (☎ **800/777-0707** or 305/521-2200).

BY BUS

Greyhound-Trailways or its affiliates (☎ **800/229-9424** or 402/330-8552; www.greyhound.com) offers service from around the United States to the Mexican border, where passengers disembark, cross the border, and buy a ticket for travel into the interior of Mexico. At many border crossings there are scheduled buses from the U.S. bus station to the Mexican bus station.

8 The Pros & Cons of Package Tours

For popular destinations like Mexico's beach resorts, package tours are often the smart way to go, because they can save you a ton of money. In many cases, a package that includes airfare, hotel, and transportation to and from the airport will cost you less than just the hotel alone if you booked it yourself. That's because packages are sold in bulk to tour operators, who resell them to the public.

WHERE TO BROWSE

• For one-stop shopping on the Web, go to **www.vacationpackager. com**, an extensive search engine that'll link you up with more than 30 packagers offering Mexican beach vacations—and even let you custom design your own package.

- Check out **www.2travel.com** and find a page with links to a number of the big-name Mexico packagers, including several of the ones listed here.

PACKAGERS PACKIN' A PUNCH

- **Aeromexico Vacations** (☎ 800/245-8585; www.aeromexico. com) sells year-round packages for Acapulco, Ixtapa/Zihuatanejo, and Huatulco. Aeromexico has a large selection of resorts in these destinations in a variety of price ranges. The best deals are from Houston, Dallas, San Diego, Los Angeles, Miami, and New York, in that order.

- **Alaska Airlines Vacations** (☎ 800/426-0333; www. alaskaair.com) sells packages to Ixtapa/Zihuatanejo. Alaska flies direct to Mexico from Los Angeles, San Diego, San Jose, San Francisco, Seattle, Vancouver, Anchorage, and Fairbanks.

- **American Airlines Vacations** (☎ 800/321-2121; www. americanair.com) has seasonal packages to Acapulco. You don't have to fly with American if you can get a better deal on another airline; land-only packages include hotel, airport transfers, and hotel room tax. American's hubs to Mexico are Dallas/Fort Worth, Chicago, and Miami, so you're likely to get the best prices—and the most direct flights—if you live near those cities.

- **America West Vacations** (☎ 800/356-6611; www.americawest. com) has deals to Acapulco and Ixtapa, mostly from its Phoenix gateway.

- **Apple Vacations** (☎ 800/365-2775; www.applevacations. com) offers inclusive packages to all the beach resorts, and has the largest choice of hotels. Scheduled carriers booked for the air portion include American, United, Mexicana, Delta, TWA, US Airways, Reno Air, Alaska Airlines, AeroCalifornia, and Aeromexico. Apple perks include baggage handling and the services of an Apple representative at the major hotels.

- **Continental Vacations** (☎ 800/634-5555; www.flycontinental. com) has year-round packages available to Acapulco and Ixtapa, and the best deals are from Houston; Newark, New Jersey; and Cleveland.

- **Friendly Holidays** (☎ 800/344-5687; www.friendlyholidays. com), a major player in the Mexico field, is based in upstate

New York, but also has offices in California and Houston, so they've got their bases covered. They offer trips to all the resorts, including Ixtapa and Acapulco. Although they don't have the largest variety of hotels from which to choose, the ones they work with are high quality. In addition, their Web site is very user-friendly, listing both a starting price for 3 nights' hotel room and a figure for air add-ons, so at least you have a rough idea of what your trip is likely to cost you.

- **Funjet Vacations** (bookable through travel agents or online at **www.funjet.com**), one of the largest vacation packagers in the United States, has packages to Acapulco, Huatulco, and Ixtapa. You can choose a charter or fly on American, Continental, Delta, Aeromexico, US Airways, Alaska Air, TWA, or United.

- **Mexicana Vacations (or MexSeaSun Vacations)** (☎ 800/ 531-9321; www.mexicana.com) offers getaways to all the resorts, buttressed by Mexicana's daily direct flights from Los Angeles to Acapulco and Ixtapa/Zihuatanejo.

REGIONAL PACKAGERS

FROM THE EAST COAST: Liberty Travel (☎ 888/ 271-1584; www.libertytravel.com), one of the biggest packagers in the Northeast, often runs a full-page ad in the Sunday papers, with frequent Mexico specials. You won't get much in the way of service, but you will get a good deal.

FROM THE WEST COAST: Sunquest Holidays (☎ 800/ 357-2400 or 888/888-5028 for departures within 14 days) is one of the largest packagers for Mexico on the West Coast, with a large selection of hotels.

FROM THE SOUTHWEST: Town and Country (bookable through travel agents) packages regular deals to Ixtapa and Acapulco with America West, from the airline's Phoenix and Las Vegas gateways.

RESORTS

The biggest hotel chains and resorts also sell packages. The Mexican-owned Fiesta Americana/Fiesta Inns, for example, run **Fiesta Break** deals that include airfare from New York, Los Angeles, Dallas, or Houston, airport transfers, optional meal plans, and more. Call ☎ **800/9-BREAK-9** for details, or ☎ 800/ FIESTA-1 for land-only packages.

9   Getting Around

An important note: If your travel schedule depends on an important connection, say a plane trip between points or a ferry or bus connection, use the telephone numbers in this book or other information resources mentioned here to find out if the connection you are depending on is still available. Although we've done our best to provide accurate information, transportation schedules can and do change.

BY PLANE

To fly from point to point within Mexico, you'll rely on Mexican airlines. Mexico has two privately owned large national carriers: **Mexicana** (☎ **800/366-5400,** toll-free within Mexico) and **Aeromexico** (☎ **800/021-4000,** toll-free within Mexico). Mexicana and Aeromexico both offer extensive connections to the United States as well as within Mexico.

Several of the new regional carriers are operated by or can be booked through Mexicana or Aeromexico. Regional carriers are **Aerolitoral** (see "Aeromexico," above) and **Aero Mar** (see "Mexicana," above). For points inside the state of Oaxaca only— Oaxaca City, Puerto Escondido, and Huatulco—contact **Zapotec Tours** (☎ **800/44-OAXACA,** or 773/506-2444 in IL). The regional carriers are expensive, but they go to difficult-to-reach places. In each applicable section of this book, we've mentioned regional carriers with all pertinent telephone numbers.

Because major airlines can book some regional carriers, read your ticket carefully to see if your connecting flight is on one of these smaller carriers—they may leave from a different airport or check in at a different counter.

AIRPORT TAXES   Mexico charges an airport tax on all departures. Passengers leaving the country on an international departure pay $18—in dollars or the peso equivalent. It has become a common practice to include this departure tax in your ticket price, but double check to make sure you're not caught by surprise at the airport upon leaving. Taxes on each domestic departure you make within Mexico cost around $12.50, unless you're on a connecting flight and have already paid at the start of the flight, in which case you shouldn't be charged again.

Starting in May 1999, Mexico also charges an additional $18 "tourism tax," the proceeds of which go into a tourism promotional fund. This may or may not be included in your ticket price, so be sure to set aside this amount in either dollars or pesos to pay at the airport upon departure.

RECONFIRMING FLIGHTS   Although Mexican airlines say it's not necessary to reconfirm a flight, it's still a good practice. To avoid getting bumped on popular, possibly overbooked flights, check in for an international flight the required hour and a half in advance of travel.

BY CAR

Most Mexican roads are not up to U.S. standards of smoothness, hardness, width of curve, grade of hill, or safety marking. Driving at night is dangerous—the roads aren't good and are rarely lit; trucks, carts, pedestrians, and bicycles usually have no lights; and you can hit potholes, animals, rocks, dead ends, or bridges out with no warning.

CAR RENTALS   You'll get the best price if you reserve a car a week in advance in the United States. U.S. car-rental firms include **Avis** (☎ **800/331-1212** in the U.S., 800/TRY-AVIS in Canada), **Budget** (☎ **800/527-0700** in the U.S. and Canada), **Hertz** (☎ **800/654-3131** in the U.S. and Canada), and **National** (☎ **800/CAR-RENT** in the U.S. and Canada). For European travelers, **Kemwel Holiday Auto** (☎ **800/678-0678**) and **Auto Europe** (☎ **800/223-5555**) can arrange Mexican rentals, sometimes through other agencies. You'll find rental desks at airports, all major hotels, and many travel agencies.

Cars are easy to rent if you have a major credit card, are 25 or over, and have a valid driver's license and passport with you. Without a credit card you must leave a cash deposit, usually a big one. Rent-here/leave-there arrangements are usually simple to make but more costly.

Car-rental costs are high in Mexico, because cars are more expensive here. The condition of rental cars has improved greatly over the years, however, and clean, comfortable, new cars are the norm. The basic cost of a 1-day rental of a Volkswagen Beetle, with unlimited mileage (but before 17% tax and $15 daily insurance), is about $48 in Puerto Escondido and $37 in Acapulco. Renting by the week gives you a lower daily rate. Prices may be considerably higher if you rent in these same cities around a major holiday.

Deductibles   Be careful—these vary greatly in Mexico; some are as high as $2,500, which comes out of your pocket immediately in case of car damage. Hertz's deductible is $1,000 on a VW Beetle; Avis's is $500 for the same car.

Insurance   Insurance is offered in two parts: **Collision and damage** insurance covers your car and others if the accident is your fault, and **personal accident** insurance covers you and anyone in your car. Read the fine print on the back of your rental agreement and note that insurance may be invalid if you have an accident while driving on an unpaved road.

Damage   Always inspect your car carefully and note every damaged or missing item, no matter how minute, on your rental agreement, or you may be charged.

BY TAXI

Taxis are the preferred way to get around in almost all of the resort areas of Mexico, and also around Mexico City. Short trips within towns are generally charged by preset zones, and are quite reasonable compared with U.S. rates. For longer trips, or excursions to nearby cities, taxis can generally be hired for around $10 to $15 per hour, or for a negotiated daily rate. Even drops to different destinations, say between Huatulco and Puerto Escondido, can be arranged. A negotiated one-way price is usually much less than the cost of a rental car for a day, and service is much faster than traveling by bus. For anyone who is uncomfortable driving in Mexico, this is a convenient, comfortable alternative. An added bonus is that you have a Spanish-speaking person with you in case you run into any car or road trouble. Many taxi drivers speak at least some English. Your hotel can assist you with the arrangements.

BY BUS

Mexican buses are frequent, readily accessible, and can get you to almost anywhere you want to go. They're often the only way to get from large cities to other nearby cities and small villages. Don't hesitate to ask questions if you're confused about anything.

Travel Tip

Little English is spoken at bus stations, so come prepared with your destination written down, then double-check the departure.

Bus Hijackings

The U.S. State Department notes that bandits target long-distance buses traveling at night, but there have been daylight robberies as well. Avoid Highway 200 south from Acapulco to Huatulco, if at all possible.

Dozens of Mexican companies operate large, air-conditioned, Greyhound-type buses between most cities. Travel class is generally labeled second (*segunda*), first (*primera*), and deluxe (*ejecutiva*), which is referred to by a variety of names. The deluxe buses often have fewer seats than regular buses, show video movies en route, are air-conditioned, and have few stops; some have complimentary refreshments. Many run express from origin to the final destination. They are well worth the few dollars more that you'll pay. In rural areas, buses are often of the school-bus variety, with lots of local color.

Whenever possible, it's best to buy your reserved-seat ticket, often via a computerized system, a day in advance on many long-distance routes and especially before holidays. Schedules are fairly dependable, so be at the terminal on time for departure. Current information may be obtained from local bus stations. See the Appendix for a list of helpful bus terms in Spanish.

FAST FACTS: Mexico

Abbreviations   Dept. (apartments); Apdo. (post office box); Av. (*Avenida;* avenue); c/ (*calle;* street); Calz. (*Calzada;* boulevard). "C" on faucets stands for *caliente* (hot), and "F" stands for *fría* (cold). PB (*planta baja*) means ground floor, and most buildings count the next floor up as the first floor (1).

Business Hours   In general, businesses in larger cities are open between 9am and 7pm; in smaller towns many close between 2 and 4pm. Most are closed on Sunday. In resort areas it is common to find more stores open on Sundays, as well as extended business hours for shops, often until 8pm or even 10pm. Bank hours are Monday through Friday from 9 or 9:30am to 5 or 6pm. Increasingly, banks are offering Saturday hours for at least a half day.

Cameras/Film   Film costs about the same as in the United States.

Customs   See "Visitor Information, Entry Requirements & Money," earlier in this chapter.

Doctors/Dentists   Every embassy and consulate is prepared to recommend local doctors and dentists with good training and modern equipment; some of the doctors and dentists even speak English. See the list of embassies and consulates under "Embassies/Consulates," below. Hotels with a large foreign clientele are often prepared to recommend English-speaking doctors. Almost all first-class hotels in Mexico have a doctor on call.

Drug Laws   To be blunt, don't use or possess illegal drugs in Mexico. Mexican officials have no tolerance for drug users, and jail is their solution, with very little hope of getting out until the sentence (usually a long one) is completed or heavy fines or bribes are paid. Remember, in Mexico the legal system assumes you are guilty until proven innocent. (*Important note:* It isn't uncommon to be befriended by a fellow user, only to be turned in by that "friend," who's collected a bounty.) Bring prescription drugs in their original containers. If possible, pack a copy of the original prescription with the generic name of the drug.

U.S. Customs officials are also on the lookout for diet drugs sold in Mexico but illegal in the United States, possession of which could also land you in a U.S. jail. If you buy antibiotics over the counter (which you can do in Mexico)—say, for a sinus infection—and still have some left, you probably won't be hassled by U.S. Customs.

Drugstores   See "Pharmacies" below.

Electricity   The electrical system in Mexico is 110 volts AC (60 cycles), as in the United States and Canada. However, in reality it may cycle more slowly and overheat your appliances. To compensate, select a medium or low speed for hair dryers. Many older hotels still have electrical outlets for flat two-prong plugs; you'll need an adapter for any modern electrical apparatus that has an enlarged end on one prong or that has three prongs. Many first-class and deluxe hotels have the three-holed outlets (*trifásicos* in Spanish). Those that don't may have loan adapters, but to be sure, it's always better to carry your own.

Embassies/Consulates   They provide valuable lists of doctors and lawyers, as well as regulations concerning marriages in Mexico. Contrary to popular belief, your embassy cannot get you out of a Mexican jail, provide postal or banking services, or fly you home when you run out of money. Consular officers can provide you with advice on most matters and problems, however. Most countries have a representative embassy in Mexico City and many have consular offices or representatives in the provinces.

The Embassy of **Australia** in Mexico City is at Ruben Darío 55 Col. Polanco (☎ **5/531-5225;** fax 5/531-9552; www.immi. gov.au; e-mail dfat@ozemb.org.mx.); it's open Monday through Friday from 9am to 1pm.

The Embassy of **Canada** in Mexico City is at Schiller 529, in Polanco (☎ **5/724-7900**); it's open Monday through Friday from 9am to 1pm and 2 to 5pm (at other times the name of a duty officer is posted on the embassy door). In Acapulco, the Canadian consulate is located in the Centro Comercial Marbella, Local 23, Prolongacíon Farallón S/N, at the corner of Costera Miguel Aleman (☎ **74/84-1305;** www.canada.org.mx); it's open Monday through Friday from 9am to 5pm.

Irish and **South African** citizens should go to the British Consulate.

The Embassy of **New Zealand** in Mexico City is at José Luis Lagrange 103, 10th floor, Col. Los Morales Polanco (☎ **5/ 281-5304** or 5/281/5486; kiwimexico@compuserve.com.mx); it's open Monday through Thursday from 9am to 2pm and 3 to 5pm and Friday from 9am to 2pm.

The Embassy of the **United Kingdom** in Mexico City is in Río Lerma 71, Col. Cuahutemoc (☎ **5/207-2089** or 5/207-7672; www.embajadabritanica.com.mx); it's open Monday through Friday from 8:30am to 3:30pm.

The Embassy of the **United States** in Mexico City is next to the Hotel María Isabel Sheraton at Paseo de la Reforma 305, at the corner of Río Danubio (☎ **5/209-9100**). There are consular agencies in Acapulco (☎ **74/84-0300** or 74/69-0556) and Oaxaca (☎ **951/4-3054**).

Emergencies   The 24-hour **Tourist Help Line** in Mexico City is ☎ **800/903-9200** or 5/250-0151. A tourist legal assistance office (Procuraduria del Turista) is located in Mexico City (☎ **5/625-8153** or 5/625-8154). They offer 24-hour service and there is always an English-speaking person available.

Internet Access In large cities and resort areas, a growing number of five-star hotels offer business centers with Internet access. You'll also find cybercafes in destinations that are popular with expats and business travelers. Note that many ISPs will automatically cut off your Internet connection after a specified period of time (say, 10 minutes), because telephone lines are at a premium. Some Telmex offices also have free-access Internet kiosks in their reception areas.

Legal Aid   International Legal Defense Counsel, 111 S. 15th St., 24th Floor, Packard Building, Philadelphia, PA 19102 (☎ **215/977-9982**), is a law firm specializing in legal difficulties of Americans abroad. See also "Embassies/ Consulates" and "Emergencies," above.

Liquor Laws The legal drinking age in Mexico is 18; however, it is extremely rare that anyone will be asked for ID or denied purchase (often, children are sent to the stores to buy beer for their parents). Grocery stores sell everything from beer and wine to national and imported liquors. You can buy liquor 24 hours a day; but during major elections, dry laws often are enacted for as much as 72 hours in advance of the election—and those laws apply to foreign tourists as well as local residents. Mexico also does not have any "open container" laws for transporting liquor in cars, but authorities are beginning to target drunk drivers more aggressively. It's a good idea to drive defensively.

It is not legal to drink in the street; however, many tourists do so. Use your better judgment—if you are getting too drunk you shouldn't drink in the street because you are more likely to get stopped by the police. As is the custom in Mexico, it is not so much what you do, it is how you do it.

Newspapers/Magazines Two English-language newspapers, the *News* and the *Mexico City Times,* are published in Mexico City, distributed nationally, and carry world news and commentaries, plus a calendar of the day's events, including concerts, art shows, and plays. Newspaper kiosks in larger Mexican cities will carry a selection of English-language magazines.

Pharmacies *Farmacias* will sell you just about anything you want, with a prescription or without one. Most pharmacies are open Monday through Saturday from 8am to 8pm. There are generally one or two 24-hour pharmacies now located in the major resort areas. Pharmacies take turns staying open during off-hours, so if you are in a smaller town and need to buy medicines after normal hours, ask for the *farmacia de turno.*

Police   In Mexico City, police are to be suspected as frequently as they are to be trusted; however, you'll find many who are quite honest and helpful. In the rest of the country, especially in the tourist areas, the majority are very protective of international visitors. Several cities, including Acapulco, have gone as far as to set up a special corps of English-speaking Tourist Police to assist with directions, guidance, and more.

Taxes   There's a 15% IVA (value-added) tax on goods and services in most of Mexico, and it's supposed to be included in the posted price. There is an exit tax of around $17.25 imposed on every foreigner leaving the country, usually included in the price of airline tickets.

Telephone/Fax   Telephone area codes are gradually being changed all over the country. The change may affect the area code and first digit or only the area code. Some cities are even adding exchanges and changing whole numbers. Courtesy messages telling you that the number you dialed has been changed do not exist. You can call operator assistance for difficult-to-reach numbers. Many fax numbers are also regular telephone numbers; you have to ask whomever answers your call for the fax tone (*"tono de fax, por favor"*). Cellular phones are becoming more and more popular for small businesses in resort areas and smaller communities. To dial a cellular number inside the same area code, dial 044 and then the number. To dial the cellular phone from anywhere else in Mexico, first dial 01, and then the eight-digit number. To dial it from the United States, just dial 011-52 plus the eight-digit number.

The **country code** for Mexico is **52.** For instructions on how to call Mexico from the United States, call the United States from Mexico, place calls within Mexico, or use a pay phone, consult "Telephones & Mail" in the Appendix.

Time Zone   Central standard time prevails throughout most of Mexico, and all of the areas covered in this book. Mexico observes **daylight saving time.**

Water   Most hotels have decanters or bottles of purified water in the rooms, and the better hotels have either purified water from regular taps or special taps marked *agua purificada.* Some hotels will charge for in-room bottled water. Virtually any hotel, restaurant, or bar will bring you purified water if you specifically request it, but you'll usually be charged for it. Bottled purified water is sold widely at drugstores and grocery stores. Some popular brands are Santa María, Ciel, Agua Pura, and Pureza.

2

Acapulco

*T*hough most beach resorts were made for relaxing, Acapulco has a nonstop, 24-hours-a-day energy. Its perfectly sculpted bay is an adult playground filled with water-skiers in tanga swimsuits and darkly tanned, mirror-shaded studs on WaveRunners. Golf and tennis are also played with intensity, but the real participant sport is the nightlife, which has made this city famous for decades. Back in the days when there was a jet set, they came to Acapulco— filmed it, sang about it, wrote about it, and lived it.

It's not hard to understand why: The view of Acapulco Bay, framed by mountains and beaches, is breathtaking day or night. And I dare anyone to take in the lights of the city and not feel the pull to go out and get lively.

Though Acapulco has fallen out of favor with travelers over the past decade, it's experiencing a renaissance, in a style reminiscent of Miami's South Beach district. Classic hotels are being renovated and areas gentrified. Clean-up efforts have put a whole new face on a place that was once aging less than gracefully.

International travelers began to reject Acapulco when it became clear that the cost of development was the pollution of the bay and surrounding areas. The catalyst for change was Hurricane Paulina, which hit in October of 1997, exposing the poorly constructed parts of the city and taking 400 lives as it swept through the bay. Since then, over $1.2 billion has been invested in public and private infrastructure improvements that include hotel upgrades, new roads, and a new water and waste treatment facility. In addition, a program called "ACA-Limpia" ("Clean Acapulco") was instituted in the early 1990s, and has cleaned up the water— whales have even been sighted offshore recently for the first time in years. Today, 80% of Acapulco's visitors come from within Mexico, most by way of the express toll road that links the city with the capital.

A city that never sleeps, Acapulco tries hard to hold on to her image as the grande dame of resorts and the ultimate, extravagant party town. It's still the place for those who want to have dinner at midnight, dance until dawn, and sleep all day on a sun-soaked beach.

Where else do bronzed men dive from cliffs into the sea at sunset, and where else does the sun shine 360 days a year? I like to think of Acapulco as a diva—maybe a little past her prime, perhaps overly made up, but still able to captivate an audience.

1 Essentials

Acapulco is 229 miles (366km) S of Mexico City; 170 miles (272km) SW of Taxco; 612 miles (979km) SE of Guadalajara; 158 miles (253km) SE of Ixtapa/ Zihuatanejo; 470 miles (752km) NW of Huatulco

GETTING THERE & DEPARTING

BY PLANE   See chapter 1, "Planning a Trip to Southern Pacific Mexico," for information on flying from the United States or Canada to Acapulco. Local numbers for major airlines with non-stop or direct service to Acapulco are: **Aeromexico** (☎ 7/485-1600 or 7/481-1766), **American** (☎ 7/466-9232 or 01-800/904-6000 inside Mexico for reservations), **Continental** (☎ 7/466-9063), **Mexicana** (☎ 7/466-9121 or 7/486-7586), and **America West** (☎ 7/466-9257).

Within Mexico, **Aeromexico** flies from Guadalajara, Mexico City, and Tijuana; **Mexicana** flies from Mexico City. Check with a travel agent about **charter flights.**

The airport (ACA) is 14 miles southeast of town, over the hills east of the bay. Private **taxis** are the fastest option to get to downtown Acapulco, running from $18 to $50. The major **rental-car** agencies all have booths at the airport. **Transportes Terrestres** has desks at the front of the airport where you can buy tickets for minivan *colectivo* transportation into town ($10). Return service to the airport must be reserved through your hotel.

BY CAR   From Mexico City, you can take either the curvy toll-free Highway 95D south (6 hr.), or scenic Highway 95, the four-to six-lane toll highway (3$1/2$ hr.) that costs around $50 one way. The free road from Taxco is in good condition; you'll save around $40 in tolls from there through Chilpancingo to Acapulco. From points north or south along the coast, the only choice is Highway 200, but be aware that it is one of the most dangerous roads to travel in Mexico, especially the road south from Acapulco—travel only by day if you take it at all.

Acapulco Bay Area

ATTRACTIONS ●
Catedral **22**
Centro Acapulco (Convention Center) **15**
Centro Internacional de
  Convivencia Infantil **16**
Cliff Divers **9**
Fort San Diego/Museo Histórico
  de Acapulco **23**

Jai Lai Frontón Stadium **6**
Mágico Mundo Marino **4**
Plaza de Toros **5**
Zócalo/Plaza Álvarez **21**

ACCOMMODATIONS ■
Calinda Acapulco Quality Inn **12**
Camino Real **19**

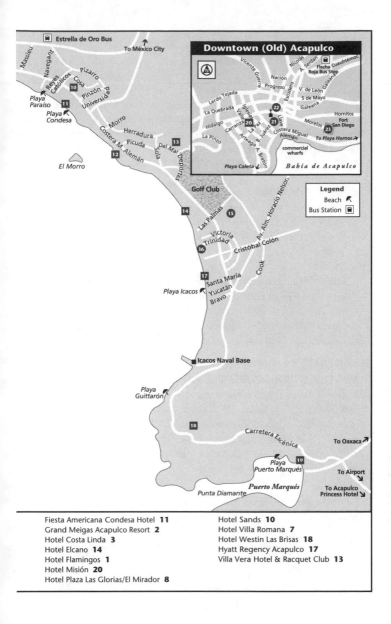

Downtown (Old) Acapulco

To México City

Massieu
Navegant
Reyes Católicos
Cosa
Pizarro
Pinzón
Universid
Playa Paraíso
Playa Condesa
Morro
Herradura
Picuda
Del Mar
Sola
Costera M. Alemán
Deportes

El Morro

Golf Club
Las Palmas

Victoria
Trinidad
Cristóbal Colón
Av. Alm. Horacio Nelson
Cook
Santa María
Playa Icacos
Yucatán
Bravo

Icacos Naval Base

Playa Guittarón

Carretera Escénica
To Oaxaca

Playa Puerto Marqués
To Airport
To Acapulco Princess Hotel

Puerto Marqués
Punta Diamante

Downtown (Old) Acapulco

Vicente Guerra
Nicolás
A. Serdán
Flecha Roja Bus Stop
Cuauhtémoc
Galeana
Nación
Progreso
Escudero
V. de León
5 de Mayo
Galeana
Lerdo Tejada
Hornitos
Fort San Diego
La Quebrada
Hidalgo
Iglesias
Valle
Carranza
La Paz
J. Juárez
Morelos
To Playa Hornos
La Pinza
Arteaga
A. Breton
Costera Miguel Alemán

commercial wharfs

Playa Caleta

Bahía de Acapulco

Legend
Beach
Bus Station

Fiesta Americana Condesa Hotel **11**
Grand Meigas Acapulco Resort **2**
Hotel Costa Linda **3**
Hotel Elcano **14**
Hotel Flamingos **1**
Hotel Misión **20**
Hotel Plaza Las Glorias/El Mirador **8**

Hotel Sands **10**
Hotel Villa Romana **7**
Hotel Westin Las Brisas **18**
Hyatt Regency Acapulco **17**
Villa Vera Hotel & Racquet Club **13**

Important Car & Bus Travel Warning

Car robberies and bus hijackings on Highway 200 south of Acapulco on the way to Puerto Escondido and Huatulco are frequent,
making this an unsafe route for both bus and car travel, even
though occasional military checkpoints have been installed. If
you're going to either place from Acapulco, it's safer to fly; flight
routing will take you from Acapulco to Mexico City and then to
Puerto Escondido or Huatulco.

BY BUS   The **Ejido/Central Camionera station** is on the far
northern end of the bay and north of downtown (Old Acapulco)
at Ejido 47. It's far from the hotels; however, it has the widest
choice of bus lines served from one terminal and the widest array
of routes of any Acapulco bus station. It also has a hotel-
reservation service.

From this station, **Turistar, Estrella de Oro,** and **Estrella
Blanca** have almost hourly service for the five- to seven-hour trip
to Mexico City and daily service to Zihuatanejo. Buses also travel
to/from other points in Mexico including Chilpancingo, Cuernavaca, Iguala, Manzanillo, Puerto Vallarta, and Taxco.

ORIENTATION

VISITOR INFORMATION   The **State of Guerrero Tourism
Office** operates the **Procuraduría del Turista** on street level in
front of the **International Center** (☎/fax **7/484-4583** or
7/484-4416), a convention center set far back from the main
avenida Alemán, down a lengthy walkway with fountains. The
office offers maps and information about the city and state, as
well as police assistance for tourists; it's open daily from 9am to
10pm.

CITY LAYOUT   Acapulco stretches for more than four miles
around the huge bay so trying to take it all in by foot is imprac-
tical. The tourist areas are roughly divided into three sections:
Old Acapulco (Acapulco Viejo) is the original town that attracted
the jet setters of the 1950s and 1960s—and today it looks like it's
still locked in that era, though a sort of a renaissance is underfoot.
The second section is known as the **Hotel Zone** (Zona Hotelera);
it follows the main boulevard, **Costera Miguel Alemán** (or just

"the Costera"), as it runs east along the bay from downtown. The street is lined with towering hotels, restaurants, shopping centers, and strips of open-air beach bars. At the far eastern end of the Costera lie the golf course and the International Center (a convention center).

Avenida Cuauhtémoc is the major artery inland, running roughly parallel to the Costera. The third major area begins just beyond the Hyatt Regency Hotel, where the Costera changes its name to **Carretera Escénica** (Scenic Highway), which continues all the way to the airport. Along this section of the road, the hotels are their most lavish, and extravagant private villas, gourmet restaurants, and flashy nightclubs built into the hillside offer dazzling views. The area fronting the beach here is called **Acapulco Diamante,** Acapulco's most desirable address.

Street names and numbers in Acapulco can be confusing and hard to find—many streets either are not well marked or change names unexpectedly. Fortunately, there's seldom a reason to be far from the Costera, so it's hard to get lost. Street numbers on the Costera do not follow logic, so don't assume that similar numbers will necessarily be close together.

GETTING AROUND   By Taxi   Taxis are more plentiful than tacos in Acapulco—and practically as inexpensive if you're traveling in the downtown area only. Just remember that you should always establish the price with the driver before starting out. Hotel taxis may charge three times the rate of a taxi hailed on the street, and nighttime taxi rides cost extra, too. Taxis are also more expensive if you're staying in the Diamante section or south. The minimum fare is $1.50 per ride for a roving VW bug-style taxi in town, with the fare from Puerto Marqués to the hotel zone costing $8, or $10 into downtown. Sitio taxis are nicer cars, but are more expensive, with a minimum fare of $3.

The fashion among Acapulco taxis is to decorate them with flashy, Las Vegas–style lights—the more colorful and pulsating, the better. It appears to be almost a local competition. And there's no extra charge for the added embellishment.

By Bus   Even though the city has a confusing street layout, it's amazingly easy and inexpensive to use city buses. Two kinds of buses run along the Costera: pastel color-coded buses and regular "school buses." The difference is the price: New air-conditioned tourist buses (Aca Tur Bus) are 35¢; old buses, 3¢. Covered bus stops are located all along the Costera, with handy maps on the walls showing bus routes to major sights and hotels.

The best place near the zócalo to catch a bus is next to Sanborn's, 2 blocks east. "Caleta Directo" or "Base-Caleta" buses will take you to the Hornos, Caleta, and Caletilla beaches along the Costera. Some buses return along the same route; others go around the peninsula and return to the Costera.

For expeditions to more distant destinations, there are buses to **Puerto Marqués** to the east (marked PUERTO MARQUÉS–BASE) and **Pie de la Cuesta** to the west (marked ZÓCALO–PIE DE LA CUESTA). Be sure to verify the time and place of the last bus back if you hop on one of these.

By Car Rental cars are available both at the airport and at hotel desks along the Costera. Unless you plan on exploring outlying areas, you're better off taking taxis or using the easy and inexpensive public buses. Traffic can get tangled, and it's much easier to leave the driving to someone else.

FAST FACTS: Acapulco

American Express The main office is in the "Gran Plaza" shopping center at Costera Alemán 1628 (☎ **7/469-1166** or 7/469-1167); it's open Monday to Saturday from 10am to 7pm.

Area Code The telephone area code is **7.**

Climate Acapulco boasts sunshine 360 days a year, with average daytime temperatures of 80°F. Humidity varies, with approximately 59 inches of rain per year. June through October is the rainy season, though July and August are relatively dry. Tropical showers are brief and usually occur at night.

Consular Agents The **United States** has an agent at the Hotel Club del Sol on Costera Alemán at Reyes Católicos (☎ **7/481-1699** or 7/469-0556), across from the Hotel Acapulco Plaza; the office is open Monday to Friday from 10am to 2pm. The **Canadian** office is at the Centro Comercial Marbella, Local 23 (☎ **7/484-1305**) and is open Monday to Friday from 9am to 5pm. The **United Kingdom** has an office at the Las Brisas Hotel on Carretera Escénica near the airport (☎ **7/484-6605**); it's open Monday to Friday from 9am to

6pm. Most other countries in the European Union also have consulate offices in Acapulco.

Currency Exchange   Numerous banks are located along the Costera and are open Monday to Friday from 9am to 6pm and Saturday from 10am to 1:30pm. They, and their automatic teller machines, generally have the best rates. *Casas de cambio* (currency exchange booths) along the street may have better exchange rates than hotels.

Hospital   Try **Hospital Magallanes,** avenida Wilfrido Massieu #2 Fracc Magallanes (☎ **7/485-6194** or 7/485-6096), which has an English speaking staff and doctors, or **Hospital Pacífico,** calle Fraile y Nao #4 Fracc La Bocana, (☎ **7/487-7180** or 7/487-7161).

Internet Access   Cyber-café on Costera Miguel Alemán #93, in the Torres Gemelas building (☎ **7/484-7010** or 7/484-4828; ask for the cybercafe extension) is open daily from 10am until 8pm. The charge for 15 minutes online is just $1.

Parking   It is illegal to park on the Costera at any time.

Pharmacy   One of the largest drugstores in town is **Farmacia Daisy** (☎ 7/484-7664).

Post Office   The **central post office** (*correo*) is located next door to Sears, close to the Fideicomiso office. Other branches are located in the Estrella de Oro bus station on Cuauhtémoc, inland from the Acapulco Qualton Hotel, and on the Costera near Caleta Beach.

Safety   Riptides claim a few lives every year, so pay close attention to warning flags posted on Acapulco beaches. Red or black flags mean stay out of the water, yellow flags signify caution, and white or green flags mean it's safe to swim.

As is the case anywhere, tourists are vulnerable to thieves. This is especially true when shopping in a market, lying on the beach, wearing jewelry, or visibly carrying a camera, purse, or bulging wallet.

Telephone   Phone numbers seem to change frequently in Acapulco—the most reliable source for telephone numbers is the **Procuraduría del Turista** at ☎ **7/484-4583,** where the exceptionally friendly staff can help you locate what you need.

Tourist Police   If you see policemen in uniforms of white and light blue, they belong to a special corps of English-speaking police established to assist tourists.

2   Where to Stay

The listings below begin with the very expensive resorts south of town (nearest the airport) and continue along the famous main avenue, Costera Miguel Alemán, to the less-expensive, more traditional hotels north of town, in what is considered the downtown or "Old Acapulco" part of the city. Especially in the "very expensive" and "expensive" categories, inquire about promotional rates or check airlines to see what air and hotel packages are available. During Christmas and Easter weeks some hotels double their normal rates.

Private, ultra-secluded **villas** are available for rent all over the hills south of town; staying in one of these luxurious and palatial homes is an unforgettable Acapulco vacation experience.

SOUTH OF TOWN

Acapulco's most exclusive and renowned hotels, restaurants, and villas are nestled in the steep forested hillsides south of town, between the naval base and Puerto Marquéz. This area is several miles from the heart of Acapulco; a $12 to $20 round-trip taxi fare will be required every time you venture off the property into town.

VERY EXPENSIVE

✪ **Camino Real Acapulco Diamante.** km 14 Carretera Escénica, Baja Catita s/n, Pichilingue, 39867 Acapulco, Guerrero. ☎ **800/7-CAMINO** in the U.S. and Canada, or 7/466-1010. Fax 7/466-1111. www.caminoreal.com/acapulco. E-mail: aca@caminoreal.com. 157 units. A/C MINIBAR TV TEL. High season $250 double; $410 master suite (includes American breakfast). Ask about low-season and midweek discounts and "Mischief Club" for children. AE, MC, V.

This relaxing, self-contained resort is an ideal choice for families, or for those who already know Acapulco and don't care to explore much. I consider this to be one of Acapulco's finest places in terms of contemporary decor, services, and amenities. The Camimo Real is tucked in a secluded location on 81 acres; it's part of the enormous Acapulco Diamante project. I like its location on the clean and safe-for-swimming Playa Marquéz, but you do miss out on the compelling views of Acapulco Bay. From the Carretera Escénica, you wind down a handsome brick road to the site of the hotel, overlooking Puerto Marquéz Bay. The lobby has an enormous terrace facing the water. The spacious rooms have balconies or terraces, small sitting areas, marble floors, comfortable, classic furnishings, ceiling fans in addition to newly updated air conditioning with remote control, and a safe-deposit box in the closet.

Dining/Diversions: La Vela is a casual yet stylish outdoor seafood grill overlooking the bay. The semiformal **Cabo Diamante** features both Mexican and international food. The open-air lobby bar facing the bay is a great spot for evening cocktails. There's also excellent, 24-hour in-room dining, with prices in line with Acapulco restaurants—saving you the cab fare into town.

Amenities: Three pools including one for children, tennis court, beauty salon, and shopping arcade. The health club offers aerobics, spa treatments, massage, and complete workout equipment, available for an extra charge. Room and laundry service, travel agency, car rental.

✪ **Westin Las Brisas.** Apdo. Carretera Escénica 5255, Las Brisas, 39868 Acapulco, Guerrero. ☎ **800/228-3000** in the U.S., or 7/469-6900. Fax 7/484-6071. E-mail: lasbrisas@infosel.net.mx. 263 units. A/C MINIBAR. High season $385 share pool; $500 private pool, $630 Royal Beach Club. Low season $230 share pool, $345 private pool; $380 Royal Beach Club. $20 per day service charge extra (in lieu of all tips) plus 17% tax. Rates include continental breakfast. AE, DC, MC, V.

The Westin Las Brisas is a local landmark, and often considered Acapulco's finest hotel. Perched on a hillside overlooking the bay, Las Brisas is known for its tiered pink stucco facade, private pools, and 175 pink Jeeps rented exclusively to Las Brisas guests. If you stay here, you ought to like pink, because the color scheme extends to practically everything.

The hotel is a community unto itself: The simple, marble-floored rooms are like separate villas sculpted from a terraced hillside, with panoramic views of Acapulco bay from a balcony or terrace. Each room has a private (or semiprivate) swimming pool. Altogether, there are 250 swimming pools here. The spacious Regency Club rooms are located at the apex of the property and offer the best views. You stay at Las Brisas more for the panache and setting than for the amenities, though rooms have been

Acapulco, Queen of the Silver Screen

Along with hosting some of the legendary stars of the silver screen, Acapulco has also had a few starring roles herself. Over 250 films have been shot here, including 1985's *Rambo II*, which used the Pie de la Cuesta lagoon as its backdrop.

recently upgraded. TVs were just added last year in the Royal Beach rooms (local channels only) and Junior Suites (cable), but have strict volume control so as not to disturb other guests. Early each morning, continental breakfast arrives in a discreet cubbyhole, so your coffee is ready when you are. The mandatory service charges take care of the courtesy shuttle service from the hillside rooms to the lobby, and all other service tips. The hotel is located on the southern edge of the bay, overlooking the road to the airport and close to the hottest nightclubs in town.

Dining: Complimentary breakfast of fruit, rolls, and coffee served in each room daily. **Bella Vista** is the reservations-only (but open to the public) panoramic-view restaurant, open 6:30 to 10:30pm daily. **El Mexicano Restaurant,** on a terrace open to the stars, receives guests Saturday to Thursday evenings from 5 to 11pm. **La Concha Beach Club** offers seafood daily from 12:30 to 4:30pm. **The Deli Shop** is open from 11am to 7pm daily. All restaurants now offer no-smoking sections.

Amenities: Private or shared pools with each room, with fresh floating flowers daily; private La Concha Beach Club at the bottom of the hill, with both fresh- and salt-water pools (the hotel provides transportation); five tennis courts; pink Jeeps for rent. Concierge, travel agency, gas station, express checkout with advance notice, 24-hour shuttle transportation around the resort, laundry, dry cleaning, room service, newspaper delivery, beauty and barber shops, in-room massage service, shopping arcade, babysitters upon request, safe-deposit box, money exchange, car-rental desk, jogging track, walking paths, sauna, access to a nearby gym.

COSTERA HOTEL ZONE

The following hotels are all found along the main boulevard, Costera Alemán, extending from the Convention Center (Centro Internacional) in the east to Papagayo Park, just before reaching Old Acapulco. One of the most familiar images of Acapulco is that of the twinkling lights of these hotels stretching for miles along Acapulco Bay.

EXPENSIVE

Fiesta Americana Condesa Acapulco. Costera Miguel Alemán 97, 393690 Acapulco, Guerrero. ☎ **800/FIESTA1** in the U.S., or 7/484-2355. Fax 7/484-1828. www.fiestamericana.com. Email: nsalgado@fiestaamericana.com.mx. 500 units. A/C MINIBAR TV TEL. High season $112–$150 double;

$253 suite. Low season $93–$124 double; $253 suite. Ask about "Fiesta Break" packages, which include meals. AE, DC, MC, V.

Once the Condesa del Mar, the Fiesta Americana Condesa Acapulco is a long-standing favorite deluxe hotel. The 18-story structure towers above Condesa Beach, just east and up the hill from the Glorieta Diana. The recently remodeled, attractive, and very comfortable rooms have marble floors and a private terrace or balcony with ocean view. The more expensive rooms have the best bay views, and all have purified tap water. The location is great for enjoying the numerous beach activities, shopping, and more casual nightlife of Acapulco.

Dining/Diversions: La Trattoria restaurant serves Italian specialties in a casual atmosphere. There's also a coffee shop, pool-side restaurant, and lobby bar with live entertainment most nights. During high season, look for theme nights—including Tex-Mex, Caribbean, and Mexican Fiesta nights—that combine buffet dinners, drinks, and entertainment.

Amenities: The dramatic adults-only swimming pool is perched atop a hill with the land dropping off toward the bay, affording swimmers the finest pool view of Acapulco in the city. A smaller pool for children has a sundeck. Two wheelchair-accessible rooms, beauty shop, boutiques, pharmacy, laundry and room service, travel agency.

✪ **Hotel Elcano.** Costera Alemán 75, 39690 Acapulco, Guerrero. ☎ **800/ 972-2162** in the U.S., or 7/484-1950. Fax 7/484-2230. http://hotel-elcano. com. E-mail: elcano@hotel-elcano.com.mx. 180 units. A/C TV TEL. $132 studio and standard room; $155 junior suite; $213 master suite. Ask about promotional discounts. AE, DC, MC, V.

An Acapulco classic, the Elcano was gutted and remodeled a few years back, returning it to favored status. Its appeal is enhanced by its exceptional service and prime location near the convention center on a broad stretch of golden sand beach in the heart of the hotel zone. Rooms are bright and very comfortable, and feature classic navy-and-white tile accents, ample oceanfront balconies, tub/shower combinations, and ceiling fans in addition to the central air-conditioning. The very large junior suites, all located on corners, have two queen-size beds and huge closets. Studios are quite small, with king-size beds and small sinks outside the bathroom area. In the studios, a small portion of the TV armoire serves as a closet and there are no balconies, only full sliding doors open to let in the breeze. All rooms have purified tap water.

Dining: The informal **Bambuco** restaurant, by the pool and beach, is open from 2 to 11pm daily, and is a great place for fresh seafood with a beach view. The more formal **Victoria** specializes in Spanish cuisine, and is located on an outdoor terrace overlooking the pool and beach. It's open from 9am to 2pm daily during high season only. A third restaurant, overlooking the Costera, was under construction at press time, with plans for a Spanish cuisine menu. They also have 24-hour room service.

Amenities: One beachside pool, small workout room, gift shop, boutiques, travel agency, beauty shop, massages, video-game room, baby-sitting, newspaper delivery, and laundry service.

✪ **Hyatt Regency Acapulco.** Costera Miguel Alemán 1, 39869 Acapulco, Guerrero. ☎ **800/233-1234** in the U.S. and Canada, 01-800/005-0000 in Mexico, or 7/469-1234. Fax 7/484-3087. www.hyattacapulco.com.mx. E-mail: ggarcia@acabtu.com.mx. 645 units. A/C TV TEL. High season $165 double; $175 Regency Club; $250–$575 suite. Low season $140 double; $150 Regency Club; $225–$575 suite. AE, DC, MC, V.

The Hyatt is one of the most modern of Acapulco's hotels. Its lobby is a sophisticated oasis in this mainly dated city. Several years of remodeling and a multimillion-dollar face-lift have given it an edge even over pricier options, especially in amenities and common areas. Its free-form pool fronts a broad stretch of beautiful beach, one of the most inviting in Acapulco. The sleek lobby has an inviting sitting area/bar that hosts live music every evening. Room decor is stylish, with rich greens and deep blues. All rooms are large, with sizable balconies overlooking the pool and ocean, in addition to security boxes and purified tap water. Robes, hair dryers, and remote-control TVs are standard in deluxe rooms and the Regency Club. Regency Club guests receive complimentary continental breakfast and afternoon canapés, separate check-in and checkout, and a paperback-exchange library. Children are not allowed in Regency Club rooms. In addition, this hotel caters to a Jewish clientele, with a full-service kosher restaurant, on-premises synagogue, and a special Sabbath elevator.

Dining/Diversions: The **Zapata, Villa & Co. Cantina,** which features Mexican specialties and mariachi music; the landmark seafood-specialty restaurant, **El Pescador;** and the poolside **El Isleño,** featuring full kosher service from December through March. Vegetarian options are available at all three.

Amenities: Two large, shaded free-form pools, three outdoor tennis courts lit for night play, sundeck, laundry, dry cleaning, room service, in-room massage, concierge, newspaper delivery for Regency Club rooms, business center, conference room, babysitting, travel agency, car rental, direct-dial telephone, money exchange, express checkout, safe-deposit box in the lobby, shopping arcade, boutiques, beauty shop, children's programs, access to a nearby gym, car rental desk, tour desk. Synagogue services are held on the premises. Wheelchair access is available, and kitchenettes are options in a limited number of rooms for an extra charge.

Villa Vera Hotel & Racquet Club. Lomas del Mar 35, Fracc. Club Deportivo, Acapulco, 39693, Guerrero. ☎ **800/710-9300** inside Mexico or 7/484-0334, 7/484-0335. Fax 7/484-7479. E-mail: hotel_villavera_aca@clubregina.com. 69 rooms, including suites, villas and 2 houses. A/C MINIBAR TEL TV. High season $150 studio; $195–$250 double; $300–$400 suite; $365 villa; $865 Casa Teddy for 4 people; $1,095 Casa Julio for 6 people. AE, MC, V.

The legendary Villa Vera started off as a private home with adjacent villas serving as accommodations for houseguests. After a while it became a popular hangout for stars such as Liz Taylor, who married Mike Todd here. This hotel is also where Richard and Pat Nixon celebrated their 25th wedding anniversary and Elvis's film *Fun in Acapulco* was shot. Lana Turner even made it her home for 3 years.

Under new ownership by Starwood Hotels, Villa Vera has undergone significant renovations and upgrades in facilities that have transformed it into an exclusive boutique-style hotel. A new spa offers world-class services 7 days a week. Each room has been tastefully decorated in sophisticated light tones of white and off-white, with details in blue. A total of 14 pools include 8 private pools for the six villas and two houses. Most of the other rooms share pools, except for standard rooms, which have the use of the large public pool, located across from the restaurant. The hotel is a couple of blocks from the Condesa beach, and offers the closest experience to Acapulco villa life in a public property that you'll find.

Dining/Diversions: The **Palma Real** restaurant is open for breakfast, lunch, and dinner, and the pool bar serves drinks and cocktails from 7am to 10:30pm.

Amenities: There are two clay tennis courts, two lighted racquet ball courts, gymnasium, spa, boutique, pool, travel agency, car-rental desk, money exchange. Safe-deposit boxes are in each room.

MODERATE

Calinda Beach Acapulco. Costera Miguel Alemán 1260, 39300 Acapulco, Guerrero. ☎ **800/228-5151** in the U.S., or 7/484-0410. Fax 7/484-4676. E-mail: calinda@acnet.net. 357 units. A/C TV TEL. $110–$120 double. AE, DC, MC, V. Limited free parking.

You'll see this tall cylindrical tower rising at the eastern edge of Condesa Beach. Each room has a view, usually of the bay. Though not exceptionally furnished, the guest rooms are large and comfortable; most have two double beds. Package prices are available; otherwise the hotel is high-priced for what it provides. Three restaurants offer a choice of poolside snacks or informal indoor dining. The lobby-bar party gets going around 9pm and shuts down at 2am; there's a happy hour from 4 to 9pm when drinks are two-for-one, and live music or a show from 9pm to 1am. Laundry and room service, money exchange and a travel agency round out the services. There's also a swimming pool, concierge, safe deposit box, conference rooms, several lobby boutiques, a pharmacy, laundry, beauty shop, two wheelchair-accessible rooms, babysitting on request, and four no-smoking floors.

Hotel Sands. Costera Alemán 178, 39670 Acapulco, Guerrero. ☎ **7/484-2260.** Fax 7/484-1053. www.sands.com.mx. E-mail: sands@sands.com.mx. 93 units. A/C TV TEL. $55 double all year except Christmas, Easter, and other major Mexican holidays. AE, MC, V. Limited free parking.

This is a great option for budget-minded families. This unpretentious and comfortable hotel is nestled away on the inland side, opposite the giant resort hotels, away from the din of Costera traffic. From the street, you enter the hotel lobby through a stand of umbrella palms and a pretty garden restaurant. The rooms are light and airy in the style of a good modern motel, with basic furnishings and wall-to-wall carpeting. Some units have kitchenettes, and all have a terrace or balcony. There are two swimming pools (one for children), a squash court, and volleyball and Ping-Pong areas. Services include a concierge, laundry and dry cleaning, babysitting, and complimentary coffee service in the lobby. The rates here are more than reasonable, the accommodations satisfactory, and the location is excellent.

DOWNTOWN (ON LA QUEBRADA) & OLD ACAPULCO BEACHES

Numerous budget hotels dot the streets fanning out from the zócalo (Acapulco's official and original downtown). They're among the best values in Acapulco, but be sure to check your room first to see that it has the basic comforts you desire. Several in this area are found close to the beaches of Caleta and Caletilla, or on the back side of the hilly peninsula, at Playa La Angosta. These were the standards of luxury in the 1950s, and many have gorgeous views of the city and bay. Recent renovations are bringing this area back to its original charm.

MODERATE

○ **Grand Meigas Acapulco Resort.** Cerro San Martín 325, Fracc. Las Playas, Acapulco, Guerrero, 39390. ☎ **7/483-9940** or 7/483-9140. Fax 7/483-9125. E-mail: meigaca@pordigy.net.mx. 255 units. A/C FAN TV TEL. Low season $50–$80 per person, all inclusive; high season $120–$150 per person, all-inclusive. Room-only prices are sometimes available upon request. AE, DC, MC, V. Free private parking.

The Meigas is known more to Mexican travelers than to their U.S. counterparts. The values are excellent at this high quality, nine-floor resort, located adjacent to one of the liveliest beaches in old Acapulco. Stay here if you prefer the authentic feel of a Mexican holiday, with all its boisterous, family-friendly, and spirited charms. The Meigas is built into a cliff on the Caleta peninsula, overlooking the beach. The rooms surround a central plant-filled courtyard, topped by a glass ceiling. All rooms have large terraces with ocean views, although some lack separation from your neighbor's terrace. Recently remodeled, the rooms are very clean and comfortable, with a large closet, desk, and simple decor. Each room has two queen beds with firm mattresses, cable TV, and access to an elevator.

A succession of terraces are home to tropical gardens, three restaurants, various snack bars, and large freshwater and saltwater pools. A private beach and boat dock are located down a brief flight of stairs. As is traditional in all-inclusive resorts, meals and drinks are available at almost any hour, and the resort has a changing agenda of theme nights and evening entertainment.

Plaza Las Glorias/El Mirador. Quebrada 74, Acapulco, 39300 Guerrero. ☎ **800/342-AMIGO** in the U.S., or 7/483-1221, reservations: 7/484-0909. Fax 7/482-4564. 132 units. A/C TV TEL. High season $120 double; Low season $98 double. Suites with whirlpool $140. An extra charge of $10 applies to use the kitchenette. AE, MC, V. Parking on street.

One of the landmarks of "Old Acapulco," the former El Mirador Hotel overlooks the famous cove where the cliff divers perform. Renovated with tropical landscaping and lots of handsome Mexican tile, this romantic hotel offers attractively furnished rooms with double or queen-size beds, a small kitchenette area with minifridge and coffee makers, and large bathrooms with marble counters. Most have separate living-room areas, some have whirlpool tubs, and all are accented with colorful Saltillo tile and other Mexican decorative touches. Ask for a room with a balcony (there are 42) and ocean view (95).

The evening set-price dinner ($27) offers great views of the cliff-diving show, and there's also a diner-style coffee shop. The large and breezy lobby bar is a favorite spot to relax as day fades into night on the beautiful cove and bay. There are three pools, including one saltwater pool reached via mountainside elevator, a protected cove with good snorkeling, room service for breakfast and lunch, laundry service, and a travel agency.

Inexpensive

Hotel Costa Linda. Costera Miguel Alemán 1008, Acapulco, Guerrero, 39390. ☎ **7/482-5277** or 7/482-2549. Fax 7/483-4017. 45 units. A/C MINIBAR TV TEL. High season $60 double; Low season $35 double. 2 children under 8 free. MC, V. Free parking.

Budget-minded American and Mexican couples are drawn to the clean, sunny, and well-kept rooms of the Costa Linda, one of the best values in the area. All rooms have individually controlled air-conditioning and a minifridge, and some have a small kitchenette (during low season there is a $5 extra charge for using the kitchenette). Both the closets and bathrooms are ample in size, and mattresses are firm. The hotel has a small pool surrounded by lounges and tropical plants, a tennis court, and a restaurant/bar. Cozy as the Costa Linda is, it is situated adjacent to one of the busier streets in old Acapulco, so traffic noise can be bothersome. It's just a short 1-block walk down to lively Caleta beach.

✪ **Hotel Los Flamingos.** López Matéos s/n, Fracc. Las Playas, Acapulco, Guerrero. ☎ **7/482-0690.** Fax 7/483-9806. 40 rooms. FAN. High season $65 double, $85 with A/C; $100 junior suite. Low season $52 double, $68 with A/C, $80 junior suite. AE, MC, V.

An Acapulco landmark, this hotel perched on a cliff 500 feet above Acapulco Bay was frequently visited by John Wayne—he liked it so much that at one point he owned it. The place is a real find—it's in excellent shape and very clean, and offers visitors a totally different perspective of Acapulco, as it maintains all the charm of a grand era gone by. Photos of movie stars grace the lobby, especially those of Wayne, Cary Grant, and Johnny Weissmuller— who was also an owner, and constructed the large "Tarzan Suite" as his part-time residence. All rooms have dramatic ocean views with either a balcony or terrace but most of them are not air-conditioned, but the constant seabreeze is cooling enough. Rooms that have air-conditioning also have TVs. Rooms are colorful, with mosaic tile-tables and mirrors, and brightly painted walls. It also has a pool, restaurant, and bar. Thursdays at Los Flamingos are especially popular, with a weekly pozole party, accompanied by live music, played by a classic Mexican combo that was probably around in the era of Wayne and Weissmuller—note the pink bass. Even if you don't stay here, plan to come for a margarita at sunset, and a walk along their lookout point.

Hotel Misión. Felipe Valle 12, 39300 Acapulco, Guerrero. ☎ **7/482-3643.** Fax 7/482-2076. 27 units. $40 double. No credit cards.

Enter this hotel's plant-filled brick courtyard, shaded by two enormous mango trees, and you'll retreat into an earlier, more peaceful Acapulco. This tranquil 19th-century hotel lies 2 blocks inland from the Costera and the zócalo. The original L-shaped building is at least a century old. The rooms have colonial touches, such as colorful tile and wrought iron, and come simply furnished, with a fan and one or two beds with good mattresses. Unfortunately, the promised hot water is not reliable—request a cold-water only room and receive a discount. Breakfast is served on the patio. The hotel is located 2 blocks inland from the fishermen's wharf, main square, and la Quebrada.

Hotel Villa Romana. Av. López Matéos 185, Fracc. Las Playas, 39300 Acapulco, Guerrero. ☎ **7/482-3995.** 9 units. A/C TV. High season $40 double. Low season $35 double. MC, V. Parking on street.

This is one of the most comfortable inns in the area for a long stay. Some rooms are tiled and others carpeted; nine have small kitchens with refrigerators. Terraces face Playa la Angosta. There is a small plant-filled terrace on the second floor with tables and chairs and a fourth-floor pool with a great view of the bay.

3 Where to Dine

Diners in Acapulco enjoy stunning views and fresh seafood. The quintessential experience is being seated at a candlelit table with the glittering bay spread out before you. If it's a romantic place you're looking for, Acapulco fairly brims over with such inviting places, most located along the southern coast, with views of the bay. If, however, you're looking for simple, good food, or an authentic local dining experience, you're best off in Old Acapulco.

A deluxe establishment in Acapulco may not be much more expensive than a mass-market restaurant. The proliferation of U.S. franchise restaurants (Subway, Shakey's Pizza, Tony Roma's) has increased competition in Acapulco, and even the more expensive places have reduced prices in response. Trust me—the locally owned restaurants offer both the best food and best value.

SOUTH OF TOWN: LAS BRISAS AREA
VERY EXPENSIVE

Casa Nova. Carretera Escénica 5256. ☎ **7/484-6815/19.** Reservations required. Main courses $12–$22. Fixed-price 4-course meal $30. AE, MC, V. Mon–Fri 7–11pm, Sat–Sun 7–11:30pm. GOURMET ITALIAN.

Enjoy an elegant meal and a fabulous view of glittering Acapulco Bay at this spot east of town on the scenic highway before the Las Brisas hotel. The restaurant is set in a cliff, and offers several elegantly appointed dining rooms awash in marble and stone accents, or outdoor terrace dining with a stunning view. If you arrive before your table is ready, have a drink in the comfortable lounge. This is a long-standing favorite of Mexico City's elite; dress tends toward fashionable tropical attire. The best dishes include veal scaloppini and homemade pastas, such as linguini with fresh clams. A changing "tourist menu" offers a sampling of the best selections for a fixed price. There's also an ample selection of reasonably priced national and imported wines. And there's live piano music nightly.

Mezzanotte Acapulco. Plaza La Vista, Carretera Escénica a Puerto Marquez 28-1, 39880 Acapulco, Guerrero. ☎ **7/484-7874,** 7/446-5727 or 7/446-5728. Reservations required. Main courses $20–$30. AE, MC, V. Daily 6:30pm–midnight. Closed Sun during the low season. ITALIAN/FRENCH/MEXICAN.

Acapulco's current hot spot, the Mezzanotte offers a contemporary blending of classic cuisines. Until recently, this place housed the stuffily formal Miramar, but it has turned upscale and chic while relaxing the atmosphere a bit. The view of the bay remains

Dining with a View

Restaurants with unparalleled views of Acapulco include **Madeiras, Spicey, Mezzanotte,** and **Casa Nova** in the Las Brisas area; **El Olvido** along the Costera; **Su Casa** on a hill above the Convention Center; and the **Bella Vista Restaurant** (now open to the public) at the Las Brisas hotel.

outstanding, though the food still strives for consistency. Dress up a bit for dining here. Mezzanotte is in the La Vista complex near the Las Brisas hotel.

✪ **Spicey.** Carretera Escénica. ☎ **7/446-6003** or 7/446-5991. Reservations recommended on weekends. Main courses $15–$30. AE, CB, DC, MC, V. Daily 7–11:30pm. Valet parking available. CREATIVE CUISINE.

For original food with flair, you can't beat this restaurant in the Las Brisas area, next to Kookaburas. Once considered trendy, it's become a contemporary classic. Diners can enjoy the air-conditioned indoor dining room or the completely open rooftop terrace with a sweeping view of the bay. To begin, try the shrimp Spicey, in a fresh coconut batter with an orange-marmalade-and-mustard sauce. Among the main courses, the grilled veal chop in pineapple and papaya chutney is a winner, as is the beef tenderloin, prepared Thai- or Santa Fe-style, or blackened. The chiles rellenos in mango sauce win raves. There's also an exceptional selection of premium tequilas for sipping. Attire is on the dressy side of casual.

COSTERA HOTEL ZONE
Very Expensive

El Olvido. Diana Circle, Plaza Marbella. ☎ **7/481-0203,** 7/481-0256, 7/481-0214, or 7/481-0240. Reservations recommended. Main courses $11–$29. AE, DC, MC, V. Daily 6pm–2am. NUEVA COCINA.

Once in the door of this handsome terrace restaurant, you'll almost forget that it's tucked in a shopping mall. It gives you all the glittering bay-view ambiance of the posh Las Brisas restaurants without the taxi ride. The menu is one of the most sophisticated in the city. It's expensive, but each dish is delightful in both presentation and taste. Start with one of the 12 house-specialty drinks such as Olvido, made with tequila, rum, Cointreau, tomato juice, and lime juice. Soups include a delicious cold melon and a thick black-bean and sausage. Among the innovative entrees are quail with honey and pasilla chiles and thick sea bass with a mild sauce of cilantro and avocado. For dessert try the chocolate fondue or the *guanabana* (a tropical fruit) mousse in a rich *zapote negro* (black-colored tropical fruit) sauce. El Olvido is in the same shopping center as La Petite Belgique (see below), fronting Diana Circle. Walk into the passage to the left of Aca-Joe and bear left; it's at the back.

○ **La Petite Belgique.** Diana Circle, Plaza Marbella. ☎ **7/484-7725.** Fax 7/484-0776. Reservations recommended. Main courses $5.50–$15. AE, MC, V. Daily 5pm–midnight (or until the last customer is satisfied). SEAFOOD, NORTHERN EUROPEAN.

An intimate and exceptional restaurant known principally to locals, La Petite Belgique is noted more for its food than its ambiance. Although the old-styled dining room overlooks Acapulco Bay, the view is dominated by an adjacent parking lot. But never mind that—your attention will be focused on the plates in front of you. The European owner was a former food and beverage director for a premier hotel chain, but chose to settle in Acapulco years ago and devote his talents to his own restaurant; we're the luckier for it. Although the menu boasts an impressive selection of pâtés, continental classics, and fresh fish, I'm hooked on their mussels, flown in fresh daily from a mussel farm in Baja, California, also owned by the proprietor. The huge pot of perfectly steamed mussels I enjoyed here could possibly be one of my top five dining experiences of my life. Great espresso drinks, cordials, and sumptuous sweets—there's a full French bakery on site—provide a fitting close to a truly special dinner. The restaurant is in the shopping center fronted by the Aca-Joe clothing store on Diana Circle. Walk into the passage to the left of Aca-Joe; it's at the back.

Su Casa/La Margarita. Av. Anahuac 110. ☎ **7/484-4350** or 7/484-1261. Fax 7/484-0803. Reservations recommended. Main courses $8–$18. MC, V. Daily 6pm–midnight. INTERNATIONAL.

Relaxed elegance and terrific food at moderate prices are what you get at Su Casa. Owners Shelly and Ángel Herrera created this pleasant and breezy open-air restaurant on the patio of their hillside home overlooking the city. Both are experts in the kitchen and stay on hand nightly to greet guests on the patio. The menu changes often, so each time you go there's something new to try. Some items are standard, such as shrimp a la patrona in garlic; grilled fish, steak, and chicken; and flaming *fillet al Madrazo,* a delightful brochette first marinated in tropical juices. Most entrees come with garnishes of cooked banana or pineapple. The margaritas are big and delicious. Su Casa is the hot-pink building on the hillside above the Convention Center.

MODERATE

El Cabrito. Costera M. Alemán 1480. ☎ **7/484-7711.** Main courses $2–$8. AE, MC, V. Mon–Sat 2pm–1am, Sun 2–11pm. NORTHERN MEXICAN.

With its hacienda-inspired entrance, waitresses in white dresses with charro-styled neckties, and location in the heart of the Costera, this restaurant targets the tourists. But its authentic and well-prepared specialties attract Mexicans in the know—a comforting stamp of approval. Among its specialties are *cabrito al pastor* (roasted goat), charro beans, and Oaxaca-style molé. It's on the ocean side of the Costera, south of the Convention Center.

INEXPENSIVE

✪ **Ika Tako.** Costera M. Aleman 99. No phone. Main courses $2.50–$5. No credit cards. Daily 6pm–5am. SEAFOOD TACOS.

Very simply, this is my favorite place to eat in Acapulco, and I never miss it. Perhaps I have simple tastes, but these fresh fish, shrimp, and seafood tacos served in combinations that include grilled pineapple, fresh spinach, grated cheese, garlic, and bacon are so tasty they're addicting. Unlike most inexpensive places to eat, the setting here is also lovely, with its handful of tables overlooking tropical trees and the bay below. The lighting may be bright, the atmosphere occasionally hectic, and the service dependably slow, but the tacos are delectable. You can also get beer, wine, soft drinks, and a dessert of the day. This restaurant is located along the Costera, next to Beto's lobster restaurant. A second branch of Ika Taco is located across from the Hyatt Regency hotel.

DOWNTOWN: THE ZÓCALO AREA

The old downtown area of Acapulco is loaded with simple, inexpensive restaurants serving up tasty eats. It's easy to pay more elsewhere in Acapulco and not get such consistently good food as what you'll find in this part of town. To explore this area, start right at the zócalo and stroll west along Juárez. After about 3 blocks you'll come to Azueta, lined with small seafood cafes and street-side stands.

MODERATE

✪ **El Amigo Miguel.** Juárez 31, at Azueta. ☎ **7/483-6981.** Main courses $2.70–$10. AE, MC, V. Daily 10am–11pm. MEXICAN/SEAFOOD.

Locals know that El Amigo Miguel is a standout among downtown seafood restaurants—you can easily pay more but not eat

If There's Pozole, It Must Be Thursday

If you're visiting Acapulco on a Thursday, indulge in the local cus-tom of eating *pozole,* a bowl of white hominy and meat in a broth, garnished with sliced radishes, shredded lettuce, onions, oregano, and lime. The truly traditional version is served with pork, but a newer chicken version has also become a standard. You can also find green pozole, which is made by adding a paste of roasted pumpkin seeds to the traditional pozole base; this gives the broth a green color.

better elsewhere. Impeccably fresh seafood reigns here; the large open-air dining room, 3 blocks west of the zócalo, is usually brimming with seafood lovers. When it overflows, head to a sec-ond branch with the exact same menu, across the street. Try the delicious *camarones borrachos* (drunken shrimp) in a sauce made with beer, applesauce, ketchup, mustard, and bits of fresh bacon—its whole tastes nothing like the individual ingredients. The *filete Miguel* is red-snapper fillet stuffed with seafood and covered in a wonderful chipotle-pepper sauce. Grilled shrimp with garlic and whole red snapper (*mojo de ajo*) is served at its classic best.

Mariscos Pipo. Almirante Breton 3. ☎ **7/482-2237.** Main courses $2–$25. AE, MC, V. Daily noon–8pm. SEAFOOD.

Check out the photographs of Old Acapulco on the walls while relaxing in this airy dining room, decorated with hanging nets, fish, glass buoys, and shell lanterns. The English-language menu lists a wide array of seafood, including ceviche, lobster, octopus, crayfish, and baby-shark quesadillas. This local favorite is 2 blocks west of the zócalo on Breton, just off the Costera. Another branch, open daily from 1 to 9:30pm, is at Costera M. Alemán and Canadá (☎ 7/484-0165).

INEXPENSIVE

Mi Parri Pollo. Jesus Carranza 2B, Zocalo. ☎ **7/483-7427.** Breakfast $1.50–$2.50; sandwiches $1–$2; fresh-fruit drinks $1.25; daily specials $2–$4. No credit cards. Daily 7am–11pm. MEXICAN/INTERNATIONAL.

This little restaurant has umbrella-covered tables on one of the coolest and shadiest sections of the zócalo. It's especially popular for breakfast, with specials that include a great fresh-fruit salad with mango, pineapple, and cantaloupe, and coffee refills. Other specials include fish burgers, tortas, a special rotisserie-grilled chicken, and steak milanesa. Fruit drinks, including fresh mango juice, come in schooner-size glasses. To find the restaurant, enter the zócalo from the Costera and walk toward the kiosk. On the right, about midway into the zócalo, you'll see a wide, shady passageway that leads onto avenida Jesus Carranza and the umbrella-covered tables under the shady tree.

4 Activities on & off the Beach

Acapulco is known for its great beaches and water sports, and, sadly, few visitors bother to explore its traditional downtown area. But it's worth a trip there, to the shady **zócalo** (also called Plaza Álvarez), to experience a true glimpse of local life and color. Inexpensive cafes and shops border the plaza, and at its far north end is the **cathedral Nuestra Señora de la Soledad**—with its blue, onion-shaped domes and Byzantine towers. Though reminiscent of a Russian Orthodox church, it was originally (and perhaps appropriately) built as a movie set, then later adapted to be the house of worship. From the church, turn east along the side street going off at a right angle (calle Carranza, which doesn't have a marker) to find an arcade with newsstands and more shops. The hill behind the cathedral provides an unparalleled view of Acapulco. Take a taxi up to the top of the hill from the main plaza, and follow the signs leading to **El Mirador** (lookout point).

City tours, day-trips to Taxco, cruises, and other excursions and activities are offered through local travel agencies. Taxco is about a three-hour drive inland from Acapulco (see chapter 5 for more information).

THE BEACHES

Here's the rundown, from west to east around the bay. **Playa la Angosta** is a small, sheltered, and often deserted cove just around the bend from **La Quebrada** (where the cliff divers perform).

South of downtown on the Peninsula de las Playas lie the beaches **Caleta** and **Caletilla.** They're separated by a small outcropping of land that contains the new aquarium and water park, **Mágico Mundo Marino** (open daily, 9am to 7pm). You'll find thatched-roofed restaurants, water-sports equipment for rent, and brightly painted boats that ferry passengers to **Roqueta Island.** You can rent beach chairs and umbrellas for the day. Mexican families favor these beaches because they're close to several

A Masterpiece of a House

Acapulco is as well known for its exclusive villas as its nightlife, but one house in particular stands out. Though not as elegantly impressive as the villas of Las Brisas, the **home of Dolores Olmedo,** in Acapulco's traditional downtown area, is a veritable work of art. In 1956, the renowned Mexican artist Diego Rivera covered its outside wall with a mural of colorful mosaic tiles, shells, and stones. The work is unique, and one of the last he created.

Rivera is considered one of Mexico's greatest artists, and is credited with being one of the founders of the 20th century Mexican muralist movement. The Olmeda mural, which took him 18 months to complete, features Aztec deities such as Quetzacoatl and Tepezcuincle, the Aztec dog. Rivera and Olmeda were lifelong friends, and Rivera once asked Olmeda to marry him but she refused. He lived in this house for the last 2 years of his life, during which time he also covered the interior with murals. However, since this home is not a museum, you'll have to settle for enjoying the masterpiece of its exterior.

The house is located a few blocks behind the Casablanca Hotel, a short cab ride from the central plaza, at #6 Calle Cerro de la Pinzona. Have the driver wait while you look around, as there's not much traffic, and it's a steep climb back to the plaza.

inexpensive hotels. In the late afternoon, fishermen pull their color-ful boats up on the sand; you can buy the fresh catch of the day and, occasionally, oysters on the half shell.

Pleasure boats dock at **Playa Manzanillo,** just south of the zócalo. Charter fishing trips sail from here. In the old days, the downtown beaches—Manzanillo, Honda, Caleta, and Caletilla—were the focal point of Acapulco. Today the beaches and the resort developments stretch along the four-mile length of the shore.

East of the zócalo, the major beaches are **Hornos** (near Papa-gayo Park), **Hornitos, Condesa,** and **Icacos,** followed by the naval base (La Base) and **Punta del Guitarrón.** After Punta del Guitarrón, the road climbs to the legendary Las Brisas hotel (see above), where many of the 300 *casitas* (bungalow-type rooms) have their own swimming pools (the hotel has a total of 250

To Swim or Not to Swim in the Bay?

In the past decade, the city has gone to great lengths (and great expense) to clean up the waters off Acapulco. Nevertheless, this is an industrial port that was once heavily polluted, so many choose to stick to the hotel pool for a refreshing dip. You may also notice the fleet of more than 20 power-sweeper boats that skim the top of the bay each morning to remove debris and oil film.

Among the bay beaches that remain popular with visitors and locals alike are **Las Caletas** and **Playa Puerto Marqués.**

---

pools). Past Las Brisas, the road continues to the small, clean, and separate bay of Puerto Marqués, followed by **Punta Diamante,** about 12 miles from the zócalo. The fabulous Acapulco Princess, the new Quinta Real, and the Pierre Marqués hotels dominate the landscape here, which fronts the open Pacific.

Playa Marqués, located in the bay of Puerto Marqués, is an attractive area for swimming. The water is calm and the bay sheltered. Water-skiing can also be arranged. Past the bay lie **Revolcadero Beach** and a fascinating jungle lagoon.

Other beaches are found further north, and are best reached by car, though buses also make the trip. **Pie de la Cuesta** is 8 miles west of town (buses that regularly run along the Costera leave every 5 or 10 min.; a taxi will cost about $18). The water is too rough to swim here, but it's a great spot for checking out big waves and the spectacular sunset, especially over *coco locos* (drinks served in a fresh coconut with the top whacked off) at one of the rustic beachfront restaurants hung with hammocks.

If driving, continue west along the peninsula, passing **Coyuca Lagoon** on your right, until you have almost reached the small air base at the tip. Along the way, you'll be invited to park near different sections of beach by various private entrepreneurs, mostly young boys. You'll also find colectivo boat tours of the lagoon offered for about $8.

BAY CRUISES & ROQUETA ISLAND

A boat deck rocking gently in the ocean is a great spot for viewing the entire bay, and Acapulco has virtually every kind of boat to choose from—yachts, catamarans, and trimarans, single- and double-decker. Cruises run morning, afternoon, and evening.

Tide Warning

Each year in Acapulco at least one or two unwary swimmers drown because of deadly riptides and undertow (see "Safety" in "Fast Facts," above). Swim only in Acapulco Bay or Puerto Marqués Bay—but be careful of the undertow no matter where you go.

Some offer buffets, open bars, and live music; others just snacks, drinks, and taped music. Prices range from $20 to $50. Cruise operators come and go, and their phone numbers change so frequently from year to year that it's pointless to list them here; to find out what cruises are currently operated, contact any Acapulco travel agency or your hotel's tour desk and ask for brochures or recommendations.

Having said that, there is still one cruise that stands out—it's the **Aca Tiki** (☎ 7/484-6140 or 7/484-6786), with its heart-shaped strand of red lights visible from the boat's tall masts. The moonlight cruise, known as the "love boat," has live music, dancing, snacks, and open bar each evening from 10:30pm to 1am. Aca Tiki also offers sunset cruises, with departure times depending upon the time of sunset. Both cruises leave from the *malecon* across from the central plaza downtown and each costs $15.

Boats from Caletilla Beach to **Roqueta Island**—a good place to snorkel, sunbathe, hike to a lighthouse, visit a small zoo, or have lunch—leave every fifteen minutes from 7am until the last one returns at 7pm. There are also glass-bottom boats that circle the bay as you look down at a few fish, until a diver swims down to a statue of the Virgin of Guadalupe, patron saint of Mexico. You can purchase tickets (which cost approximately $3) directly from any boat that's loading or at a discount from the **information booth** on Caletilla Beach (☎ 7/482-2389).

WATER SPORTS & BOAT RENTALS

An hour of **waterskiing** can cost as little as $35 or as much as $65. Caletilla Beach, Puerto Marqués Bay, and Coyuca Lagoon have waterskiing facilities. There's also the **Club de Esquis** located at Costera Alemán no. 100 (☎ 7/482-2034); it charges $40 per hour.

Scuba diving costs $30 for $1\frac{1}{2}$ hours of instruction if you book directly with the instructor on Caleta Beach. It costs $35 to

$45 if you make arrangements through a hotel or travel agency. Dive trips start around $30 per person for one dive.

Boat rentals are least expensive on Caletilla Beach, where an information booth rents inner tubes, small boats, canoes, paddle-boats, and beach chairs. It can also arrange waterskiing and scuba diving (see "Bay Cruises & Roqueta Island," above).

For **deep-sea fishing** excursions, go to the pale-pink building of the boat cooperative opposite the zócalo, or book a day in advance (☎ 7/482-1099). Charter fishing trips run from $150 to $200 for six hours, tackle and bait included. Credit cards aren't accepted and ice, drinks, and lunch are extra. The fishing license is $9. The boats leave at 8am and return at 3pm. If you book through a travel agent or hotel, fishing trips start around $200 to $280 for four people. Fishing license, food, and drinks are extra.

Parasailing, though not free from risk (the occasional thrill-seeker has collided with a palm tree or even a building), can be brilliant. The pleasure of floating high over the bay hanging from a parachute towed by a motorboat costs about $35. Most of these rides operate on Condesa Beach, but they also can be found independently operating on the beach in front of most hotels along the Costera.

OTHER OUTDOOR ACTIVITIES

A round of 18 holes of **golf** at the Acapulco Princess Hotel (☎ 7/469-1000) is $63 for guests and $84 for nonguests; American Express, Visa, and MasterCard are accepted. Tee-times begin at 7:35am, and reservations should be made 1 day in advance. Club rental is $21. At the **Club de Golf Acapulco,** off the Costera next to the Convention Center (☎ 7/484-0781), you can play 9 holes for $45 and 18 holes for $55, with equipment renting for $12.

Tennis at one of the tennis clubs open to the public goes for about $11 an hour. One option is the **Club de Golf Acapulco** (☎ 7/484-0781), open daily from 7am to 9pm. Outdoor courts cost $15 during the day and $22 per hour at night; the indoor courts costs $25. Rackets rent for $4 and a set of balls for $2. Many of the hotels along the Costera have tennis facilities for their guests.

You can go **horseback riding** along the beach. Independent operators stroll the Hotel Zone beachfront offering rides for about $20 to $40, for one to two hours. Horses for riding are also commonly found on the beach in front of the Acapulco Princess Hotel. There is no phone; you have to go directly to one of the beaches to make arrangements.

Traditionally called Fiesta Brava, **bullfights** are held during Acapulco's winter season at a ring up the hill from Caletilla Beach. Tickets purchased through travel agencies cost around $35 and usually include transportation to and from your hotel. The festivities begin at 5:30pm each Sunday from December to March.

MUSEUMS & WATER PARKS

The original **Fuerte de San Diego,** Costera Alemán, east of the zócalo, was built in 1616 to protect the town from pirate attacks. At that time, the port reaped considerable wealth from trade with the Philippine Islands (which, like Mexico, were part of the Spanish empire). The fort you see today was rebuilt after extensive earthquake damage in 1776. The structure houses the **Museo Histórico de Acapulco (Acapulco Historical Museum),** with exhibits that tell the story of Acapulco from its role as a port in the conquest of the Americas to a center for local Catholic conversion campaigns and for exotic trade with the Orient. Other exhibits chronicle Acapulco's pre-Hispanic past, the coming of the conquistadors (complete with Spanish armor), and the subsequent Spanish imperial activity. Temporary shows are also held here.

To reach the fort, follow Costera Alemán past old Acapulco and the zócalo; the fort is on a hill on the right. The museum is open Tuesday to Sunday from 10am to 5pm, but the best time to go is in the morning, since the air-conditioning is minimal. The $1.60 admission is waived on Sunday.

The **Centro Internacional de Convivencia Infantil (CICI),** Costera Alemán, at Colón (☎ 7/484-8033), is a sea-life and water park east of the Convention Center. It has swimming pools with waves, water slides, and water toboggans. The park is open daily from 10am to 6pm. There are **dolphin shows** at noon, 2:30, and 5pm (in Spanish), and there's also a dolphin swim program, which includes 30 minutes of introduction and 30 minutes of swim time. Minimum age is 6 years. Amenities include a cafeteria and rest rooms. General admission is $5; children under 2 are admitted free.

Death-Defying Divers

High divers perform at La Quebrada each day at 12:30, 7:15, 8:15, 9:15, and 10:15pm for a $1 admission. From a spot-lighted ledge on the cliffs, divers (holding torches for the final performance) plunge into the roaring surf 130 feet below—after wisely praying at a small shrine nearby. To the applause of the crowd, divers climb up the rocks and accept congratulations and gifts of money from onlookers.

Great views are available in the public areas, but arrive early, as all performances quickly fill up. Another option is to watch from the lobby bar and restaurant terraces of the **Hotel Plaza Las Glorias/El Mirador.** At the bar you'll have to pay a $9.50 cover charge, which includes two drinks. You could get around the cover by having dinner at the hotel's **La Perla restaurant.** Dinner is $27. Reservations (☎ 7/483-1155) are recommended during the high season.

5 Shopping

Acapulco is not among the best places to buy Mexican crafts, but it does have a few interesting shops. The best are the **Mercado Parazal** (often called the Mercado de Artesanías) on calle Velázquez de León near Cinco de Mayo in the downtown zócalo area (when you see Sanborn's, turn right and walk behind it for several blocks; ask directions if you need to). Here you'll find stall after covered stall of curios from around the country, including silver, embroidered cotton clothing, rugs, pottery, and papier-mâché. As they wait for patrons, artists paint ceramics with village folk scenes. The market is a pleasant place to spend a morning or afternoon.

The shopkeepers here aren't pushy, but they'll test your bargaining mettle. The starting price will be steep, and dragging the price down may take more time than you have. As always, acting uninterested often brings down prices in a hurry. Before buying silver, examine it carefully and looked for ".925" stamped on the back (this supposedly signifies that the silver is 92.5% pure, but often, the less expensive silver metal called "alpaca" will also have this stamped on it). The market is open daily from 9am to 6pm.

For a well-known department store with fixed prices, try **Arte-sanías Finas de Acapulco** (☎ 7/484-8039), called AFA-ACA for short. Tour guides bring their groups to this mammoth air-conditioned place. Merchandise includes a mix of mass-produced, tacky junk, along with some fairly good folk art among the clothes, marble-top furniture, saddles, luggage, jewelry, pottery, papier-mâché, and more. The store is open Monday through Saturday from 9am to 6pm and Sunday from 9am to 2pm. To find it, go east on the Costera until you see the Hotel Romano Days Inn on the seaward side. Then take avenida Horacio Nelson, across the street, and on the right, half a block up, you'll see AFA-ACA. **Sanborn's,** another good department store, offers an array of staples, including cosmetics, drugstore, electronics, music, clothing, books, and magazines.

The Costera Alemán is crowded with boutiques selling resort wear. These stores have ample attractive summer clothing at prices lower than what you generally pay in the United States. If there's a sale, you can find incredible bargains. One of the nicest air-conditioned shopping centers on the Costera is **Plaza Bahía,** Costera M. Alemán 125 (☎ 7/485-6939 or 7/485-6992), which has four stories of shops, movie theaters, a bowling alley, and small fast-food restaurants. The center is located just west of the Costa Club Hotel. The bowling alley, **Bol Bahía** (☎ 7/485-0970 or 7/485-6446) is open Monday to Saturday from 12pm to 1:30am, Sundays from 10am to 12am. Another popular shopping strip is the **Plaza Condessa,** adjacent to the Fiesta Americana Condessa, with shops that include Guess, Izod, and Bronce Swimwear. **Olvida Plaza,** near the restaurant of the same name, has Tommy Hilfiger and Aca-Joe.

6 Acapulco After Dark

SPECIAL ATTRACTIONS

The **"Gran Noche Mexicana,"** combines a performance by the Acapulco Ballet Folklórico with one by Los Voladores from Papantla. It's held in the plaza of the Convention Center every Monday, Wednesday, and Friday night at 7pm. With dinner and open bar, the show costs $40; general admission (including three drinks) is $25. Call for reservations (☎ 7/484-7046) or consult a local travel agency. Many major hotels also host Mexican fiestas and other theme nights that include dinner and entertainment. Local travel agencies will have information.

NIGHTCLUBS & DISCOS

Acapulco is even more famous for its nightclubs than for its beaches. Because clubs are always opening and closing, it's extremely difficult to give specific and accurate recommendations. But some general tips will help. Every club seems to have a cover charge of around $20 in high season and $10 in low season; drinks can cost anywhere from $3 to $10. Women can count on paying less, or entering for free. Don't even think about going out to one of the hillside discos before 11pm, and don't expect much action until after midnight. But it will keep going until 4 to 5am.

Many discos periodically waive their cover charge or offer some other promotion to attract customers. Another popular option is to have a higher cover charge but an open bar. Look for promotional materials displayed in hotel reception areas, at travel desks or concierge booths, and in local publications. You'll also be hit up with promotions for nightclubs as you take in the sun at the local beaches.

The high-rise hotels have their own bars, and sometimes discos. Informal lobby or poolside cocktail bars often offer free live entertainment.

THE BEACH BAR ZONE   Prefer a little fresh air with your nightlife? The young and hip crowd is favoring the growing number of open-air oceanfront dance clubs along Costera Alemán, most featuring techno or alternative rock. There's a concentration of them between the Fiesta Americana and Continental Plaza hotels. These clubs are an earlier and more casual option to the glitzy discos, and include the jamming **Disco Beach, El Sombrero** (you'll know it when you see it), **Tabu,** and the pirate-themed **Barbaroja.** These mainly offer open bar with cover charge (around $10) options. Women frequently drink for free with a lesser charge. Men may pay more, but then, this is where the young and tanned beach babes are. And if you are brave enough, a new bungee jump has recently opened in the midst of the beach bar zone.

Shorts Short

When the managers of local discos say no shorts, they mean no shorts for men; they welcome (no doubt encourage) them for women.

Alebrijes. Costera M. Alemán #3308 (across the street from the Hyatt Regency Acapulco). ☎ **7/484-5902.** Cover (including open bar) for women $5–$19, for men $5–$25. On Mon the open bar is for Tequila drinks only.

Formerly called "The News," this high-tech club boasts an exterior of reflection pools, gardens, and flaming torches. Inside, booths and round tables that can seat up to 1,200 surround the vast dance floor—the disco doubles as a venue for concerts and live performances by some of Mexico's most notable singers. Dress code states no shorts, T-shirts, tennis shoes, sandals, or jeans. It's open nightly from 11pm to 5am.

Baby-0. Costera Alemán. ☎ **7/484-7474.** Cover for women, $5–$10; for men, $10–$15, includes 2 national drinks.

Baby-O is a long-time favorite in Acapulco and still serves as a throwback to the town's heavy disco days. The mid- to late-twenties crowd dances to everything from swing to hip-hop and rock 'n' roll. Located across from the Romano Days Inn, this intimate disco has a small dance floor surrounded by several tiers of tables and sculpted, cavelike walls. Drinks run from $4 to $5. Open from 10:30pm to 5am.

Carlos 'n' Charlie's. Costera Alemán 999. ☎ **7/484-1285** or 7/484-0039. No cover.

For fun, danceable music and good food, you can't go wrong with this branch of the Carlos Anderson chain. It's always packed. Come early and get a seat on the terrace overlooking the Costera. This is a great place to go for late dinner and a few drinks before going to one of the "true" Acapulco clubs. It's located east of the Diana traffic circle, across the street from the Fiesta Americana Condesa. Open nightly from 1pm to midnight.

Enigma. Carretera Escénica. ☎ **7/484-7154** or 7/484-7164. Cover $15–$20. AE, DC, DISC, MC, V.

Venture into this stylish chrome-and-neon extravaganza perched on the side of the mountain for a true Acapulco nightlife experience. It's located between Los Rancheros Restaurant and La Vista Shopping Center—you can't miss the neon lights. The plush, dim interior dazzles patrons, with a sunken dance floor and panoramic view of the lights of Acapulco Bay. The club has been totally remodeled and has added a new, intimate salsa room with live Cuban music. The updated decor includes baroque-style murals and granite floors. There's also pumped-in mood smoke, alternating with fresh oxygen to keep you dancing. The door attendants wear tuxedos, indicating that they encourage a more sophisticated dress—tight and slinky is the norm for ladies, no shorts for gentlemen. The club opens nightly at 10:30pm; fireworks rock the usually full house at 3am. Call to find out if reservations are needed.

Fantasy. Carretera Escénica #28. ☎ **7/484-6727** or 7/484-6764. Cover $5–$10. AE, DC, MC, V.

This club, located in the La Vista Shopping Center, has a fantastic bay view. It's particularly popular with the moneyed Mexico City set. Musically, it caters to patrons in their mid-twenties to mid-thirties. Periodically during the evening the club projects a laser show across the bay. The dress code prohibits shorts, jeans, T-shirts, or sandals. Reservations are recommended. It's open nightly from 10:30pm to 2:30am, but stays open later (until 4am) on weekends or when the crowd demands it. The cover charge is occasionally waived.

Hard Rock Cafe. Costera Alemán 37. ☎ **7/484-0047.** No cover.

If you like your music loud, your food trendy, and your entertainment *à la internationale,* you'll feel at home in Acapulco's branch of this chain bent on world domination. Elvis memorabilia greets you in the entry area, and among other numerous framed or encased mementos is the Beatles' gold record for "Can't Buy Me Love." There's a bandstand for the live music—played every night between 10pm and 2am—and a small dance floor. It's on the seaward side toward the southern end of the Costera, south of the Convention Center and opposite El Cabrito. It's open daily from noon to 2am.

✪ **Pepe's Piano Bar.** Carretera Escenica, Comercial La Vista, Local 5. ☎ **7/484-8060.** No cover.

Pepe's is one of the most famous piano bars in the hemisphere. Its setting of red velvet banquettes and its eclectic mix of art has inspired patrons of all ages to sing their hearts out for more than 40 years—and it still draws a crowd. This isn't karaoke, but authentic vocals, accompanied by a pianist you'd have to think has seen it all by now. The music ranges from Mexican boleros to English-language love songs. I've witnessed men in the parking lot practicing their lyrics before getting up the nerve to sing before the fun-loving crowd. Open nightly from 10pm to 4am. Only in Acapulco.

Salon Q. Costera Miguel Alemán 3117. ☎ **7/481-0114.** $10 cover.

This place bills itself as "the cathedral of salsa," and it's a fairly accurate claim—Salon Q is now known as the place to get down among the Latin rhythm. Frequently, management raises the cover and features impersonators doing the top Latin American musical acts.

Tequila's Le Club. 20 Calle Urdaneta. ☎ **7/485-8623.** $10 cover, Tues and Thurs; $22 cover includes drinks on Mon, Wed, and Fri.

They say that female impersonator shows used to be considered fun for the whole family in old Acapulco—and this club is a throwback to that time. The early show features international (English lip-syncing) "ladies," while the later show stars Mexican drag divas.

3

Northward to Zihuatanejo
& Ixtapa

*I*xtapa and Zihuatanejo are side-by-side beach resorts that share a common geography, but that in character couldn't be more different. Ixtapa is a model of modern infrastructure, services, and luxury hotels, while Zihuatanejo—or Zihua, to the locals—is the quintessential Mexican beach village. For travelers, this offers the intriguing possibility of visiting two distinct destinations in one vacation. Those looking for luxury should opt for Ixtapa and take advantage of well-appointed rooms in this pristine setting of great natural beauty. You can easily and quickly make the 4-mile trip into Zihuatanejo for a sampling of the simple life in this *pueblo* by the sea. Those who prefer a more rustic retreat with real personality, however, should settle in Zihuatanejo. It's noted for its long-standing community of Swiss and Italian immigrants, and its legendary beach playboys. Those who enjoy Zihua seem to return year after year.

The area, with a backdrop of the Sierra Madre mountains and a foreground of Pacific Ocean waters, provides a full range of activities and diversions. Scuba diving, deep-sea fishing, bay cruises to remote beaches, and golf are among the favorites. Nightlife in both towns borders on the subdued, but Ixtapa is the livelier.

This dual destination is the choice for the traveler looking for a little of everything, from resort-styled indulgence to unpretentious simplicity. These two resorts are more welcoming to couples and adults than families, with a number of places off-limits to children under 16—something of a rarity in Mexico.

1 Essentials

Zihuatanejo & Ixtapa are 360 miles (576km) SW of Mexico City; 353 miles (565km) SE of Manzanillo; 158 miles (253km) NW of Acapulco

GETTING THERE & DEPARTING

BY PLANE These destinations tend to be even more seasonal than most resorts in Mexico. Flights are available year-round from U.S. gateways, though the frequencies are generally reduced in summer months. See chapter 1, "Planning a Trip to Southern Pacific Mexico," for information on flying to Ixtapa/Zihuatanejo from the United States and Canada. Both **Aeromexico** and **Mexicana** fly daily into Ixtapa via Mexico City and Guadalajara, and with less frequency from Acapulco. Here are the local numbers of some international carriers: **Aeromexico** (☎ **7/554-2018** or 7/554-2019), **Alaska Airlines** (☎ **7/554-8457**), **America West** (☎ **7/554-8634**), **Continental** (☎ **7/554-4219**), **Mexicana** (☎ **7/554-2208,** 7/554-2209, or 7/554-2227). Ask your travel agent about charter flights and packages, which are becoming the most efficient and least expensive way to get here.

Arriving: The **Ixtapa-Zihuatanejo airport** is 15 minutes (about 7 miles) south of Zihuatanejo. Taxi fares range from $12 to $19. **Transportes Terrestres** colectivo minivans transport travelers to hotels in Zihuatanejo, Ixtapa, and Club Med; tickets are sold just outside the baggage-claim area and run between $3 and $6. There are also several car-rental agencies with booths in the airport. These include **Dollar** (☎ **800/800-4000** in the U.S., 7/554-2314, 7/553-1858, or 7/554-5366) and **Hertz** (☎ **800/ 654-3131** in the U.S., 7/554-2590, or 7/554-2952).

BY CAR   From Mexico City, the shortest route is Highway 15 to Toluca, then Highway 130/134 the rest of the way—be advised that on the latter road, highway gas stations are few and far between. The other route is the four-lane Highway 95D to Iguala, then Highway 51 west to Highway 134. It's about a 7-hour drive from Mexico City.

From Acapulco or Manzanillo, the only choice is the coastal Highway 200. The ocean views along the winding,

---

Motorist Advisory

Motorists planning to follow Highway 200 northwest up the coast from Ixtapa or Zihuatanejo toward Lázaro Cárdenas and Manzanillo should be aware of reports of car and bus hijackings on that route, especially around Playa Azul, with bus holdups more common than car holdups. Before heading in that direction, ask locals and the tourism office about the status of the route. Don't drive at night. According to tourism officials, police and military patrols of the highway have recently been increased, and the number of incidents has dropped dramatically.

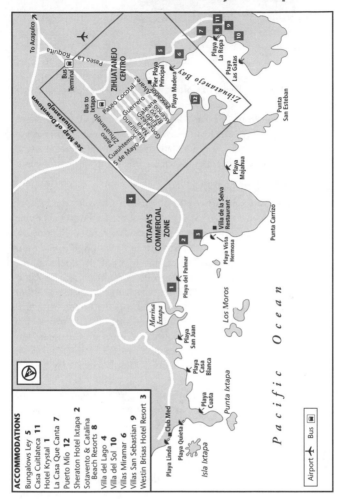

Zihuatanejo & Ixtapa Area

ACCOMMODATIONS
Bungalows Ley **5**
Casa Cuitlateca **11**
Hotel Krystal **1**
La Casa Que Canta **7**
Puerto Mio **12**
Sheraton Hotel Ixtapa **2**
Sotavento & Catalina Beach Resorts **8**
Villa del Lago **4**
Villa del Sol **10**
Villas Miramar **6**
Villas San Sebastian **9**
Westin Brisas Hotel Resort **3**

Airport ✈   Bus ▣

mountain-edged drive from Manzanillo can be spectacular (trip time from Manzanillo is about 11 hours).

BY BUS There are two bus terminals in Zihuatanejo: the **Central de Autobuses** (☎ 7/554-3477), from which most lines operate (it's opposite the Pemex station and IMSS Hospital on Paseo Zihuatanejo at Paseo la Boquita), and the new **Estrella de**

Oro station (☎ 7/554-2175), a block away. At the Central de Autobuses, several companies offer daily service to/from Acapulco, Puerto Escondido, Huatulco, Manzanillo, Puerto Vallarta, and other cities. At the other station, first-class Estrella de Oro buses run daily to Acapulco. Advance tickets with seat assignments can be purchased at **Turismo Caleta** in the La Puerta shopping center in Ixtapa.

The trip from Mexico City to Zihuatanejo takes 5 hours (bypassing Acapulco); from Acapulco, 4 to 5 hours. From Zihuatanejo, it's 6 or 7 hours to Manzanillo, and an additional 6 to Puerto Vallarta, which doesn't include time spent waiting for buses.

VISITOR INFORMATION

The **State Tourism Office** (☎ **888/248-7037** from the U.S., or ☎/fax 7/553-1967 or 7/553-1968) is in the **La Puerta** shopping center in Ixtapa across from the Presidente Inter-Continental Hotel; it's open Monday to Friday from 8am to 8:30pm. This is mainly a self-service office where you may collect brochures; the staff is less helpful than in other offices in Mexico. The **Zihuatanejo Tourism Office Module** (www.cdnet.com.mx/turismo/ixtapa_zihuatanejo.html) is on the main square by the basketball court at Álvarez; it's open Monday to Friday from 9am to 8pm (no phone), and serves basic tourist-information purposes. The actual administrative office is located in City Hall, (☎ **7/554-2355,** ask for Turismo), and is open Monday to Friday 8am to 4pm.

Note: According to recent regulations, the very few time-share sales booths that exist in both towns must be clearly marked according to business names and cannot carry signs claiming to be tourist-information centers.

CITY LAYOUT

The fishing village and resort of **Zihuatanejo** spreads out around the beautiful Bay of Zihuatanejo, framed by downtown to the north and a beautiful long beach and the Sierra foothills to the east. The heart of Zihuatanejo is the waterfront walkway **Paseo del Pescador** (also called the **Malecón**), bordering the Municipal Beach. The town centerpiece is, rather than a plaza as in most Mexican villages, Zihuatanejo's **basketball court,** which fronts the beach. It's a useful point of reference for directions. The main thoroughfare for cars is **Juan Álvarez,** a block behind the Malecón. Sections of several of the main streets are designated as *zona* *peatonal* (pedestrian zone, blocked off to cars). The area is zig-zagged, however, and seems to block parts of streets haphazardly.

A cement-and-sand walkway runs from the Malecón in downtown Zihuatanejo along the water to **Playa Madera**, making it much easier to walk between the two points. The walkway is lit at night. Access to Playa La Ropa ("clothing beach") is via the main road, **Camino a Playa La Ropa.** Playa La Ropa and Playa Las Gatas are connected only by boat.

A good highway connects "Zihua," as the resort is often called, to **Ixtapa,** 4 miles to the northwest. The 18-hole **Ixtapa Golf Club** marks the beginning of the inland side of Ixtapa. Tall hotels line Ixtapa's wide beach, **Playa Palmar,** against a backdrop of lush palm groves and mountains. Access is by the main street, **bulevar Ixtapa.** On the opposite side of the main boulevard lies a large expanse of small shopping plazas (many of the shops are air-conditioned) and restaurants. At the far end of bulevar Ixtapa, **Marina Ixtapa** has excellent restaurants, private yacht slips, and an 18-hole golf course. Condominiums and private homes surround the marina and golf course, and more developments of exclusive residential areas are rising in the hillsides past the marina en route to Playa Quieta and Playa Linda. Ixtapa also has a paved bicycle track that begins at the marina and continues around the golf course and on towards Playa Linda. There are plans to extend it to the Ixtapa entrance near the Ixtapa Golf Club.

GETTING AROUND

BY TAXI   Taxi rates are reasonable, but from midnight to 5am rates increase by 50%. The average fare between Ixtapa and Zihuatanejo is $3. A **shuttle bus** goes back and forth between Zihuatanejo and Ixtapa every 15 or 20 minutes from 5am to 11pm daily, but is almost always very crowded with commuting workers. In Zihuatanejo it stops near the corner of Morelos/Paseo Zihuatanejo and Juárez, about 3 blocks north of the market. In Ixtapa it makes numerous stops along bulevar Ixtapa.

Special note: The highway leading from Zihuatanejo to Ixtapa is now a broad, four-lane highway, which makes driving between the towns easier and faster than ever. Street signs are becoming more common in Zihuatanejo, and good signs now lead you in and out of both towns. However, both locations have an area called the *Zona Hotelera* (Hotel Zone), so if you're trying to reach Ixtapa's Hotel Zone, you may be confused by signs in Zihuatanejo pointing to that village's own Hotel Zone.

FAST FACTS: Zihuatanejo & Ixtapa

American Express   The main office is in the commercial promenade of the Krystal Ixtapa Hotel (☎ 7/553-0853; fax 7/553-1206). It's open Monday to Saturday from 9am to 6pm.

Area Code   The telephone area code is 7.

Banks   Ixtapa's banks include **Bancomer,** in the La Puerta Centro shopping center. The most centrally located of Zihuatanejo's banks is **Banamex,** Cuauhtémoc 4. Banks change money during normal business hours, which are now generally 9am to 6pm Monday to Friday and Saturday from 9am to 1pm. Automated tellers and currency exchanges are available during these and other hours.

Climate   Summer is hot and humid, though tempered by sea breezes and brief showers; September is the peak of the tropical rainy season, with showers concentrated in the late afternoons.

Doctors   Medica Ixtapa, Plaza Tulares #13 (☎ 7/553-0280), provides doctors who speak English and French.

Internet Access   Two cybercafes are located in the Los Patios Shopping Center in Ixtapa. **Comunicación Mundial** is found in Local 105, and **Dolfy's Internet Café** is in Local 108. Go to the back of the shopping center and take the stairs to the second level: Comunicación Mundial is to your right, and Dolfy's is located across from the stairs, next to the Golden Cookie Shop.

Pharmacy   Farmacias Coyuca are open 24 hours a day, and will deliver. The Ixtapa branch doesn't have a phone number; in Zihuatanejo call ☎ 7/554-5390.

Post Office   The post office is in the SCT building (called Edificio SCT), behind El Cacahuate (☎ 7/554-2192). It's open Monday to Friday from 8am to 3pm and Saturday from 9am to 1pm.

2 Where to Stay

Accommodations in Ixtapa and Playa Madera are dominated by larger, more expensive hotels, including many of the well-known chains. There are only a few choices in the budget and moderate price ranges. If you're looking for lower-priced rooms, Zihuatanejo will offer the best selections and the best values. Many long-term guests in Ixtapa and Zihuatanejo search out apartments and condos to rent. **Lilia Valle** (☎ 7/554-2084) is an excellent source for apartment and villas rentals.

IXTAPA
VERY EXPENSIVE

✪ **Westin Brisas Resort.** Boulevar Ixtapa, 40880 Ixtapa, Guerrero. ☎ **800/228-3000** in the U.S., or 7/553-2121. Fax 7/553-1091. 423 units. A/C MINIBAR TV TEL. High season $250 deluxe; $280 Royal Beach Club. Low season $175 deluxe; $202 Royal Beach Club. AE, CB, DC, MC, V. Free parking.

Set above the high-rise hotels of Ixtapa on its own rocky promontory, the Westin is clearly the most stunning of Ixtapa's hotels, and the most noted for gracious service. The austere but luxurious public areas, all in stone and stucco, are bathed in sweeping breezes and an air of exclusivity. A minimalist luxury also characterizes the rooms—all redone in the past year—which have Mexican-tile floors and private, plant-decked patios with hammocks and lounges. All rooms face the hotel's cove and private beach, which although attractive, is dangerous for swimming. The six master suites come with private pools, the 16th floor is reserved for nonsmokers, and three rooms on the 18th floor are equipped for travelers with disabilities.

Dining/Diversions: Five restaurants, from elegant indoor dining to casual open-air restaurants, allow you to relax entirely; you might never even go out for a meal. The airy lobby bar is one of the most popular places to enjoy sunset cocktails while a soothing trio croons romantic Mexican songs.

Amenities: Shopping arcade, barber and beauty shop, four swimming pools (one for children), four lit tennis courts with pro on request, elevator to secluded beach, laundry and room service, travel agency, car rental, massage, baby-sitting.

EXPENSIVE

Barceló Ixtapa. Bulevar Ixtapa, 40880 Ixtapa, Guerrero. ☎ **800/325-3535** in the U.S. and Canada, or 7/553-1858. Fax 7/553-2438. 331 units. A/C MINIBAR TV TEL. High season $144 double. Low season $100 double. Ask for packages that include breakfast and welcome cocktails. AE, DC, MC, V. Free parking.

This grand, 12-story resort hotel (formerly the Sheraton) has large, handsomely furnished public areas facing the beach; it's an inviting place to sip a drink and people-watch. Rooms are as nice as the public areas. Most have balconies with views of either the ocean or the mountains. Thirty-six rooms on the fifth floor are no-smoking. Rooms equipped for travelers with disabilities are available. Gardens surround the large pool, which has a swim-up bar and separate section for children.

Dining/Diversions: There are four restaurants, a nightclub, a lobby bar, and a weekly Mexican fiesta with buffet and live entertainment outdoors.

Amenities: One beachside pool, four tennis courts, a fitness room, beauty and barber shop, boutiques, pharmacy/gift shop, room and laundry service, travel agency, concierge, car rental.

✪ **Krystal.** Bulevar Ixtapa s/n, 40880 Ixtapa, Guerrero. ☎ **800/231-9860** in the U.S., or 7/553-0333. Fax 7/553-0216. 255 units. A/C MINIBAR TV TEL. High season $190 double; $240 suite. Low season $150 double; $215 suite. 2 children under 12 stay free in parents' room. Ask for special packages. AE, DC, MC, V. Free parking.

Krystal hotels are known in Mexico for quality rooms and service, and this was the original hotel in the chain. As such, it is also their hallmark of welcoming, exceptional service. Many of the staff members, who have been with the hotel for its more than 20 years of operation, are on hand to greet return guests. It is probably the best hotel in the area for families. This large, V-shaped hotel has ample grounds and a pool area. Each spacious and nicely furnished room has a balcony with an ocean view, game table, and tile bathrooms. Master suites have large, furnished, triangular-shaped balconies. Some rates include a daily breakfast buffet. The eighth floor is no-smoking, and there's one room equipped for travelers with disabilities.

Dining/Diversions: Among the hotel's five restaurants is the superelegant, evening-only **Bogart's.** There's live music nightly in the lobby bar, and the center of Ixtapa nightlife is found here, at Krystal's famed **Christine Disco,** the one and only true nightclub in the area.

Amenities: Swimming pool, one tennis court, racquetball court, gym, beauty and barber shop, massage, laundry, room service, travel agency, car rental.

ZIHUATANEJO

The more economical hotels are in Zihuatanejo and its nearby beach communities. The term "bungalow" is used loosely in Zihuatanejo, as it is elsewhere in Mexico. Thus a bungalow may be an individual unit with a kitchen and bedroom, or a mere bedroom. It may also be hotel-like, in a two-story building with multiple units, some of which have kitchens. It may be cozy or

Downtown Zihuatanejo

Legend
Bus
Post Office

To Ixtapa

Main Bus Terminal

Avenida Morelos

Paseo Zihuatanejo

I. Altamirano

Avenida Nava

Cuauhtémoc

5 de Mayo

Galeana

Vicente Guerrero

C. González

Benito Juárez

Tres Estrellas Bus Terminal

Paseo del Palmar

Municipal Market

Kioto Plaza

Camino a la Playa la Ropa

Ejido

Paseo de la Boquita

Canal

Calle Adelita

Artisan's Market

Las Salinas

N. Bravo
Pedro Ascencio

J.N.

Álvarez

Paseo del Pescador

Calle Mateos

Playa Municipal

Playa Municipal

Playa La Ropa

Muelle Pier

Bahía de Zihuatanejo

Punta Godomia

Playa Las Gatas

ACCOMMODATIONS
Apartamentos Amueblados Valle **6**
Bungalows Ley **8**
Hotel Ávila **3**
Hotel Imelda **1**
Hotel Raúl 3 Marias **2**
Hotel Susy **4**
La Casa Que Canta **10**

Posada Citlali **5**
Sotavento & Catalina
  Beach Resorts **11**
Villas Miramar **9**
Villas San Sebastián **12**
Villa del Sol **13**
ATTRACTIONS
Museo de Arqueología **7**

rustic, with or without a patio or balcony. Accommodations in town are generally very basic, though clean and comfortable.

Playa Madera and Playa La Ropa, separated from each other only by a craggy shoreline, are both accessible by road. Prices here tend to be higher than those in town, but the value is much better—and generally people find that the beautiful and tranquil setting is worth the extra cost. The town is just 5 to 20 minutes away, depending on whether you walk or take a taxi.

IN TOWN

✪ **Apartamentos Amueblados Valle.** Vincente Guerrero 14, 40880 Zihuatanejo, Guerrero. ☎ **7/554-2084.** Fax 7/554-3220. 8 units. TV. High season $60 1-bedroom apt; $90 2-bedroom apt. Low season $40 1-bedroom apt; $60 2-bedroom apt. Ask for special rates during low season and for prolonged stays. No credit cards.

Here you can rent a well-furnished apartment for the price of an inexpensive hotel room. Five one-bedroom apartments accommodate up to three people; the three two-bedroom apartments can fit four comfortably. Request an apartment that does not face the street, as they are not as noisy. Each apartment is different, but all are clean and airy, with ceiling fans, private balconies, and kitchenettes. Maid service is provided daily, and there's a paperback-book exchange in the office. Guadalupe Rodríguez, the owner, or her son Luis Valle, are good sources of information for cheaper apartments elsewhere for guests who want to stay several months. Reserve well in advance during high season. It's on Guerrero about 2 blocks in from the waterfront between Ejido and N. Bravo.

Hotel Raul 3 Marias. Juan Alvarez 52, 40880 Zihuatanejo, Guerrero. ☎ **7/554-6706.** www.cdnet.com.mx/r3marias. E-mail: garroboscrew@cdnet.com.mx. 17 units. A/C. High season $40 double, variable prices in low season. AE, MC, V.

A small hotel known for its guest services, the Raul has small, basic rooms that are clean and functional. Nine rooms have a balcony overlooking the street, and the small office offers telephone and fax service to guests. Downstairs is the landmark Zihuatanejo seafood restaurant, Garrobos, open for lunch and dinner. The hotel also offers deep-sea fishing and diving charters.

Hotel Susy. Juan Álvarez 3 (at Guerrero), 40880 Zihuatanejo, Guerrero. ☎ **7/554-2339.** 18 units. TV. High season $35 double. Low season $25 double. MC, V.

Consistently clean, with lots of plants along a shaded walkway set back from the street, this two-story hotel offers small rooms with fans and louvered glass windows with screens. Upper-floor rooms have balconies overlooking the street. Facing away from the water at the basketball court on the Malecón, turn right and walk 2 blocks; the hotel is on your left at the corner of Guerrero.

Posada Citlali. Vicente Guerrero 3, 40880 Z
☎ 7/554-2043. 19 units. $35 double. No credit car

In this pleasant, three-story hotel, small ro
arranged around a shaded plant-filled courtya
comfortable rockers and chairs; it's a good v̲a̲   price.
Bottled water is in help-yourself containers on the patio. The
stairway to the top two floors is narrow and steep. The hotel is
near the corner of Álvarez and Guerrero.

PLAYA MADERA

Madera Beach is a 15-minute walk along the street, a 10-minute
walk along the beach pathway, or a cheap taxi ride from Zihuatanejo. Most of the accommodations are on calle Eva S. de
López Matéos, the road overlooking the beach. Most hotels are
set against the hill and have steep stairways.

✪ **Bungalows Ley**. Calle Eva S. de López Matéos s/n, Playa Madera (Apdo.
Postal 466), 40880 Zihuatanejo, Guerrero. ☎ 7/554-4087. Fax 7/554-4563.
8 units. TV. $45 double with fan, $50 double with A/C; $80 for 2-bedroom
suite with kitchen and fan for up to 4 persons, $120 with A/C; $140 for up to
6 persons. AE, MC, V.

No two suites are the same at this small complex, one of the
nicest on Playa Madera. If you're traveling with a group, you may
want to book the most expensive suite (called Club Madera),
which comes with a rooftop terrace with tiled hot tub, outdoor
bar and grill, and a spectacular view. All the rooms are immacu-
late; the simplest are studios with one bed and a kitchen in the
same room. All rooms have terraces or balconies just above the
beach, and all are decorated in Miami Beach colors. Bathrooms,
however, tend to be small and dark. Clients praise the management and the service. To find the complex, follow Matéos to the
right up a slight hill; it's on your left.

✪ **Villas Miramar**. Calle Adelita, Lote 78, Playa Madera (Apdo. Postal 211),
40880 Zihuatanejo, Guerrero. ☎ 7/554-2106 or 7/554-3350. Fax 7/554-
2149. 18 units. A/C TV TEL. High season $95 suite for 1 or 2, $100 with ocean
view; $130 2-bedroom suite. Low season $60 suite for 1 or 2, $70 with ocean
view; $90 2-bedroom suite. AE, MC, V. Free parking.

This lovely hotel with beautiful gardens offers a welcoming
atmosphere, attention to detail, and superb cleanliness. Some of
the elegant suites are built around a shady patio that doubles as a
restaurant. Those across the street center on a lovely pool and
have private balconies and sea views. A new terrace with a view to

bay was added last year, and has a bar that features a daily happy hour from 5 to 7pm. TVs (with cable channels) were also added recently, as was a new restaurant serving a basic menu for breakfast, lunch, and dinner. Parking is enclosed. To find Villas Miramar, follow the road leading south out of town toward Playa La Ropa, then take the first right after the traffic circle, then left on Adelita.

PLAYA LA ROPA

Some travelers consider Playa La Ropa to be the most beautiful of Zihuatanejo's beaches. It's a 20- to 25-minute walk south of town on the east side of the bay or a $2 taxi ride.

Casa Cuitlateca. Calle Playa La Ropa, Apartado Postal 124, Zihuatanejo, 40880, Guerrero. ☎ **7/554-2448;** U.S. reservations office ☎ 877/541-1234 or 406/252-2834, fax: 406/252-4692. www.cuitlateca.com. E-mail: casacuitlateca@cdnet.com.mx. 4 suites. A/C FAN TEL. $425 double. $50 each extra person. Rates include round-trip transfers to the airport and breakfast. No children under 15. AE, MC, V.

This exclusive bed & breakfast is done in the architectural style that has made Zihua famous, with its palapa roofs and earthy colors. Built on the hillside across from La Ropa beach, each one of the rooms offers a stunning view. This is the perfect place for a romantic holiday. There are two smaller rooms, each with its own private terrace and a small sitting area. There is also a suite with a large terrace, and a second suite with no view but a very nice sitting area and small private garden. The bar is on the first level behind the pool, serving cocktails to the public from 4:30 to 8pm. Guests can help themselves to soft drinks and beers when the bar is closed, on the honor system. The small pool, like everything else in this property, is beautifully designed. Each room is carefully decorated with handcrafts and textiles from all over Mexico, especially from Michoacán, Puebla, and Oaxaca. On the top level is a sundeck and a hot tub for all guests. From the entrance you have to climb a well designed, yet steep staircase with 150 steps. The driveway, also very steep, has parking for six cars. The parking lot connects to the house through a hanging bridge. The inn is a short walk from La Ropa beach.

✪ **La Casa Que Canta.** Camino Escénico a la Playa La Ropa, 40880 Zihuatanejo, Guerrero. ☎ **888/523-5050** in the U.S., or 7/554-2722, or 7/554-6529. 24 suites. A/C MINIBAR. High season $320–$350 double. Low season $290–$320 double. AE, MC, V. No children under 16.

La Casa Que Canta ("The House that Sings") opened in 1992, and in looks alone, it's a very special hotel. Located on a mountainside overlooking Zihuatanejo Bay, it was designed with striking molded-adobe architecture, the first of a rustic-chic style of architecture known as Mexican Pacific. Rooms, all with handsome natural-tile floors, are individually decorated in unusual painted Michoacán furniture, antiques, and stretched-leather equipales, with hand-loomed fabrics used throughout. All units have large, beautifully furnished terraces with bay views. Hammocks under the thatched-roof terraces, supported by rough-hewn vigas, are perfectly placed for watching yachts sail in and out of the harbor. The four categories of rooms are all spacious; there are three terrace suites, four deluxe suites, nine grand suites, and two private-pool suites. Rooms meander up and down the hillside, and while stairs aren't extensive on the property, there are no elevators. La Casa Que Canta is a member of the "Small Luxury Hotels of the World" group. Technically it's not on Playa La Ropa, nor any beach; it's on the road leading there. The closest stretch of beach (still not yet Playa La Ropa) is down a steep hill.

Dining/Diversions: There's a small restaurant/bar on a shaded terrace overlooking the bay.

Amenities: Freshwater pool on the main terrace, saltwater pool on the bottom level, laundry and room service.

○ Sotavento and Catalina Beach Resorts. Playa La Ropa, 40880 Zihuatanejo, Guerrero. ☎ **7/554-2032.** Fax 7/554-2975. 126 units. TEL in 85 units. $58–$85 standard room; $65–$110 bungalow or terrace suites; $50 small terrace doubles. AE, CB, DC, MC, V.

Perched on a hill above the beach, these hotels are meant for people who want to relax near the ocean in a beautiful and simple setting and don't want to be bothered by televisions closed up in air-conditioned rooms. The Catalina consists of a collection of bungalows tucked away in tropical vegetation. The Sotavento consists of two multi-story buildings that are placed so as not to intrude on the bungalow dwellers. Between the two hotels, there are quite a variety of rooms to choose from, and you should ask to see a few different categories to find something that suits you. My favorites are the doubles on the upper floors of the Sotavento. These rooms are three times the size of normal doubles. They are simply and comfortably furnished with little decoration and have an ocean-view terrace that is half-sheltered and half-open with chaises for taking the sun and hammocks for enjoying the shade.

Screened windows catch the ocean breezes, and ceiling fans keep the rooms airy even when the breeze is absent. One curious feature of the Sotavento is that the floors are always slightly slanted in one direction or another—by design of the owner.

The bungalows in the Catalina are more decoratively furnished with Mexican tile floors, wrought iron furniture, and artwork. Some come with ocean-view terraces. The restaurant serves good food. The lobby terrace has a little bar high above the water that is ideal for having cocktails and enjoying the sunset. There is a lovely pool with whirlpool down by the beach, surrounded by lounge chairs.

This hotel is on the side of a hill and is not for people who mind climbing stairs. Take the highway south of Zihuatanejo about a mile, turn right at the hotels' sign, and follow the road to the hotels.

Villa del Sol. Playa la Ropa (Apdo Postal 84), Zihuatanejo, Guerrero, 40880. ☎ **7/554-2239** or 7/554-3239. Fax 7/554-2758. www.hotelvilladelsol.com. E-mail: hotel@villasol.com.mx. 45 individually designed rooms and suites. A/C MINIBAR TV TEL. High season $230–$900 double. Low season $160–$750 double. Meal plan, including breakfast and dinner, for $60 per person per day is mandatory during the winter season. AE, MC, V.

This exquisite inn is known as much for its unequivocal attention to luxurious detail as it is for its exacting German owner, Helmut Leins. It's a tranquil spot that caters to guests looking for complete privacy and serenity, with each room exhibiting a harmony of magnificent design and decor. Spacious, split-level suites have one or two bedrooms, plus a living area and a large terrace, some with private minipool. King-size beds are draped in white netting, and comfy lounges and hammocks beckon to you at siesta time. Standard rooms are smaller, and sans TV or telephone, though still artfully appointed with Mexican artistic details. Nine beachfront suites have recently been added, but I still prefer the original rooms. No two are alike, but amenities in all include thick bathrobes, hairdryers, and fine toiletries. Suites also have CD players and private fax. This is one of only two hotels in Mexico to meet the demanding standards of the French Relais and Châteaux, and is also a member of the "Small Luxury Hotels of the World." No children under 14 during high season, and in general, this inn has a "no children" and "no excess noise" feel to it. This may make it less enjoyable for those travelers who relish a more typically welcoming Mexican ambiance.

Dining/Diversions: Open-air beachfront restaurant and bar serves continental cuisine (nothing with garlic is permitted). A new restaurant serving Mediterranean/seafood in a casual setting was recently added. Room service is available.

Amenities: The hotel sits on a private, 600-foot-long palm-shaded beach. Three pools (including one 60-foot lap pool!), two tennis courts, massage service, beauty salon, art gallery, gift shop, tour desk, car rental, doctor on call.

Villas San Sebastián. Bulevar Escénico Playa La Ropa (across from the Dolphins Fountain). ☎ 7/554-2084. 9 units. A/C. High season $155 1-bedroom; $190 2-bedroom. Low season $105 1-bedroom; $155 2-bedroom. No credit cards.

Nestled on the mountainside above Playa La Ropa, this nine-villa complex offers great views of Zihuatanejo's bay (two of the units are new additions). The villas surround tropical vegetation and a central swimming pool. Each comes complete with kitchenette and its own spacious, private terrace. The personalized service is one reason these villas come so highly recommended; owner Luis Valle, whose family dates back decades in this community, is always available to help guests with any questions or needs.

ZIHUATANEJO BEACH

Puerto Mío. Paseo del Morro 5, Zihuatanejo, 40880, Guerrero. ☎ 888/633-3295 in the U.S., 800/711-2080 inside Mexico, or 7/554-3344. Fax 7/554-3535. www.puertomio.com.mx. E-mail: puertomio@puertomio.com.mx. 22 rooms and suites. A/C MINIBAR TV TEL. High season $225–$275 double; $425–$450 suite; $600 top level suite with pool; $750 master suite. Low season prices drop by $25 per room. AE, MC, V.

Located on 25 acres of beautifully landscaped grounds, this resort sits apart from the rest of the hotels in Zihuatanejo, on the furthest end of the bay, almost directly across from Las Gatas beach. The rooms are divided in three main areas: Casa de Mar, the cliffside mansion closer to the main entrance, where most of the rooms are located; the Peninsula, located on the tip of the bay; and a more secluded area with only two suites with ample sitting areas to enjoy the beautiful view. (These two suites have no TVs to disturb the tranquility.) Three new suites are located between Casa de Mar and the Peninsula and have private pools, with the upper level suite the largest in size. All rooms are nicely decorated with handcrafted details from around Mexico, and all enjoy beautiful views of either Zihuatanejo's bay or the Pacific Ocean. Golf carts provide transportation to all the different areas.

Dining/Diversions: There are two restaurants: La Cala is open to the public, and serves international fare, with a specialty of fresh seafood. Reservations are recommended. La Terraza serves breakfast, lunch, and dinner to guests only.

Amenities: A private beach that can be reached only through the hotel is available for guests only. There is a small marina with a sailboat, the *Nirvana*, available for charters. At the marina you can also arrange for fishing trips and other tours designed to your needs.

All rooms have safe deposit boxes and plush bathrobes. A concierge service can help with tour services, car rentals, and other special needs. Children under 16 are welcome only during the summer, and it's recommended that you call in advance to make sure that children are welcome even then.

3 Where to Dine

IXTAPA

VERY EXPENSIVE

Villa de la Selva. Paseo de la Roca. ☎ 7/553-0362. Reservations recommended during high season. Main courses $15–$35. AE, MC, V. Daily 6–11pm. MEXICAN/CONTINENTAL.

Clinging to the edge of a cliff overlooking the sea, this elegant, romantic restaurant enjoys the most spectacular sea and sunset view in Ixtapa. The candlelit tables are arranged on three terraces; try to come early in hopes of getting one of the best vistas, especially on the lower terrace. The cuisine is delicious, artfully appointed, and classically rich; Filet Villa de la Selva is red snapper topped with shrimp and hollandaise sauce. The cold avocado soup or hot lobster bisque makes a good beginning; finish with chocolate mousse or bananas Singapore.

EXPENSIVE

✪ **Beccofino.** Marina Ixtapa. ☎ 7/553-1770. Breakfast $4–$6; main courses $12–$25. AE, MC, V. Daily 9:30am–midnight. NORTHERN ITALIAN.

This restaurant is a standout in Mexico. Owner Ángelo Rolly Pavia serves up the flavorful northern Italian specialties he grew up knowing and loving. The breezy marina location has a menu that's strong on pasta. Ravioli, a house specialty, comes stuffed with seafood in season. The garlic bread is terrific, and there's an extensive wine list. A popular place, the restaurant tends to be loud when it's crowded, which is often. It's also increasingly becoming a popular breakfast spot.

MODERATE

Golden Cookie Shop. Los Patios Center. ☎ 7/553-0310. Breakfast $4–$6; sandwiches $4–$6; main courses $6–$8. No credit cards. Daily 8am–3pm. PASTRIES/INTERNATIONAL.

Although the name is misleading—there are more than cookies here—Golden Cookie's freshly baked goods beg for a detour, and the coffee menu is the most extensive in town. Although the prices are high for the area, the breakfasts are particularly noteworthy, as are their deli sandwiches. The large sandwiches, made with fresh soft bread, come with a choice of sliced deli meats. Chicken curry is among the other specialty items. To get to the shop, walk to the rear of the shopping center as you face Mac's Prime Rib; walk up the stairs, turn left, and you'll see the restaurant on your right. They have a new air-conditioned area, reserved for nonsmokers.

ZIHUATANEJO

Zihuatanejo's **central market,** located on avenida Benito Juárez (about 5 blocks inland from the waterfront), will whet your appetite for cheap and tasty food. It's best at breakfast and lunch before the market activity winds down in the afternoon. Look for what's hot and fresh. The market area is one of the best on this coast for shopping and people-watching.

Two excellent **bakeries** should quell cravings for something freshly baked. Try **El Buen Gusto,** at Guerrero 4, a half a block inland from the museum (☎ 7/554-3231), where you'll find banana bread, French bread, doughnuts, and cakes. It's open daily from 7:30am to 10pm. For more fresh-baked bread aroma, head for **Panadería Francesa,** González 15, between Cuauhtémoc and Guerrero (☎ 7/554-2742). Here you can buy sweet pastries or grab a long baguette or loaf of whole-wheat bread for picnic supplies. It's open daily from 7am to 9pm.

EXPENSIVE

♻ **Coconuts.** Augustín Ramírez 1 (at Vicente Guerrero). ☎ 7/554-2518 or 7/554-7980. Main courses $9–$25. AE, MC, V. High season daily 6pm–11pm. Closed during rainy season. INTERNATIONAL/SEAFOOD.

What a find! Not only is the food innovative and delicious, but the restaurant is set in a historic building—the oldest in Zihuatanejo. This popular restaurant set in a tropical garden was the former weigh-in station for Zihua's coconut industry in the late 1800s. Fresh is the operative word on this creative, seafood-heavy menu. Chef Patricia Cummings checks what's fresh at the market, then uses only top-quality ingredients to prepare dishes like seafood pâté and grilled fillet of snapper Coconuts. Their Bananas Flambé has earned a loyal following of its own, with good reason. Expect friendly, efficient service here.

El Patio. Cinco de Mayo 3 at Álvarez. ☎ **7/554-3019.** Breakfast $3–$5; Mexican platters $5–$11; seafood $7–$18. AE, MC, V. Daily 8am–11pm. SEAFOOD/MEXICAN.

Casually elegant, this romantic patio restaurant is decorated with baskets and flickering candles. It's a good choice for those wanting to experience a truly Mexican meal in an attractive atmosphere. Whatever you crave, you're likely to find it here, whether it's fajitas, steak, chicken, chiles rellenos, green or red enchiladas, or lobster in garlic sauce. In the evenings, musicians often play Latin American favorites. It's a block inland from Álvarez and next to the church.

Kau-Kan. Camino a Playa La Ropa. ☎ **7/554-8446.** Main courses $8–$25. AE, MC, V. Daily 1–11:30pm. NUEVA COCINA/SEAFOOD.

A stunning view of the bay is one of the many attractions of this refined restaurant. The architecture is open, and uses stucco and whitewashed walls to frame the simply understated furniture. Head chef Ricardo Rodriguez supervises every detail from the ultra-smooth background music that invites after-dinner conversation to the spectacular presentation of all the dishes. The baked potato with baby lobster and the mahi mahi carpaccio are two of my favorites, but I recommend you consider the daily specials— Ricardo always gets the freshest seafood available and prepares it with great care. For dessert the pecan and chocolate cake, served with a dark chocolate sauce, is simply delicious. On the road to La Ropa it is on the right hand side, past the first curve coming from downtown.

⭐ **Restaurant Paul's.** Benito Juárez s/n. ☎ **7/554-6528.** Main courses $9–$25. MC, V. Mon–Sat noon–2am. INTERNATIONAL/SEAFOOD.

This is sure to be the only place in town that serves fresh artichokes as an appetizer, and their fish fillet is covered with a smooth, delicately flavored shrimp-and-dill sauce. From thick and juicy pork chops and beef medallions, to vegetarian main courses such as pasta with fresh artichoke hearts and sun-dried tomatoes, Chef Paul's offerings are consistently exceptional. Neither the ambiance nor the service quite lives up to the food, but that's okay—what really matters is that you'll enjoy an exceptional meal here. Paul's is on Benito Juárez, half a block from the Bancomer and Serfin banks. Taxi drivers all know how to get here.

INEXPENSIVE

Casa Puntarenas. Calle Noria, Colonia Lázaro Cárdenas. No phone. Main courses $3.50–$7. No credit cards. Daily 6:30–9pm. MEXICAN/SEAFOOD.

A modest spot with a tin roof and nine wooden tables, Puntarenas is one of the best spots in town for fried whole fish served with toasted *bolillos* (crusty, white bread mini-loaves), sliced tomatoes, onions, and avocado. They are renowned for their chile rellenos, mild and stuffed with plenty of cheese; the meat dishes are less flavorful. Although it may appear a little too rustic for less experienced travelers to Mexico, it is very clean and the food is known for its freshness. To get to Puntarenas from the pier, turn left on Álvarez and cross the footbridge on your left. Turn right after you cross the bridge; the restaurant is on your left.

La Sirena Gorda. Paseo del Pescador. ☎ 7/554-2687. Breakfast $2–$4; main courses $3–$6. MC, V. Thurs–Tues 7am–10pm. MEXICAN.

For one of the most popular breakfasts in town, head to La Sirena Gorda for a variety of eggs and omelets, hotcakes with bacon, or fruit with granola and yogurt. The house specialty is seafood tacos—fish in a variety of sauces, plus lobster—but I consider these overpriced at $3 and $20, respectively. After all, a taco is a taco is a taco. Instead, I'd recommend something from their short list of daily specials, such as blackened red snapper, steak, or fish kebabs. The food is excellent and patrons enjoy the casual sidewalk-cafe atmosphere. To get here from the basketball court, face the water and walk to the right; La Sirena Gorda is on your right just before the town pier.

Nueva Zelanda. Cuauhtémoc 23 at Ejido. ☎ 7/554-2340. Tortas $2.50–$3.50; enchiladas $2.50–$4; fruit-and-milk *licuados* (milkshakes) $1.80; cappuccino $1.50. No credit cards. Daily 8am–10pm. MEXICAN.

One of the most popular places in town, this clean open-air snack shop welcomes diners with rich cappuccinos sprinkled with cinnamon, fresh fruit liquados, and pancakes with real maple syrup. The mainstays of the menu are tortas and enchiladas, and everything is offered with friendly, efficient service. You'll find Nueva Zelanda by walking 3 blocks inland from the waterfront on Cuauhtémoc; the restaurant is on your right. There's a second location (☎ 7/553-0838) in Ixtapa in the back section of the Los Patios shopping center.

✪ **Ruben's.** Calle Adelita s/n. ☎ **7/554-4617.** Burgers $2.50–$3.50; vegetables $1.50; ice cream $1. No credit cards. Daily 6–11pm. BURGERS/ VEGETABLES.

The choices are easy here—you can order either a big juicy burger made from top sirloin beef grilled over mesquite, or a foil-wrapped packet of baked potatoes, chayote, zucchini, or sweet corn. Ice cream, plus beer and soda, fill out the menu, which is posted on the wall by the kitchen. It's kind of a do-it-yourself place: Guests snare a waitress and order, grab their own drinks from the cooler, and tally their own tabs. Still, because of the ever-present crowds, it can be a slow process. Rolls of paper towels hang over the tables on the open porch and shaded terrace. Ruben's is a popular fixture in the Playa Madera neighborhood, though the customers come from all over town. To get here from Matéos, turn right on Adelita; Ruben's is on your right.

PLAYA MADERA & PLAYA LA ROPA

La Perla. Playa La Ropa. ☎ **7/554-2700.** Breakfast $2.50–$5; main courses $6–$11. AE, MC, V. Daily 9am–10pm; breakfast served 10am–noon. SEAFOOD.

There are many palapa-style restaurants on Playa La Ropa, but La Perla, with tables under the trees and thatched roof, is the most popular. The long stretch of pale sand and group of wooden chairs under palapas are part of what makes La Perla a local tradition—despite a reputation for mediocre food and slow service. There are rumors to the effect that it is so hard to get a waiter's attention, you can get take out food from a competitor, bring it here, and they'll never notice. Still, it's considered the best spot for tanning and socializing. It's near the southern end of La Ropa Beach. Take the right fork in the road; there's a sign in the parking lot.

Ziwok. Juan N. Alvarez s/n. ☎ **7/554-3136.** Main courses $7.50–$15. MC, V. Mon–Sat 4pm–midnight. ASIAN.

A cool and funky restaurant with only eight tables, Ziwok has a colorful decor of bright Rosa Mexicana (pink) and purple, with Frida Kahlo's art all over. Background music is an eclectic mix of Willie and Lobo, Otmar Liebert, Gypsy Kings, and other nuevo flamenco artists. Owner Juan Pablo has created hand-painted replicas of works by Frida for his menus, which feature fresh Asian-style seafood and vegetables, accompanied by pasta or rice. Your bill is delivered in a small wooden box, accompanied by fresh cut flowers for the ladies. Friendly service in a captivating atmosphere makes this restaurant a refreshing option.

4 Activities on & off the Beach

The **Museo de Arqueología de la Costa Grande** traces the history of the Costa Grande (the area from Acapulco to Ixtapa/Zihuatanejo) from pre-Hispanic times, when it was known as Cihuatlán, through the colonial era. Most of the museum's pottery and stone artifacts give evidence of extensive trade with far-off cultures and regions, including the Toltec and Teotihuacán cultures near Mexico City, the Olmec culture on both the Pacific and Gulf coasts, and areas known today as the states of Nayarit, Michoacán, and San Luis Potosí. Local indigenous groups gave the Aztecs tribute items, including cotton *tilmas* (capes) and *cacao* (chocolate), representations of which can be seen here. This museum, near Guerrero at the east end of Paseo del Pescador, easily merits the half hour or less it takes to stroll through; information signs are in Spanish, but an accompanying brochure is available in English. Admission is 50¢, and it's open Tuesday to Sunday from 10am to 6pm.

THE BEACHES

IN ZIHUATANEJO At Zihuatanejo's town beach, **Playa Municipal,** the local fishermen pull their colorful boats up onto the sand, making for a fine photo-op. The small shops and restaurants lining the waterfront here are great for people-watching and absorbing the flavor of daily village life. **Playa Madera (Wood Beach),** just east of Playa Municipal, is open to the surf but generally peaceful. A number of attractive budget lodgings overlook this area from the hillside.

South of Playa Madera is Zihuatanejo's largest and most beautiful beach, **Playa La Ropa,** a long sweep of sand with a great view of the sunset. Some lovely small hotels and restaurants nestle in the hills; palm groves edge the shoreline. Although it's also open to the Pacific, waves are usually gentle. A taxi from town costs $2. The name "Playa La Ropa" (*ropa* means clothing) comes

Beach Safety

All beaches in Zihuatanejo are safe for swimming, as undertow is rarely a problem, and the municipal beach is protected from the main surge of the Pacific. Beaches in Ixtapa are more dangerous for swimming, with frequent undertow problems.

from an old tale of the sinking of a *galeón* during a big storm. The silk clothing that it was carrying back from the Philippines all washed ashore on this beach—hence the name.

The nicest beach for swimming, and the best for children, is the secluded **Las Gatas (Cats Beach),** which can be seen across the bay from Playa Ropa and Zihuatanejo. The small coral reef just offshore is a nice spot for snorkeling and diving, and a little dive shop on the beach rents gear. Shop owner Jean Claude is a local institution—and the only full-time resident of Las Gatas. He claims to offer special rates for female divers, and has a collection of bikini tops on display, which are surpassed only by his stories. The waters at Las Gatas are exceptionally clear, and there's no undertow or big waves. Open-air seafood restaurants on the beach make it an appealing lunch spot. Small launches with shade run to Las Gatas from the Zihuatanejo town pier, a 10-minute trip; the captains will take you across whenever you wish between 8am and 4pm. Usually the last boat back leaves Las Gatas at 6:30pm, but check to be sure.

Playa Larga is a beautiful, sparsely crowded beach, located between Zihuatanejo and the airport, with several small palapa restaurants, hammocks, and wading pools for children. The main attraction here is the beach club, Splendido's, open daily from 10am to 6pm. Owner Edmond Benloulou and his young daughter Carly make guests feel like family, and serve excellent food to boot. A specialty is the *abulón rasurado*, paper-thin slices of abalone marinated in Worcestershire and soy sauces, with lime juice and chopped onion. Batter-fried shrimp with tartar sauce is equally popular. Prices range from $3.50 to $18 for entrees, cash only. With bathrooms and showers available, this is a comfortable place for a daylong stay.

IN IXTAPA Ixtapa's main beach, **Playa Palmar,** is a lovely white sand arc on the edge of the Hotel Zone, with dramatic rock formations silhouetted in the sea. The surf here can be rough; use caution and don't swim when a red flag is posted. Several of the nicest beaches in the area are essentially closed to the public, as resort developments rope them off exclusively for their guests. Although by law all Mexican beaches are open to the public, it is a common practice for hotels to create artificial barriers (such as rocks or dunes) to preclude entrance to their beaches. **Playa Quieta,** on the mainland across from Isla Ixtapa, has been largely claimed by Club Med and Qualton Club. The remaining piece of beach was once the launching point for boats to the Isla Ixtapa, but it is gradually being taken over by a private development. Isla Ixtapa-bound boats now leave from the jetty on **Playa Linda,** about 8 miles north of Ixtapa. Inexpensive water taxis here ferry passengers to Isla Ixtapa. Playa Linda is the primary out-of-town beach, with water-sports equipment and horse rentals available. **Playa las Cuatas,** a pretty beach and cove a few miles north of Ixtapa, and **Playa Majahua,** an isolated beach just west of Zihuatanejo, are both being transformed into resort complexes. Lovely **Playa Vista Hermosa** is framed by striking rock formations and bordered by the Westin Brisas Hotel high on the hill. All of these are very attractive beaches for sunbathing or a stroll, but have heavy surf and strong undertow. Use caution if swimming here.

WATER SPORTS & BOAT TRIPS

Probably the most popular boat trip is to **Isla Ixtapa** for snorkeling and lunch at the El Marlin, one of several restaurants on the island. Though you can book this outing as a tour through local travel agencies, you can also go on your own from Zihuatanejo by following the directions to Playa Linda above and taking a boat from there. Boats leave for Isla Ixtapa every 10 minutes between 11:30am and 5pm, so you can depart and return as you like. The round trip boat ride is $2. Along the way, you'll pass dramatic rock formations and be able to see in the distance **Los Morros de Los Pericos Islands,** where a great variety of birds nest on the rocky points jutting out into the blue Pacific. On Isla Ixtapa you'll find good snorkeling; snorkeling, diving, and other water-sports gear is available for rent on the island. Be sure to catch the last water taxi back at 5pm, but double-check that time upon arrival on the island.

Day-trips to Los Morros de Los Pericos islands for **bird-watching** can usually be arranged through local travel agencies, though it's less expensive to rent a boat with a guide at Playa Linda. The islands are offshore from Ixtapa's main beach.

Sunset cruises on the trimaran *TriStar,* arranged through **Yates del Sol** (☎ 7/554-2694 or 7/554-8270), depart from the Zihuatanejo town pier at Puerto Mío. The sunset cruises cost $39 and include an open bar. There's also an all-day trip to Isla Ixtapa on this very comfortable and rarely crowded yacht; it begins at 10am, costs $49, and includes an open bar and lunch. Snorkeling gear rental is available for an additional $5. Schedules and special trips vary, so call for current information.

Fishing trips can be arranged with the **boat cooperative** (☎ 7/554-2056) at the Zihuatanejo town pier. They cost $140 to $300, depending on boat size, trip length, and so on (most trips last about 6 hours; no credit cards are accepted). The price includes 10 soft drinks and 10 beers, bait, and fishing gear. Lunch is on your own. You'll pay more for a trip arranged through a local travel agency; the least expensive trips are on small launches called *pangas;* most have shade. Both small-game and deep-sea fishing are offered, and the fishing here is adequate, though not on par with that of Mazatlán or Baja. Trips that combine fishing with a visit to the near-deserted ocean beaches that extend for miles along the coast from Zihuatanejo can also be arranged. Sam Lushinsky at **Ixtapa Sport-Fishing Charters,** 33 Olde Mill Run, Stroudsburg, PA 18360 (☎ 570/688-9466; e-mail: ixtspts@ epix.net), is a noted fishing outfitter.

Boating and fishing expeditions from the new **Marina Ixtapa,** a bit north of the Ixtapa Hotel Zone, can also be arranged. As a rule, everything available in or through the marina is more expensive, in addition to being more "Americanized."

Sailboats, Windsurfers, and other **water-sports equipment** rentals are usually available at various stands on Playa La Ropa, Playa las Gatas, Isla Ixtapa, and at the main beach, Playa Palmar, in Ixtapa. **Parasailing** can be done at La Ropa and Palmar. **Kayaks** are available for rent at the **Zihuatanejo Scuba Center** (see below), hotels in Ixtapa, and some water-sports operations on Playa La Ropa.

Scuba-diving trips are arranged through the **Zihuatanejo Scuba Center,** on Cuauhtémoc 3 (☎/fax 7/554-2147). Fees start at around $70 for two dives, including all equipment and lunch. Marine biologist and dive instructor Juan Barnard speaks excellent English and is very knowledgeable about the area, which has nearly 30 different dive sites, including walls and caves. He's also known as a very fun guide. Diving takes place year-round, though the water is clearest May to December, when visibility is 100 feet or better. The nearest decompression chamber is in Acapulco. Advance reservations for dives are advised during Christmas and Easter.

Surfing is particularly good at Petacalco Beach north of Ixtapa.

LAND SPORTS & ACTIVITIES

In Ixtapa, the **Club de Golf Ixtapa Palma Real** (☎ 7/553-1062 or 7/553-1163), in front of the Sheraton Hotel, has an 18-hole course designed by Robert Trent Jones, Jr. The greens fee is $60, caddies cost $12 for 18 holes and $8 for 9 holes, electric carts are $25, and clubs are $20. Tee-times begin at 7am, and they don't take reservations. (AE, MC, V are the credit cards accepted.) The **Marina Ixtapa Golf Course** (☎ 7/553-1410; fax 7/553-0825), designed by Robert von Hagge, has 18 challenging holes. The greens fee is $85 while cart, caddies, and clubs are $20 each. Tee-off is at 7am. Call for reservations 24 hours in advance. (AE, MC, V accepted.)

To polish your **tennis** game in Zihuatanejo, try the **Hotel Villa del Sol** at Playa La Ropa (open to guests only; ☎ 7/554-2239 or 7/554-3239). In Ixtapa, the **Club de Golf Ixtapa** (☎ 7/553-1062 or 7/553-1163) and the **Marina Ixtapa Golf Course** (☎ 7/553-1410; fax 7/553-0825) both have lit public courts and rent equipment. Fees are $10 per hour daytime, $12 per hour at night. Call for reservations. In addition, the **Dorado Pacífico** and most of the four- or five-star hotels on the main beach of Ixtapa have courts.

For riding, **Rancho Playa Linda** (☎ 7/554-3085) offers guided trail rides from the Playa Linda beach (about 8 miles north of Ixtapa). Guided rides begin at 8:30, 9:45, and 11am, and 3, 4, and 5pm. Groups of three or more riders can arrange their own tour, which is especially nice a little later in the evening around sunset (though you'll need mosquito repellent in the evening). Riders can chose to trace along the beach to the mouth of the river and back through coconut plantations, or hug the beach for the whole ride (which usually lasts 1 to 1 1/2 hours). The fee is around $25, cash only. Travel agencies in either town can arrange your trip but will charge a bit more for transportation. Reservations are suggested in the high season.

A **countryside tour** of a fishing village, coconut and mango plantations, and the **Barra de Potosí Lagoon,** which is 14 miles south of Zihuatanejo and is known for its tropical birds, is available through local travel agencies for $55 to $70. The tour typically lasts 5 1/2 hours and includes lunch and time for swimming. Because the town is very small without much to see or do, this tour is really a day at a remote beach. The beach is generally crowded around noon with people from the tour buses, but tranquil at other times.

For **off-the-beaten-track tours,** contact Alex León Pineda, the friendly and knowledgeable owner of **Fw4 Tours** in the Los Patios Center in Ixtapa (☎ 7/553-1442; fax 7/553-2014). His countryside tour ($40) goes to coconut and banana plantations, small villages of traditional brick makers and palm thatch huts, and to the beach at La Saladita, where fishers and visitors together prepare a lunch of fresh lobster, dorado, or snapper. His tour to **Petatlán** and the **Laguna de San Valentín** is also very popular, at $48. Highlights include a visit to a small museum, the local market, and town church. A stop at the lagoon is next, followed by lunch on a small island. Major credit cards are accepted with a surcharge.

5 Shopping

ZIHUATANEJO

Like other resorts in Mexico, Zihuatanejo has its quota of T-shirt and souvenir shops, but it's becoming a better place to buy Mexican crafts, folk art, and jewelry. The **artisan's market** on calle Cinco de Mayo is a good place to start your shopping before moving on to specialty shops. There's also a **municipal market** on avenida Benito Juárez (about 5 blocks inland from the waterfront), but most of the vendors offer the same things—huaraches, hammocks, and baskets—with little variety. The market area sprawls over several blocks. Spreading inland from the waterfront some 3 or 4 blocks are numerous small shops well worth exploring.

Besides the places listed below, check out **Alberto's** at Cuauhtémoc 12 and 15 for jewelry. Also on Cuauhtémoc, 2 blocks down from the Nueva Zelanda Coffee Shop, is a small shop that looks like a market stand, selling beautiful tablecloths, napkins, and other linens. All are handmade in Aguascalientes and are beautiful examples of drawn work and handmade lace from central Mexico.

Shops are generally open Monday to Saturday from 10am to 2pm and 4 to 8pm; many of the better shops close on Sunday, but some smaller souvenir stands stay open, though hours vary.

Boutique D'Xochitl. Ejido at Cuauhtémoc. ☎ **7/554-2131.**

Light crinkle-cotton clothing that's perfect for tropical climates. Hours are Monday to Saturday from 9am to 9pm and Sunday from 11am to 9pm. AE, MC. V.

Casa Marina. Paseo del Pescador 9. ☎ **7/554-2373.** Fax 7/554-3533.

This small complex extends from the waterfront to Álvarez near Cinco de Mayo and houses four shops, each specializing in handcrafted wares from all over Mexico. Items include handsome rugs, textiles, masks, colorful woodcarvings, and silver jewelry. Café Marina, the small coffee shop in the complex, has shelves and shelves of used paperback books in several languages for sale. It's open daily from 9am to 9pm during the high season and from 10am to 2pm and 4 to 8pm during the rest of the year. AE, MC, V.

⭘ **Coco Cabaña Collectibles.** Guerrero and Álvarez. ☎ **7/554-2518.**

Located next to Coconuts Restaurant, this impressive shop is filled with carefully selected crafts and folk art from all across the country, including fine Oaxacan woodcarvings. Owner Pat Cummings once ran a gallery in New York, and the inventory reveals her discriminating eye. If you make a purchase, she'll cash your dollars at the going rate. Her shop's opposite the Hotel Citali and is open Monday to Saturday from 10am to 2pm and 6 to 10pm; closed during August and September. AE, MC, V.

Hacienda Luna Azul. Paseo del Pescador 18. No phone.

This is a memorable little shop that specializes in candles and funky decorative items from curios to furniture. The style is contemporary Mexican, with burnished finishes and common motifs of the sun and moon. No credit cards; open Monday to Saturday 10am to 2pm, and 6pm to 9pm.

Viva Zapatos. Cuauhtemoc 21. ☎ **7/554-4410.**

Owner Marta Valle personally chooses every item in this store. Here you will find bathing suits to fit every shape and fashion trend, great casual and not-so-casual resort wear, sunglasses, and everything else for looking good in and out of the water. The store is three doors down from the Nueva Zelanda Coffee Shop and is open Monday to Saturday from 10am to 2pm, and 4 to 9pm. AE, MC, V.

IXTAPA

Shopping is not especially memorable in Ixtapa, with T-shirts and Mexican crafts the most usual wares. On several plazas, air-conditioned shops carry resort wear as well as T-shirts and jewelry. Brand-name sportswear is sold at **Ferroni, Bye-Bye, Aca-Joe,** and **Navale.** All of these shops are within the same area on bulevar Ixtapa, across from the beachside hotels, and most are open from 9am to 2pm and 4 to 9pm, including Sunday.

⭐ **La Fuente.** Los Patios Center on Bulevar Ixtapa. ☎ **7/553-0812.**

This terrific shop carries gorgeous Talavera pottery, wicker tables in the form of jaguars, handblown glassware, masks, tin mirrors and frames, hand-embroidered clothing from Chiapas, and wood and papier-mâché miniatures. It's open daily from 9am to 10pm during the high season and 10am to 2pm and 5 to 9pm for the low season. MC, V.

6 Ixtapa & Zihuatanejo After Dark

With an exception or two, Zihuatanejo nightlife dies down around 11pm or midnight. For a good selection of clubs, discos, hotel fiestas, special events, and fun watering holes with live music and dancing, head for Ixtapa. Just keep in mind that the shuttle bus stops at 11pm, and a taxi ride back to Zihuatanejo after midnight costs 50% more than the regular price. During off-season (after Easter or before Christmas) hours vary: Some places are open only on weekends, while others are closed completely. In Zihuatanejo the most popular hangout for local residents and expats is **Paccolo**, around the corner from Amue-blados Valle. It's the one place where you can find a lively crowd of locals almost every night.

THE CLUB & MUSIC SCENE

Many discos and dance clubs stay open until the last customers leave, so closing hours are dependent upon revelers. Most discos have a ladies night at least once a week—admission and drinks are free for women, making it easy for men to buy them a drink.

Carlos 'n' Charlie's. Bulevar Ixtapa (just north of the Best Western Posada Real), Ixtapa. ☎ **7/553-0085.** Cover after 9pm for dancing $6, including drink tokens (only on Sat during the off-season).

Knee-deep in nostalgia, bric-a-brac, silly sayings, and photos from the Mexican Revolution, this restaurant-nightclub offers party ambiance and good food. The eclectic menu includes iguana in season (with Alka-Seltzer and aspirin on the house). Out back by the beach is an open-air section (partly shaded) with a raised wooden platform for "pier-dancing" at night. The recorded rock and roll mixes with sounds of the ocean surf. The restaurant is open daily from 10am to midnight; pier dancing is nightly from 9pm to 3am.

Christine. In the Hotel Krystal, Bulevar Ixtapa, Ixtapa. ☎ **7/553-0456.** Cover varies depending on the day of the week, from "free" to $15. AE, MC, V.

This glitzy street-side disco is famous for its midnight light show, which features classical music played on a mega–sound system. A semicircle of tables in tiers overlooks the dance floor. No tennis shoes, sandals, or shorts are allowed, and reservations are advised during high season. It's open nightly during high season from 10pm to the wee hours. (Off-season hours vary.)

Señor Frog's. Bulevar Ixtapa in the La Puerta Center, Ixtapa. ☎ **7/553-2282.** No cover.

A companion restaurant to Carlos 'n' Charlie's (see above), Señor Frog's has several dining sections and a warehouse-like bar with raised dance floors. Rock and roll plays from large speakers, sometimes prompting even dinner patrons to shimmy by their tables between courses. The restaurant is open daily from 6pm to midnight; the bar is open until 3am.

HOTEL FIESTAS & THEME NIGHTS

Many hotels hold Mexican fiestas and other special events that include dinner, drinks, live music, and entertainment for a fixed price (generally $33). The **Barceló Ixtapa**—formerly the Sheraton—(☎ **7/553-1858**) continues the tradition of its popular Wednesday-night fiesta; good Mexican fiestas are also held by the **Krystal Hotel** (☎ **7/553-0333**) and **Dorado Pacífico** (☎ **7/553-2025**) in Ixtapa. The Barceló Ixtapa is the only one that offers these in the off-season. Call for reservations (travel agencies also sell tickets) and be sure you understand what the fixed price covers (drinks, tax, and tip are not always included).

4

The Oaxaca Coast: From Puerto Escondido to Huatulco

*C*oastal towns in Oaxaca are covered in this chapter. **Puerto Escondido,** noted for its stellar surf break, laid-back village ambiance, attractive and inexpensive inns, and nearby nature excursions, is by itself a worthy travel destination with exceptional value. The small village of **Puerto Ángel,** just 50 miles south of Puerto Escondido and 30 miles north of the Bahías of Huatulco, is a nice day-trip from either of those destinations. It might also serve as a quiet place to relax for several days, providing you care little for any activity beyond the beach.

Further south of Acapulco, the **Bahías de Huatulco** encompass a total of nine bays—each more lovely than the last—on a pristine portion of Oaxaca's coast. Development of the area has been gradual and well planned, with great sensitivity to preserving and protecting the natural ecosystem. The town of **Huatulco,** 80 miles south of Puerto Escondido, is building a name for itself as Mexico's most authentic adventure tourism haven. Though it has an 18-hole golf course and a handful of resort hotels, it also offers a growing array of soft adventures that range from bay tours to diving, river rafting, and rappelling. Both dining and nightlife remain limited here, but the setting is beautiful and relaxing.

1 Puerto Escondido

230 miles (368km) SE of Acapulco; 150 miles (240km) NW of Salina Cruz; 50 miles (80km) NW of Puerto Ángel

Puerto Escondido (*pwer*-toe es-con-*dee*-do) is principally known for its ranking as one of the world's top surf sites. It's a place for those whose priorities include the dimensions of the surf break (big), the temperature of a beer (cold), and the "OTA" (beach-speak for "optimal tanning angle"). Time here is measured by the tides, and the pace is relaxed for the young and very hip crowd that comes here.

Puerto Escondido

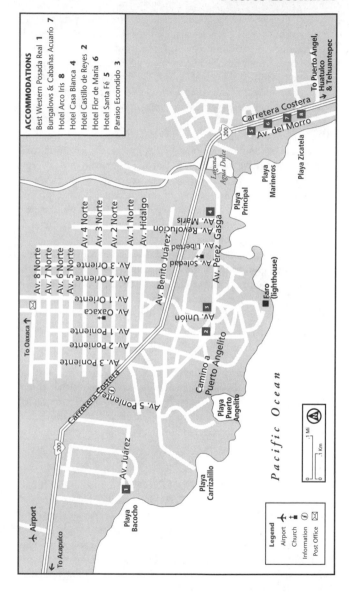

ACCOMMODATIONS

Best Western Posada Real **1**
Bungalows & Cabañas Acuario **7**
Hotel Arco Iris **8**
Hotel Casa Blanca **4**
Hotel Castillo de Reyes **2**
Hotel Flor de María **6**
Hotel Santa Fé **5**
Paraiso Escondido **3**

To Oaxaca

To Acapulco

Airport

Av. Juárez

Carretera Costera

Av. 5 Poniente

Av. 3 Poniente

Av. 2 Poniente

Av. 1 Poniente

Av. Oaxaca

Av. 1 Oriente

Av. 2 Oriente

Av. 3 Oriente

Av. 5 Norte

Av. 6 Norte

Av. 7 Norte

Av. 8 Norte

Av. 1 Norte

Av. 2 Norte

Av. 3 Norte

Av. 4 Norte

Av. Hidalgo

Av. Benito Juárez

Av. Soledad

Av. Libertad

Av. Pérez Gasga

Av. Revolución

Av. Marís

Av. Unión

Camino a Puerto Angelito

Carretera Costera

Av. del Morro

To Puerto Ángel, Huatulco & Tehuantepec

Laguna Agua Dulce

Playa Principal

Playa Marineros

Playa Zicatela

Faro (lighthouse)

Playa Puerto Angelito

Playa Carrizalillo

Playa Bacocho

Pacific Ocean

Legend
Airport
Church
Information
Post Office

1 MI
1 Km

Yet "Puerto"—as the locals call it—is broadening its appeal. Its location makes it an ideal jumping off point for ecological explorations of neighboring jungle and estuary sanctuaries, as well as indigenous mountain settlements. Increasingly, it is a place enjoyed by those seeking both spiritual and physical renewal, with abundant massage and bodywork services, yoga classes, and exceptional and varied vegetarian dining options—not to mention seaside tranquility.

People come from the United States, Canada, and Europe to stay for weeks and even months—easily and inexpensively. Expats have migrated here from Los Cabos, Acapulco, and Puerto Vallarta seeking what originally attracted them to their former homes—stellar beaches, friendly locals, and inexpensive prices. Added pleasures include an absence of beach vendors and time-share sales, an abundance of English speakers, and terrific and inexpensive dining and nightlife.

This is a real place, not a produced resort. European travelers make up a significant number of the visitors, and it's common to hear a variety of languages on the beach and in the bars. Solo travelers will probably make new friends within an hour of arriving, if they choose. No doubt about it: There are still scores of surfers here, lured by the best break in Mexico, but espresso cafes and live music are becoming just as ubiquitous, making an intriguing combo.

It's been dismissed as a colony of former hippies and settled backpackers, but it's so much more. I have a theory that those who favor "Puerto" are just trying to keep the place true to its name (*escondido* means "hidden") and undiscovered by tourists. I consider it the best overall beach value in Mexico, from hotels to dining.

ESSENTIALS

GETTING THERE & DEPARTING   By Plane   AeroCaribe and **Aerovega** (☎ **9/582-0151**) have daily flights between Oaxaca and Puerto Escondido on a small plane. AeroCaribe runs both a morning (7:50am) and evening (7:20pm) flight during high season, with tickets priced about $100 each way. The Aerovega flight leaves at 7:30am to Oaxaca, returning at 8:30am. Prices are about $75 each way. Tickets for both of these lines can be handled by **Rodimar Travel** (see below).

If flights to Puerto Escondido are booked, you have the option (possibly less expensive) of flying into the Huatulco airport via scheduled or charter flights. This is an especially viable option if your destination is Puerto Ángel, which lies between Puerto Escondido and Huatulco but is closer to the Huatulco airport. An airport taxi will cost $50 from Huatulco to Puerto Ángel or $75 between Huatulco and Puerto Escondido. If you can find a local taxi, rather than the government-chartered cabs, you can reduce these fares by about 50%, including the payment of a $5 mandatory airport exit tax. There is frequent bus service between the three destinations. **Budget Car Rental** has cars available for one-way travel to Puerto Escondido, with an added drop charge of about $10. In Puerto Escondido, the rental office is located at the entrance to Bacocho, (☎ **9/582-0312**), at the Huatulco airport, ☎ **9/587-0010.**

Arriving: The **airport (PXM)** is about 2¹/₂ miles north of the center of town near Playa Bacocho. Prices for the collective **minibus** to hotels are posted: $2.25 per person. **Aerotransportes Terrestres** sells colectivo tickets to the airport through **Rodimar Travel** on Perez Gasga St. (the pedestrian-only zone) next to Hotel Casa Blanca (☎ **9/582-1551;** fax 9/582-0737). They will pick you up at your hotel.

By Car   From Oaxaca, Highway 175 via Pochutla is the least bumpy road. The 150-mile trip takes 5 to 6 hours. Highway 200 from Acapulco is also a good road and should take about 5 hours to travel. However, this stretch of road has been plagued with car and bus hijackings and robberies in recent years—travel only during the daytime.

From Salina Cruz to Puerto Escondido is a 4-hour drive, past the Bahías de Huatulco and the turnoff for Puerto Ángel. The road is paved but can be rutty in the rainy season. The trip from Huatulco to Puerto Escondido takes just under 2 hours and can easily be made by hiring a taxi for a fixed rate (about $50).

By Bus   Buses are frequent between Acapulco and Oaxaca and south along the coast to and from Huatulco and Pochutla, the transit hub for Puerto Ángel. Puerto Escondido's several bus stations are all within a 3-block area. For **Gacela** and **Estrella Blanca,** the station is just north of the coastal highway where Pérez Gasga crosses it. First-class buses go from here to Pochutla (1 hr.), Huatulco, Acapulco, Zihuatanejo, and Mexico City (11 hr.). A block north at Hidalgo and Primera Poniente is **Transportes Oaxaca Istmo,** in a small restaurant. Several buses leave daily for Pochutla, Salina Cruz (5 hr.), or Oaxaca (10 hr. via

Salina Cruz). The terminal for **Líneas Unidas, Estrella del Valle,** and **Oaxaca Pacífico** is 2 blocks farther down on Hidalgo, just past Oriente 3. They service Oaxaca via Pochutla. At Primera Norte 207, **Cristóbal Colón** buses (☎ **9/582-1073**) serve Salina Cruz, Tuxtla Gutiérrez, San Cristóbal de las Casas, and Oaxaca.

Arriving: Minibuses from Pochutla or Huatulco will let you off anywhere en route, including the spot where Pérez Gasga leads down to the pedestrians-only zone.

VISITOR INFORMATION   The **State Tourist Office, SEDETUR** (☎ **9/582-0175**), is about a half mile from the airport at the corner of Carretera Costera and bulevar Benito Juárez. It's open Monday to Friday from 9am to 5pm and Saturday from 10am to 1pm. A kiosk at the airport is open for incoming flights during high season, and another, near the west end of the paved tourist zone, is open Monday to Saturday from 9am to 1pm.

CITY LAYOUT   Looking out on the Bahía Principal and its beach, to your left you'll see the eastern end of the bay, consisting of a small beach, **Playa Marinero,** followed by rocks jutting into the sea. Beyond this is **Playa Zicatela,** unmistakably the main surfing beach. Zicatela Beach is really coming into is own as the most popular area for visitors, with restaurants, bungalows, surf shops, and hotels, well back from the shoreline. The western side of the bay, to your right, is about a mile long, with a lighthouse and low green hills descending to meet a long stretch of fine sand. Beaches on this end are not quite as accessible by land, but hotels are overcoming this difficulty by constructing beach clubs reached by steep private roads and Jeep shuttles.

The town of Puerto Escondido has roughly an east-west orientation, with the long Zicatela Beach turning sharply southeast. Residential areas behind (east of) Zicatela Beach tend to have unpaved streets; the older town (with paved streets) is north of the Carretera Costera (Highway 200). The streets are numbered, with avenida Oaxaca the dividing line between east (oriente) and west (poniente), and avenida Hidalgo the divider between north (norte) and south (sur).

South of this is the original **tourist zone,** through which avenida Pérez Gasga makes a loop. Part of this loop is a paved pedestrians-only zone, known locally as the *Adoquin,* after the hexagonal-shaped, interlocking bricks used in its paving. Hotels, shops, restaurants, bars, travel agencies, and other services are all conveniently located here. In the morning, taxis, delivery trucks, and private vehicles are allowed. But at noon it is closed off, with chains fastened at each end.

Avenida Pérez Gasga angles down from the highway at the east end; on the west, where the Adoquin terminates, it climbs in a wide northward curve to cross the highway, after which it becomes avenida Oaxaca.

The beaches—Playa Principal in the center of town and Marinero and Zicatela southeast of the town center—are interconnected. It's easy to walk from one to the other, crossing behind the separating rocks. Puerto Ángelito, Carrizalillo, and Bacocho beaches are west of town and can be reached by road or water. Playa Bacocho hosts the few more-expensive hotels.

GETTING AROUND   Almost everything is within walking distance of the Adoquin. **Taxis** are inexpensive around town; call ☎ **9/582-0990** for service. Mountain bikes, motorcycles, and cars can be rented at **Arrendadora Express,** Pérez Gasga 605-E (☎ **800/710-6218** toll-free in Mexico, or 9/582-1355), on your right just as you enter the Adoquin on the east. Bike rentals run about $5 per day, $15 per week.

Though it's easy to hire a boat, it is possible to walk beside the sea from the Playa Principal to the tiny beach of Puerto Ángelito, but it's a bit of a hike.

FAST FACTS: Puerto Escondido

Area Code   The telephone area code is **9.**

Currency Exchange   Banamex, Bancomer, Bancrear, and Banco Bital all have branches in town, and all will change money during business hours; their individual hours vary, but you can generally find one of the above open Monday to Saturday from 8am to 7pm. Automated tellers are also available, as are currency-exchange offices.

Hospital   Try Unidad Medico-Quirurgica del Sur, avenida Oaxaca #113 (☎ **9/582-1288**), which offers 24-hour emergency services, and has an English-speaking staff and doctors.

Internet Access   There's an excellent cybercafe on the second floor of La Tigre Azul (☎ **9/582-1871**) on the Adoquin, that charges $2 per half hour, or $4 per hour for Internet access. On Zicatela beach, there's a small, extremely busy Internet service called Cyber-café, at the entrance to the Bungalows & Cabañas Acuario on Calle de Morro s/n (☎ **9/582-0357;** ask for the cybercafe). It's open daily from 8am until 9pm. They charge $1.50 for 15 minutes online, $3 for a half hour, or $5 per hour.

Pharmacy   Farmacia de Mas Ahorro (☎ **9/582-1911**) is open 24 hours a day.

Post Office   The post office is on avenida Oaxaca, at the corner of avenida 7 Norte (☎ **9/582-0959**). Open Monday to Friday 8am to 4pm, Saturday 8am to 1pm.

Safety   Depending on who you talk to, you need to be wary of potential beach muggings, primarily at night. However, the hope is that the new public lighting at Playa Principal and Playa Zicatela will go a long way in preventing these incidents. Local residents say most incidents happen after tourists overindulge and then go for a midnight stroll along the beach. It's so casual, that it's an easy place to let your guard down, so don't carry valuables, and use common sense and normal precautions.

Also, respect the power of the magnificent waves here. Drownings occur all too frequently.

Seasons   Season designations are somewhat arbitrary, but most consider high season to be mid-December to January, around and during Easter week, July and August, and during other school and business vacations.

Telephones   There are numerous businesses offering long-distance telephone service, many along the Adoquin, with several offering credit-card convenience. The best bet remains the purchase and use of a prepaid Ladatel phone card.

BEACH TIME

BEACHES   Playa Principal, where the small boats are available for fishing and tour services, and **Playa Marinero,** adjacent to the town center and on a deep bay, are the best swimming beaches. Here, beach chairs and sun shades rent for about $2, a charge which may be waived if you order food or drinks from the restaurants that offer them. **Zicatela Beach** adjoins Playa Marinero and extends southeasterly for several miles. The surfing part of Zicatela, with large curling waves, is about 1^1/2 miles from the town center. Due to the size and strength of the waves here, it's not a swimming beach, and only experienced surfers should attempt to ride Zicatela's powerful waves. New stadium-style lighting has recently been installed in both of these beach areas, in an attempt to crack down on nocturnal beach muggings. It has diminished the appeal of the Playa Principal restaurants, looking into the bright lights as you do now, rather than at the nighttime sea. Lifeguard service has recently been added to Zicatela Beach.

Barter with one of the fishermen on the main beach for a ride to **Playa Manzanillo and Puerto Angelito,** two beaches separated by a rocky outcropping. Here, and at other small coves just west of town, swimming is safe and the pace calmer than in town. You'll find palapas, hammock rentals, and snorkeling equipment. The clear blue water is perfect for snorkeling. Enjoy fresh fish, tamales, and other Mexican dishes cooked right at the beach by local entrepreneurs. Puerto Angelito is also accessible by a dirt road that's a short distance from town, so it tends to be busier. **Playa Bacocho** is on a shallow cove farther to the northwest and is best reached by taxi or boat, rather than walking. It's also the location of Coco's Beach Club at the Posada Real Hotel. They are open to the public, for a cover charge of $2.50, which gains access to their pools, food and beverage service, and facilities.

MASSAGE   There is an increasing number of services providing massage, energy, and body work. **Temazcalli,** ave. Infraganti and calle Temazcalli (☎ **9/582-1023;** ptemazcalli@yahoo.com) offers relaxation and energetic massages, as well as a herbal healing steam bath based on the ancient *temazcal* (native sweat lodge), and aqua mystical massage services.

SURFING   Zicatela Beach, $1^1/2$ miles southeast of Puerto Escondido's town center, is a world-class surf spot. A surfing competition in August, and Fiesta Puerto Escondido, held for at least three days each November, celebrate Puerto Escondido's renowned waves. The tourism office can supply exact dates and details. Beginning surfers often start out at Playa Marinero before graduating to Zicatela's awesome waves.

NESTING RIDLEY TURTLES   The beaches around Puerto Escondido and Puerto Ángel are nesting grounds for the endangered Ridley turtle. During the summer months, tourists can sometimes see the turtles laying eggs or observe the hatchlings trekking to the sea.

Escobilla Beach near Puerto Escondido and **Barra de la Cruz Beach** near Puerto Ángel seem to be the favored nesting grounds of the Ridley turtle. In 1991 the Mexican government established the Centro Mexicano la Tortuga, known locally as the **Turtle Museum,** for the study and life enhancement of the turtle. On

Ecotours & Other Adventurous Explorations

Turismo Rodimar Travel Agency, on the landward side just inside the Adoquin (☎ **9/582-0734** or 9/582-0737; open daily 8am to 10pm), is an excellent source of information and can arrange all types of tours and travel. Manager Gaudencio Díaz speaks English. He can arrange individualized tours or formal ones such as **Michael Malone's Hidden Voyages Ecotours.** Malone, a Canadian ornithologist, takes you on a dawn or sunset trip to **Manialtepec Lagoon,** a bird-filled mangrove lagoon about 12 miles northwest of Puerto Escondido. The cost is $32 and includes a stop on a secluded beach for a swim.

Another exceptional provider of ecologically oriented tour services is **Ana's Eco Tours,** located in Un Tigre Azul (on the Adoquin ☎ **9/582-1871** or 582/2001; ana@anasecotours. com). A native of the area, Anatolia Marquez was born in the small nearby mountain village of Jamiltepec, and has an intimate knowledge of the customs, people, flora, and fauna of the area. She or her expert guides lead small groups on both eco-adventures as well as cultural explorations. Tours into the surrounding mountains include a 5-hour horseback excursion up to the jungle region of the Chatino natives' **healing hotsprings,** or to **Nopala,** a Chatino mountain village and a neighboring coffee plantation. An all-day trip to **Jamiltepec,** a small, traditional Mixtex village offers the opportunity to experience day-to-day life in an authentic village. The visit includes a stop at a market, their church, and cemetery, and to the homes of local artisans.

view are examples of all species of marine turtles living in Mexico, plus six species of freshwater turtles and two species of land turtles. The center is located on **Mazunte Beach,** near the town of the same name. Hours are 10am to 4:30pm Tuesday to Saturday, and Sunday 10am to 2pm; entry is $2.50. Also found here is a unique shop that sells naturally produced shampoos, bath oils, and other personal care products. These are all made and packaged by the local community, part of a project to replace the income lost from turtle poaching. Not only are the products of excellent quality, but also purchasing them goes a long way in

One of the most popular all-day tours offered by both companies is to **Chacahua Lagoon National Park** about 42 miles west, at a cost of $35 with Rodimar, or $25 with Ana's. These are true ecotours—small groups treading lightly. You visit a beautiful sandy spit of beach, and the lagoon, which has incredible bird life and flowers including black orchids. Locals provide fresh barbecued fish on the beach. If you know Spanish and get information from the tourism office, it's possible to stay overnight under a small palapa, but bring plenty of insect repellent.

An interesting and slightly out-of-the-ordinary excursion is **Aventura Submarina,** located "on the strip" (Zicatela Beach, calle del Morro s/n, in the Acuario building near the Cafecito; ☎ 9/582-2353). Jorge, who speaks fluent English and is a certified scuba-dive instructor, guides individuals or small groups of qualified divers along the Coco trench, just offshore. Price is $55 for a two-tank dive, or $35 for a one-tank dive. They also offer refresher courses at no extra charge. The company also arranges surface activities such as deep-sea fishing, surfing, and trips to lesser-known yet nearby swimming beaches. If you want to write ahead, contact him at Apdo. Postal 159, Puerto Escondido, 71980 Oaxaca.

Fishermen keep their colorful *pangas* (small boats) on the beach beside the Adoquin. A **fisherman's tour** around the coastline in a panga costs about $35, but a ride to Zicatela or Puerto Ángelito beaches is only $5. Most hotels offer or will gladly arrange tours to meet your needs.

ensuring the cessation of poaching practices in the community. Buses go to Mazunte from Puerto Ángel about every half hour, and a taxi ride is around $4.50. You can fit this in with a trip to Zipolite Beach, the next beach closer to Puerto Ángel.

SHOPPING

The Adoquin sports a row of tourist shops selling straw hats, postcards, and Puerto Escondido T-shirts, plus a few excellent shops featuring Guatemalan, Oaxacan, and Balinese clothing and art. You can also get a tattoo, or rent surfboards and boogie boards here. Interspersed among the shops, hotels, restaurants, and bars are pharmacies and minimarkets for basic necessities. The largest of these is **Oh! Mar,** Ave. Pez Gasga 502, ☎ **9/582-0286**), that not only sells anything you'd need for a day at the beach, but also sells phone (Ladatel) cards, stamps, and Cuban cigars, plus has a mail drop box and arranges fishing tours.

Note that during high season businesses and shops are generally open all day; however, during low season they close between 2pm and 5pm. Some highlights along the Adoquin include: **Casa di Bambole,** Av. Pérez Gasga 707 (☎ **9/582-1331**), for high-quality clothing, bags, and jewelry from Guatemala and Chiapas; and **La Luna,** Av. Pérez Gasga s/n (no phone), for jewelry, Batik surf wear, and Balinese art. The store name **1000 Hamacas,** Av. Pérez Gasga s/n (no phone), says it all. Custom-made hammocks in all colors—it's the favored way to take a siesta here—may double as your bedding if you're staying in one of the numerous surfer hangouts on Zicatela beach. **Central Surf** has a shop here on the Adoquin (☎ **9/582-0568**) as well as another on Zicatela Beach, Calle Morro s/n (☎ **9/582-2285**), where they rent and sell surf boards, offer surf lessons, and all the related gear. **Un Tigre Azul,** Av. Pérez Gasga s/n (☎ **9/582-1871**), is the only true art gallery in town, with quality works of art and a cafe-bar, plus Internet services upstairs.

Also of interest is ✪ **Bazaar Santa Fe,** Hotel Santa Fe lobby, on Zicatela beach, Calle del Morro s/n (☎ **9/582-0170**), which sells antiques, including vintage Oaxacan embroidered clothing, jewelry, and religious artifacts. At **Bikini Brazil,** Calle del Morro s/n (no phone), you'll find the hottest bikinis under the sun imported from Brazil, land of the tanga. Just in front of the Rockaway Resort on Zicatela beach, there's a 24-hour **mini-super** that sells the basic necessities: beer, suntan lotion, and basic food supplies (no phone).

WHERE TO STAY
MODERATE

Best Western Posada Real. Av. Benito Juárez 1, Fracc. Bacocho, 71980 Puerto Escondido, Oax. ☎ **800/528-1234** in the U.S., or 9/582-0133 and 9/582-0237. Fax 9/582-0192. 100 units. A/C TV TEL. High season $110 double. Low season $85 double. AE, DC, MC, V.

Set on a cliff top overlooking the beach, the expanse of manicured lawn that backs the hotel is one of the most popular places in town for a sunset cocktail. A large heated swimming pool plus a wading pool for children, tennis courts, a putting green, two restaurants, and lobby bar round out the amenities on the main level. The clean but smallish standard rooms are less enticing than the hotel grounds. A big plus here is their Coco's Beach Club, with a half-mile stretch of soft-sand beach, large swimming pool, kids' playground, and bar with swing-style chairs and occasional live music. A shuttle service (or a lengthy walk down a set of stairs) will take you there. This is a great place for families, and it's open to the public ($2.50 cover for nonguests). The hotel is located only 5 minutes from the airport and about the same from Puerto Escondido's tourist zone, but a taxi is needed to get to town. Travel agency, car rental, gift shop, and laundry on-site.

✪ **Hotel Santa Fe.** Calle del Morro (Apdo. Postal 96), 71980 Puerto Escondido, Oax. ☎ **9/582-0170** or 9/582-0266. Fax 9/582-0260. E-mail: info@ hotelsantafe.com.mx. 69 units (59 rooms, 2 suites, 8 bungalows). A/C TV TEL. High season $80.50 double; $91 bungalow. Low season $56 double. AE, MC, V. Free parking.

If Puerto Escondido is the best beach value in Mexico, then the Santa Fe is without a doubt one of the best hotel values in Mexico. It's got a winning combination of unique Spanish-colonial style, a welcoming staff, and clean, comfortable rooms. The hotel has grown up over the years alongside the surfers who came to Puerto in the 1960s and 1970s—and nostalgically return today. It's located a half a mile southeast of the town center, off Highway 200, at the curve in the road where Marinero and Zicatela beaches join—a prime sunset-watching spot. The three-story hacienda-style buildings have clay-tiled stairs, archways, and blooming bougainvillea, surrounding two courtyard swimming pools (one is a lap pool). The ample but simply stylish rooms feature large tile bathrooms, colonial furnishings, handwoven fabrics, Guerrero pottery lamps, and both air-conditioning and ceiling fans, plus TVs with local channels. Most have a balcony or terrace, with ocean views on upper floors. Bungalows are next to the hotel, and each has a living room, kitchen, and bedroom with two double beds. The Santa Fe Restaurant is one of the best on the southern Pacific coast. There's also a tour service, boutique, massage, laundry, baby-sitting service, and security boxes.

○ **Paraíso Escondido.** Calle Union 10, 71980 Puerto Escondido, Oax. ☎ **9/582-0444.** 20 rooms, 5 suites. A/C. $69 double; $125 suite. No credit cards.

This eclectic inn is hidden away on a shady street a couple of short blocks from the Adoquin and Playa Principal. A curious collection of Mexican folk art, masks, religious art, and paintings on the walls make this an exercise in Mexican magic realism, in addition to a tranquil place to stay. An inviting pool is surrounded by gardens, Adirondack chairs, and a fountain, and has a commanding view of the bay. The rooms each have one double and one twin bed, built-in desks, and a cozy balcony or terrace with French doors. Each has a slightly different decorative accent, and all are very clean. The suites, newly added in 2000, have a much more deluxe decor than the rooms, with recessed lighting, desks set into bay windows with French-paned windows, a living area, and large private balconies. The Penthouse suite has its own whirlpool tub and kitchenette, plus a tile chess board inlaid in the floor, and murals adorning the walls—it is the owners' former apartment. The restaurant serves all three meals if you don't feel like leaving. There's limited free parking available in front of the hotel.

INEXPENSIVE

Bungalows & Cabañas Acuario. Calle del Morro s/n, 71980 Puerto Escondido, Oax. ☎ **9/582-0357** or 9/582-1026. 40 units. FAN. High season $25 double, $30 double with A/C; $40 bungalow (no A/C). Low season $21.50 double, $27 double with A/C; $35 bungalow, but you can probably negotiate a better deal once you're there. No credit cards.

Facing Zicatela beach, this surfer's sanctuary offers clean, cheap accommodations plus an on-site gym, surf shop, vegetarian restaurant, and Internet cafe. The two-story hotel and bungalows surround a pool shaded by a few great palms. Rooms are small and basic, but bungalows offer fundamental kitchen facilities. The cabañas are more open and have hammocks. There's parking, public telephones, money exchange, a pharmacy, and a vegetarian restaurant in the adjoining commercial area. The well-equipped gym costs an extra $1 per day, $15 per month.

Hotel Arco Iris. Calle del Morro s/n, Playa Zicatela, 71980 Puerto Escondido, Oax. ☎/fax **9/582-0432,** 9/582-1494, and 9/582-2344. www.qan.com/ Hotels/Arcoiris. E-mail: arcoiris@antequera.com. 26 rooms, including 8 bungalows. FAN. Double $33–$36, $36–$38 with kitchen, extra person $4. Rates go up by 10% to 20% for Easter and Christmas holidays. MC, V.

Rooms at the Arco Iris are built in a three-story colonial style house that faces Zicatela Beach. Each is simple yet comfortable, with either a spacious terrace or balcony with hangers for hammocks—all have great views, but the upstairs ones have the best views. Beds are draped with mosquito nets, and the bed-spreads are made with beautifully worked Oaxacan textiles. An upstairs restaurant serves all three meals, and a bar, "La Galera," has one of the most popular happy hours in town, daily from 5 to 7pm, with live music during high season. There is a swimming pool, wading pool, TV/game room with foreign channels, ample parking for cars and campers, a store that sells books and arts and crafts, and a drugstore. They can help you get in touch with travel agencies, local tour operators, and English speaking doctors, should the need arise.

Hotel Casa Blanca. Av. Pérez Gasga 905, 71980 Puerto Escondido, Oax. ☎ **9/582-0168.** 21 units. FAN TV. $26 double; $45 double with A/C. MC, V.

If you want to be in the heart of the Adoquin, this is your best bet for excellent value and clean, ample accommodations. The courtyard pool and adjacent palapa restaurant is a great place to hide away and enjoy a margarita or a book from the hotel's exchange rack. If you prefer, you can choose in-room dining, or an in-room massage. The bright, clean, and simply furnished rooms offer a choice of bed combinations, but all have at least two beds and a fan. Some rooms have both air-conditioning and a minifridge. The best rooms have a balcony overlooking the action in the street below, but light sleepers should consider a room in the back. Some rooms can sleep up to five ($60). This is an excellent and economical choice for families. Guest services include a special wading pool, safe-deposit boxes, money exchange, tour desk, and car rental.

Hotel Castillo de Reyes. Av. Pérez Gasga s/n, 71980 Puerto Escondido, Oax. ☎ **9/582-0442.** 18 units. FAN. High season $20 double; Low season $15 double. No credit cards.

Don Fernando, the proprietor here, has a gift for making his guests feel at home. Guests chat around tables on a shady patio near the office, which also offers safe deposit boxes and a money exchange. Most of the clean, bright, white-walled rooms have a special touch—perhaps a gourd mask or carved coconut hanging over the bed, plus overbed reading lights. There's hot water, and the rooms are shaded from the sun by palms and cooled by fans.

The "castle" is on your left as you ascend the hill on Pérez Gasga, after leaving the Adoquin (you can also enter Pérez Gasga off Highway 200). As this hotel is on one of Puerto's busiest streets, traffic noise is a consideration.

✪ **Hotel Flor de María.** Playa Marinero, 71980 Puerto Escondido, Oax. ☎/fax **9/582-0536.** FAN. 24 units. $35 double. MC, V.

Though not right on the beach, this is a real find. Canadians María and Lino Francato own this cheery, three-story hotel facing the ocean, which you can see from the rooftop. Built around a garden courtyard, each room is colorfully decorated with beautiful trompe l'oeil still lifes and landscapes painted by Lino. Two rooms have windows with a view, the remainder face into the courtyard. All have double beds with orthopedic mattresses and small safes. On the roof, there are, in addition to the great view, a small pool, shaded hammock terrace, and an open-air bar (open 5 to 9pm during high season) with a TV that receives American channels—all in all, a great sunset spot. I highly recommend the first-floor restaurant (see "Where to Dine," below). Ask about off-season discounts for long-term stays. The hotel is a third of a mile from the Adoquin and 200 feet up a sandy road from Marinero Beach on an unnamed street at the eastern end of the beach.

WHERE TO DINE

In addition to the places listed below, a Puerto Escondido tradition are the palapa restaurants on Zicatela beach for early morning surfer breakfasts, or casual dining and drinking by the sea at night. One of the most popular is **Los Tíos,** offering very economical prices and surfer-sized portions. After dinner, enjoy homemade Italian ice cream from **Gelateria Giardino,** with two locations—one on Calle Morro at Zicatela beach, and another on the Adoquin, at Pes Gasga #609 (☎ **9/582-2243**).

MODERATE

Art & Harry's. Av. Morro s/n. No phone. Main courses $3.50–$12. No credit cards. Daily 10am–10pm. SEAFOOD/STEAKS.

Located about three-quarters of a mile southeast of the Hotel Santa Fe, on the road fronting Zicatela Beach, this robust watering hole is great for taking in the sunset, especially if you're having one of their giant-sized hamburgers or grilled shrimp dinners. Late afternoon and early evening here amount to a portrait of

Puerto Escondido. You sit watching the surfers, tourists, and resident cat, as the sun dips into the ocean.

✪ **Cabo Blanco, "Where Legends are Born."** Calle del Morro s/n. ☎ **9/582-0337.** Main courses $4–$45. V. Dec–May Daily 6pm–2am. Closed June–Nov. INTERNATIONAL.

The local crowd at this beachfront restaurant craves Gary's special sauces that top his grilled fish, shrimp, steaks, and ribs. Favorites include his dill-Dijon mustard, wine-fennel, and Thai curry sauces. But you can't count on them, because Gary buys what's fresh, then creates from there. An added bonus is that Cabo Blanco turns into a hot bar on Zicatela beach, with live music each Thursday and Saturday after 11pm. Gary's wife Roxana and an all-female team of bartenders keep the crowd well served and well behaved.

✪ **Restaurant Santa Fe.** In the Hotel Santa Fe, Calle del Morro s/n. ☎ **9/582-0170.** Breakfast $2.50–$6; main courses $5–$15. AE, MC, V. Daily 7am–11pm. INTERNATIONAL.

The atmosphere here is classic and casual, with great views of the sunset and Zicatela Beach. Big pots of palms are scattered around, and fresh flowers grace the tables, all beneath a lofty palapa roof. The shrimp dishes are a bargain for the rest of the world, though at $15, a little higher-priced than the rest of town. Their perfectly grilled tuna, served with homemade french-fried potatoes and whole-grain bread, is an incredible meal deal at under $7. A *Nopale* (cactus leaf) salad on the side ($2) is a perfect complement. Vegetarian dishes are reasonably priced and creatively adapted from traditional Mexican and Italian dishes. A favorite is the house specialty, chiles rellenos. The bar offers an excellent selection of tequilas.

INEXPENSIVE

Arte la Galería. Av. Pérez Gasga. ☎ **9/582-2039.** Breakfast $1.80–$2; main courses $2.80–$4. No credit cards. Daily 8am–midnight. INTERNATIONAL/ SEAFOOD.

At the east end of the Adoquin, La Galería has a satisfying range of eats in a cool, creative setting. Dark-wood beams tower above, and contemporary works by local artists grace the walls while jazz music plays. Specialties are homemade pastas and brick-oven pizzas, but burgers and steaks are also available. Cappuccino and espresso, plus desserts such as baked pineapples, finish the meal.

Carmen's La Patisserie. Playa Marinero. ☎ **9/582-0005.** Pastries 50¢–$1.25; sandwiches $1.75–$2.25. No credit cards. Mon–Sat 7am–3pm; Sun 7am–noon. FRENCH PASTRY/SANDWICHES/COFFEE.

This tiny, excellent cafe/bakery has a steady and loyal clientele. Carmen's baked goods are unforgettable and go quickly, so arrive early for the best selection. She also provides space for an English-speaking AA group here. La Patisserie is across the street from the Hotel Flor de María.

✪ **El Cafecito.** Calle del Morro s/n, Playa Zicatela. No phone. Pastries 50¢–$1.25; main entrees $1.75–$4.75. No credit cards. Wed–Mon 6am–10pm. FRENCH PASTRY/SEAFOOD/VEGETARIAN/COFFEE.

Carmen's second shop opened a few years ago on Zicatela Beach, with a motto of "Big waves, strong coffee!" Featuring all the attractions of La Patisserie (see above), it's now also open for lunch and dinner. This restaurant actually spans two facing corners; the northern corner is set up more for coffee or a light snack, with oceanfront bistro-style seating. The southern corner offers a more relaxed setting with wicker chairs and Oaxacan cloth–topped tables set under a palapa roof. Giant shrimp dinners are under $5, with creative daily specials always a sure bet. An oversized mug of cappuccino is $1, a fresh and filling fruit smoothie goes for $1.50, and her mango eclairs—worth any price—are a steal at $1.

El Gota de Vida. Calle del Morro s/n, Playa Zicatela. No phone. Main entrees $1.50–$4.50. No credit cards. Daily 10am–11pm. VEGETARIAN/COFFEE.

Located just in front of the Bungalows Acuario (see above), this popular vegetarian restaurant is generally packed—known for its healthy food, ample portions, and low prices. Under a palapa roof and facing Zicatela Beach, they offer an extensive menu that includes fruit smoothies, espresso drinks, herbal teas, and a complete juice bar. They make their own tempeh, tofu, pastas, and whole grain breads. Creative vegetarian offerings are based on Mexican favorites, like chiles rellenos, cheese enchiladas, and bean tostados, and they also feature fresh seafood.

Herman's Best. Ave. Pez Gasga s/n. No phone. Main entrees $1.50–$3.50. No credit cards. Mon–Sat 5pm–10pm. MEXICAN/SEAFOOD.

This small restaurant has an atmosphere about as basic as it comes, but clearly they're putting all their attention into the simply delicious, home-style cooking. The menu changes daily, but generally includes a fresh fish fillet, rotisserie chicken, and

Mexican specials like enchiladas—all served with beans, rice, and homemade tortillas. It's located just after the "No Pedestrian" zone at the eastern end of the Adoquin.

María's Restaurant. In the Hotel Flor de María, Playa Marinero. ☎ **9/582-0536.** Breakfast $2.50; main courses $3–$5. No credit cards. Daily 8–11:30am, noon–2pm, and 6–10pm. INTERNATIONAL.

This first floor, open-air hotel dining room near the beach is popular with the locals. The menu changes daily and features specials such as María Francato's fresh homemade pasta dishes. María's is a third of a mile from the Adoquin and 200 feet up a sandy road from Marinero Beach on an unnamed street at the eastern end of the beach.

Un Tigre Azul. Av. Pérez Gasga s/n. ☎ **9/582-1871.** Breakfast $1.50–$3.50; sandwiches $1.50–$4; fruit shakes $1–$3. AE MC, V Mon–Fri 11am–11pm; Sat–Sun 3–11pm. SANDWICHES/COFFEE/MEXICAN.

It's principally known for it's lower level art gallery and Internet access, but climb on up to the third floor and enjoy the view overlooking Playa Principal and the ambiance of this casual, colorful cafe. It's near the western entrance to the Adoquin. A range of light appetizers includes quesadillas, nachos, fruit smoothies, and sandwiches. They also have excellent coffee, and full bar service. Happy hour is every night from 7 to 8pm.

PUERTO ESCONDIDO AFTER DARK

Sunset-watching is a ritual to plan your days around, and good lookout points abound. Watch the surfers at Zicatela and catch up on local gossip at **La Galera** upstairs on the third floor of the Arco Iris hotel. They have a nightly happy hour (with live music during high season) from 5 to 7pm. For another great sunset spot, head to the **Hotel Santa Fe** at the junction of Zicatela and Marinero beaches or the rooftop bar of **Hotel Flor de María.** For a more tranquil, romantic setting, take a cab or walk half an hour or so west to the **Hotel Posada Real.** The hotel's cliff-top lawn is a perfect sunset perch. Or climb down the cliff side (or take the hotel's shuttle bus) to **Coco's** on the beach below.

Puerto Escondido is beginning to develop a more cultural side to its nightlife: at **The Library,** located on the main street of Zicatela beach, a few blocks past the Santa Fe hotel, you can play chess or backgammon, browse through their selection of books for sale, take a Spanish class, or just enjoy an espresso or drink from their bar. Further down the street at the far southern end of

Calle Morro, **Surf Papaya** restaurant has an upstairs art gallery and also features occasional children's theatre. There's also a **Cine Club,** at the Rinconada movie theatre that features new releases in air-conditioned comfort. Movies are Fri, Sat, and Sun nights at 7:30pm. A free shuttle runs from El Cafecito on Zicatela beach each Sat and Sun at 7pm. Call ☎ **9/582-1723** for current movie listings.

When it comes to bars and clubs, Puerto has a nightlife that will satisfy anyone dedicated to late nights and good music. **Son y la Rumba** has live jazz featuring its house band with Andria Garcia, playing each night from 8pm to 11pm, with a $1 cover. It's located beneath the El Tigre Azul, on the western end of the Adoquin. Also downtown is **Tequila Sunrise,** a two-story, open and spacious disco overlooking the beach that plays Latino, reggae, cumbia, tropical, and salsa. It's a half a block from the Adoquin on avenida Marina Nacional. A small cover charge generally applies ($1–$2).

There's an ample selection of clubs along the Adoquin— among them, the **Bucanero Bar and Grill,** with a good-sized bar and outdoor patio fronting Playa Principal. **Bar Fly, The Blue Iguana** and **Rayos X** cater to a younger surf crowd with alternative and techno tunes. **Montezuma's Revenge** has live bands, usually playing contemporary Latin American music. **El Tubo** is an open-air beachside disco just west of Restaurant Alicia on the Adoquin.

Out on Zicatela, don't miss **Cabo Blanco** (see "Where to Dine," above), where a collection of local musicians get together and jam Thursdays and Saturdays during high season. **Split Coco,** just a few doors down, has live music on Tuesdays and Fridays, and TV sports on other nights. It has one of the most popular happy hours on the beach, and serves barbecue as well.

Most nightspots are open until 3am or until the customers leave.

2 Puerto Ángel: Backpacking Beach Haven

Fifty miles southeast of Puerto Escondido and 30 miles northwest of the Bays of Huatulco is the tiny fishing port of **Puerto Ángel** (*pwer*-toe *ahn*-hel). Puerto Ángel, with its beautiful beaches, unpaved streets, and budget hotels is popular with the international backpacking set and those seeking an inexpensive and restful vacation. Though damage from 1997's Hurricane Paulina

Important Travel Note

Highway 200 north to Acapulco has had numerous problems with car and bus hijackings; if you go, you would be wise to fly. Travel south to Puerto Ángel and Huatulco on this road only during the day.

was compounded by earthquake damage in 1999, Puerto Ángel continues to welcome guests with the simple beauty and tranquil atmosphere that has made it such an alluring place. Its small bay and several inlets offer peaceful swimming and good snorkeling. The village follows a slow and simple way of life: Fishermen leave very early in the morning and return with their catch by late before noon. Taxis make up most of the traffic, and the bus from Pochutla passes every half hour or so.

ESSENTIALS
GETTING THERE & DEPARTING

BY CAR   North or south from Highway 200, take coastal Highway 175 inland to Puerto Ángel. The road will be well marked with signs. From either Huatulco or Puerto Escondido, the trip should take about an hour.

BY TAXI   Taxis are readily available to take you to Puerto Ángel or Zipolite Beach for a reasonable price, or to the Huatulco airport or Puerto Escondido.

BY BUS   There are no direct buses from Puerto Escondido or Huatulco to Puerto Ángel; however, numerous buses leave Puerto Escondido and Huatulco for Pochutla, 7 miles north of Puerto Ángel, where you can transfer for the short ride to the village. If you arrive at Pochutla from either Huatulco or Puerto Escondido, you may be dropped at one of several bus stations that line the main street; walk one or 2 blocks toward the large sign reading POSADA DON JOSÉ. The buses to Puerto Ángel are in the lot just before the sign.

ORIENTATION

The town center is only about 4 blocks long, oriented more or less east-west. There are few signs in the village, and off the main street much of Puerto Ángel is a narrow sand-and-dirt path. The navy base is toward the far (west) end of town, just before the creek-crossing toward Playa Panteón (Cemetery Beach).

Puerto Ángel has several public (LADATEL) telephones that use the readily accessible prepaid phone cards. The closest bank is **Bancomer** in Pochutla, which will change money Monday to Friday from 9am to 6pm and Saturday from 9am to 1pm. The **post office** (correo), open Monday to Friday from 9am to 3:30pm, is on the curve as you enter town.

BEACHES, WATER SPORTS & BOAT TRIPS

The golden sands and peaceful village life of Puerto Ángel are all the attractions you'll need. Playa Principal, the main beach, lies between the Mexican navy base and the pier that's home to the local fishing fleet. Near the pier, fishermen pull their colorful boats on the beach and unload their catch in the late morning while trucks wait to haul it off to processing plants in Veracruz. The rest of the beach seems light years from the world of work and purpose and, except on Mexican holidays, it's relatively deserted. It's important to note that Pacific Coast currents deposit trash on Puerto Ángel beaches. The locals do a fairly good job of keeping it picked up, but the currents are constant.

Playa Panteón is the main swimming and snorkeling beach. "Cemetery beach," ominous as that sounds, is about a 15-minute walk from the town center, straight through town on the main street that skirts the beach. You'll see the *panteón* (cemetery) on the right, which in itself is worth a visit—with it's brightly colored tombstones backed by equally brilliant blooming bougainvillea.

In Playa Panteón, some of the palapa restaurants and a few of the hotels rent snorkeling and scuba gear and can arrange boat trips, but all tend to be rather expensive. Check the quality and condition of gear—particularly scuba gear—that you're renting.

Playa Zipolite (*see*-poh-lee-tay) and its village are 3.7 miles down a paved road from Puerto Ángel. Taxis charge around $1 to $1.50 (taxis are relatively expensive here), or you can catch a colectivo on the main street in the town center and share the cost.

Zipolite is well known as a good surf break and as a nude beach. Although public nudity (including topless sunbathing) is technically against the law throughout Mexico, it's allowed here—one of only a handful of beaches in Mexico. This sort of open-mindedness has attracted an increasing number of young European travelers. Most sunbathers concentrate beyond a large rock outcropping at the far end of the beach. Police will occasionally patrol the area, but they are much more intent on searching out drug users rather than au natural sunbathers—as throughout Mexico, the purchase, sale, or use of drugs is definitely against the law, no matter what the local custom may be (see "Fast Facts: Mexico," in chapter 1). The ocean and currents here are quite strong (of course, that's why the surf is so good!) and because of this, a number of drownings have occurred over the years—know your limits. There are places to tie up a hammock and a few palapa restaurants for a light lunch and a cold beer.

Hotels in Playa Zipolite are basic and rustic; most are made with rugged walls and palapa roofs. Prices range from $5 to $20 a night, with the highest prices being charged on Mexican holidays.

Traveling north on Highway 175, you'll come to another hot surf break and a beach of spectacular beauty: **Playa San Augustinillo.** One of the pleasures of a stay in Puerto Ángel is discovering the many hidden beaches nearby and spending the day there. Local boatmen can give details and quote rates for this service, or ask at your hotel.

A PLACE TO STAY & DINE

Accommodations are found in Puerto Ángel, both near Playa Principal in the tiny town, and at Playa Panteón. Most are basic, older, cement-block style hotels, not meriting a full-blown description. Between Playa Panteón and town are also several bungalow and guest-house setups with budget accommodations. These basic rooms are generally available without reservations, except during the Christmas and Easter holidays. The hotel noted below is the one place in town worth making advanced reservations for, and worth planning a trip to Puerto Ángel to stay there.

✪ **Posada Cañon Devata.** Playa del Panteón Apdo. Postal 10, 70902 Puerto Ángel, Oax. ☎/fax **9/584-3048.** www.posadangel.com. E-mail: lopezk@ spin.com.mx. 15 rms, 6 bungalows (only 1 without bathroom). $13–$38 double; $35–$38 bungalow or El Cielo room for 2. No credit cards. Closed May–June.

One of the most inviting places in Puerto Ángel, this hotel is a 3-minute walk almost straight up from Playa Panteón. Americans Suzanne and Mateo López, and their daughter Kali, run this ecologically sound, homey, cool, and green-and-wooded oasis set in a narrow canyon. All water is recycled for the benefit of the resident plants and critters. Rooms—completely remodeled in early 1998—are agreeably rustic-chic, with fans, beds covered in Guatemalan tie-dyed cloth, and Mateo's paintings hanging from the walls (the paintings are for sale). All rooms are configured differently, and if you tell them what type of atmosphere you prefer, they'll try to accommodate your preference. I love the Sand Room, with its expansive, sunny windows and constant breezes. Don't miss climbing to the El Cielo to see the bay bathed in the light of the setting sun—plus a small bar is set up here each evening during sunset. At other times, this rooftop terrace makes a peaceful place for sunbathing, or for enjoying a morning yoga session. New services include a tranquil, open-air massage center, safe deposit boxes, money exchange, laundry services, and fishing trip arrangements. They can also arrange for airport pick up from Huatulco at rates that are less expensive than those of Transportes Terrestres.

The Restaurant Cañon Devata requires reservations if you're not staying at the hotel. Fresh flowers on the thick wooden tables set the mood, as diners enjoy some of the healthiest cooking around. Mainly vegetarian dishes are served, made with their own organically-grown vegetables, and served with home-baked bread. Occasional fish specialties are also offered. Breakfast averages $3 to $6; sandwiches $3.50; and dinner $8. No credit cards are accepted. The restaurant is open Tuesday to Sunday 7:30am to 2pm and 7pm to 9pm. Both the hotel and restaurant are closed during the months of May and June.

To find it, walk just past the Hotel Cabaña del Puerto Ángel across from Playa Panteón, to the point at which the road more or less ends; turn right and go down the sandy path to an area with a few parked cars. Walk across the tiny bridge on your right and follow the stairs on the left until you reach the restaurant. Just beyond this is the small gift shop and check-in area.

3 Bahías de Huatulco

40 miles (64km) SE of Puerto Ángel; 425 miles (680km) SE of Acapulco

Huatulco has the same, unspoiled nature and laid-back sentiment as its neighbors to the north—Puerto Angel and Puerto Escondido—but with a difference. In the midst of such natural splendor, you'll also encounter indulgent hotels and modern roads and facilities.

Pristine beaches and jungle landscapes can make for an idyllic retreat from the stress of daily life, and when viewed from a luxury hotel balcony, it's even better. Huatulco is for those who want to enjoy the beauty of nature during the day, then retreat to well-appointed comfort by night. Slow-paced and still relatively undiscovered, the Bays of Huatulco enjoy the most modern infrastructure on Mexico's Pacific coast.

Undeveloped stretches of pure white sands and isolated coves lie in wait for the promised growth of Huatulco, but it's not catching on as rapidly as Cancún, the previous resort planned by Mexico's Tourism Development arm. FONATUR development of the Bahías de Huatulco is an ambitious but staged-in development project that aims to cover 52,000 acres of land, with over 40,000 acres to remain ecological preserves. The small local communities have been transplanted from the coast into Crucecita. The area is divided into three distinct sections: **Santa Cruz, Crucecita,** and **Tangolunda Bay** (see "City Layout," below).

Though Huatulco has increasingly become known for its eco-tourism attractions—including river rafting, rappelling, and hiking jungle trails—it has yet to develop a true personality of its own. There's little to do here in the way of shopping, nightlife, or even dining outside of hotels, and what is available is high priced for the quality. However, the service in the area shines. From taxis to bellboys, it seems that although the promise of tourism has not yet been fulfilled, this fact seems to just inspire people to work harder. There is an underlying enthusiasm and willingness to share the treasures of the area with outside visitors.

If you're especially drawn to snorkeling, diving, boat cruises to virgin bays, and simple relaxation, Huatulco fits the bill. Nine bays encompass 36 beaches and countless inlets and coves. The clear blue waters and golden beaches are enough of an attraction for many vacationers. Huatulco's main problem has been securing enough incoming flights; it relies heavily on charter service from the United States and Canada.

ESSENTIALS
GETTING THERE

BY PLANE   **Mexicana** flights (☎ **800/531-7921** in the U.S.; 9/587-0223 or 9/587-0260 at the airport) connect Huatulco with Cancún, Chicago, Guadalajara, Los Angeles, Miami, San Antonio, San Francisco, San Jose, and Toronto by way of Mexico City.

From Huatulco's international airport (HUX) (☎ **9/581-9004** or 9/581-9017), about 12 miles northwest of the Bahías de Huatulco, private **taxis** charge $10 to Crucecita, $12 to Santa Cruz, and $25 to Tangolunda. **Transportes Terrestres colectivo** minibus fares range from $6 to $10 per person. When returning, make sure to ask for a taxi, unless you have a lot of luggage. Taxis to the airport run $10, but unless specifically requested, they'll send a suburban, which costs $25 for the same trip.

Budget (☎ **800/322-9976** in U.S., or 9/587-0010 and 9/581-9000), and **Advantage** (☎ **9/587-1379**) all have offices at the airport that are open for flight arrivals. Daily rates run around $56 for a VW sedan, $79 for a Sentra or Geo Tracker, and $100 for a Jeep Ranger. Dollar also has rental offices at the Royal, Barcelo, and downtown, and offers one-way drop service if you're traveling on to Puerto Escondido. Because this destination is so spread out and has excellent roads, you may want to consider a rental car, at least for a day or two, to explore the area.

BY CAR   Coastal Highway 200 leads to Huatulco (via Pochutla) from the north and is generally in good condition. The drive from Puerto Escondido is just under 2 hours. The road is safe and well-maintained, but is windy and with no lights and little traffic, so avoid travel after sunset. Allow at least 6 hours for the trip from Oaxaca City on mountainous Highway 175.

BY BUS   Reaching Huatulco by bus has become easier. There are three bus stations in Crucecita, but none in Santa Cruz or Tangolunda. The stations in Crucecita are all within a few blocks of one another. The **Gacela and Estrella Blanca** station is at the corner of Gardenia and Palma Real with service to Acapulco, Mexico City, Puerto Escondido, and Pochutla. The **Cristóbal Colón** station (☎ **9/587-0261**) is at the corner of Gardenia and Ocotillo, 4 blocks from the Plaza Principal. Buses leaving from here service destinations throughout Mexico, including Oaxaca, Puerto Escondido, and Pochutla. The **Estrella del Valle** station, located on Jasmin, between Sabali and Carrizal, services Oaxaca.

<hr />

Important Travel Note

The stretch of Highway 200 north between Huatulco and Acapulco has seen numerous bus hijackings and occasional car robberies; only drive during the day, and if you have a choice, fly.

If you arrive by bus, you'll be dropped off in Crucecita, where you can easily find a taxi or microbus to your final destination.

VISITOR INFORMATION

The **State Tourism Office** (**Oficina del Turismo; ☎ 9/587-1542;** fax 9/587-1541; e-mail: sedetur6@oaxaca-travel.gob.mx) has an information module in Tangalundo Bay, near the Grand Pacific hotel. The **Huatulco Convention & Visitor's Bureau** (**☎ 9/587-1037;** e-mail: info@BaysofHuatulco.com) is located in the Plaza San Miguel in Santa Cruz at the corner of Santa Cruz and Monte Albán. It is open Monday to Friday from 9am to 6pm, and Saturdays from 10am to 2pm, and offers very friendly, helpful service.

CITY LAYOUT

The resort area is called Bahías de Huatulco and includes all nine bays. The town of Santa María de Huatulco, the original settlement in this area, is 17 miles inland. **Santa Cruz Huatulco,** usually called Santa Cruz, was the first area on the coast to be developed. It has a central plaza with a bandstand kiosk that has been converted into a cafe serving regionally grown coffee. It also has an artisan's market on the edge of the plaza that borders the main road, a few hotels and restaurants, and a marina where bay tours and fishing trips set sail. **Juárez** is Santa Cruz's main street, about 4 blocks long in all, anchored at one end by the Hotel Castillo Huatulco and at the other by the Meigas Binniguenda hotel. Opposite the Hotel Castillo is the marina, and beyond it are restaurants housed in new colonial-style buildings facing the beach. The area's banks are on Juárez. It's impossible to get lost; you can take in almost everything at a glance.

A mile and a half inland from Santa Cruz is **Crucecita,** a planned city that sprang up in 1985 centered on a lovely grassy plaza edged with flowering hedges. It's the residential area for the resorts, with neighborhoods of new stucco homes mixed with small apartment complexes. The town has evolved into a lovely traditional town where you'll find the area's best, and most reasonably priced, restaurants plus some shopping and several clean, less-expensive hotels.

Until other bays are developed, **Tangolunda Bay,** 3 miles east, is the focal point of bay development. Gradually, half the bays will have resorts. For now, Tangolunda has the 18-hole golf course, as well as the Club Med, Quinta Real, Barcelo Huatulco,

Royal, Casa del Mar, and Camino Real Zaachila hotels, among others. Small strip centers with a few restaurants occupy each end of Tangolunda Bay. **Chahué Bay,** between Tangolunda and Santa Cruz, is a small bay with a marina under construction as well as houses and two hotels that are slated to open mid-2001.

GETTING AROUND

It's too far to walk between any of the three destinations of Crucecita, Santa Cruz, and Tangolunda, but **taxis** are inexpensive and readily available. The fare between Santa Cruz and Tangolunda is roughly $2.00; between Santa Cruz and Crucecita, $1.50; between Crucecita and Tangolunda, $2.50.

There is **minibus service** between towns that costs 30¢. In Santa Cruz, catch the bus across the street from Castillo Huatulco; in Tangolunda, in front of the Grand Pacific; and in Crucecita, kitty-corner from the Hotel Grifer.

FAST FACTS: Bahías de Huatulco

Area Code   The area code is **9.**

Banks   All three areas have banks with automatic tellers, including the main Mexican banks, Banamex and Bancomer. They can change money during business hours, which are from 9am to 5pm Monday to Friday and 9am to 1pm on Saturday. Banks are found both along calle Juarez, in Santa Cruz, and surrounding the central plaza in Crucecita.

Doctor   Dr. Ricardo Carrillo (☎ **9/587-0687** or 9/587-0600) speaks English.

Hospital   The Centro Medica Huatulco, Flamboyant #205 La Crucecita (☎ **9/587-0104** or 9/587-0435) is very modern and clean, with English-speaking doctors.

Pharmacy   Farmacia del Carmen (☎ **9/587-0878**) is one of the largest drugstores in town, located just off the central plaza. Farmacia La Clinica (☎ **9/587-0591**) located at Sabalí 1602, in Crucecita, offers both 24-hour service and home/hotel delivery.

Post Office   The post office at Blvd. Chahué #100, Sector R (☎ **9/587-0551**) is open Monday to Friday 9am to 3pm, and Saturday 9am to 1pm.

Taxis   In Crucecita there's a taxi stand opposite the Hotel Grifer and another on the Plaza Principal. Taxis are readily available in Santa Cruz and Tangolunda through your hotel. They can also be rented by the hour (about $10 per hour) or for the day, should you want to make a more thorough exploration of the area.

BEACHES, SPORTS & OTHER THINGS TO DO

Attractions around Huatulco are concentrated around the nine bays of the area, and their related water sports. The surrounding mountains are also playing host to a growing number of ecotours and interesting side trips. Through the area doesn't have the same type of traditional town frequently found near Mexico's beach resorts, the community of Crucecita is worth visiting. Just off the central plaza is the **Iglesía de Guadalupe,** with a large mural of Mexico's patron saint gracing the entire ceiling of the chapel. The image of the Virgin is set against a deep blue night sky and includes 52 stars—a modern interpretation of the original cloak of Juan Diego.

Dining in Crucecita is available for a fraction of the price charged in Tangolunda Bay, and with the added benefit of some local color. Considering that shopping in Huatulco is generally poor, you'll find the best stores are those that surround the central plaza. They tend to stay open late, and offer a good selection of regional goods and typical tourist take-homes, including artesania, silver jewelry, Cuban cigars, and tequila. There's also a small, free trolley train that takes visitors on a short tour of the town.

GOLF & TENNIS The 18-hole, par-72 **Tangolunda Golf Course** (☎ 9/581-0037) is adjacent to Tangolunda Bay and has tennis courts as well. The greens fee is $37 and carts cost about the same. Tennis courts are also available at the **Barceló** hotel (☎ 9/581-0055).

BEACHES

A section of the beach at Santa Cruz (away from the small boats) is an inviting sunning spot, and the location of the beach clubs offered for guest use by non-oceanfront hotels. In addition, several restaurants are on the beach, and palapa umbrellas are found down to the water's edge. The most popular is **Tipsy's** (☎ 9/587-0576), with full beach bar and restaurant service, lounge chairs, towel service, and showers. All kinds of watersports equipment is available for rent here, including kayaks ($9 per hour), snorkeling equipment, catamarans, jet skis ($40 per hour), banana boats, and even water-skiing ($95 per 10 classes). They're open daily from 10am to 7pm. No credit cards.

For about $10 one way, pangas from the marina in Santa Cruz will ferry you to **La Entrega Beach,** also in Santa Cruz Bay. There you'll find a row of palapa restaurants, all with beach chairs out front. Find an empty chair and use that restaurant for your refreshment needs in return. A snorkel equipment–rental booth is about midway down the beach, and there's some fairly good snorkeling on the end away from where the boats arrive.

Between Santa Cruz and Tangolunda bays is **Chahué Bay.** A beach club here has palapas, beach volleyball, and refreshments for an entrance fee of about $2. However, a strong undertow makes this a dangerous place for swimming.

Tangolunda Bay beach, fronting the best hotels, is wide and beautiful. Theoretically all beaches in Mexico are public; however, nonguests at Tangolunda hotels may have difficulty entering the hotel to get to the beach.

BAY CRUISES & ECOTOURS

Huatulco's major attraction is its coastline—that magnificent stretch of pristine bays bordered by an odd blend of cactus and jungle vegetation right at the water's edge. The only way to really grasp its beauty is by taking a cruise of the bays, stopping at **Organo** or **Maguey Bay** for a dip in the crystal-clear water and a fish lunch from one of the palapa restaurants on the beach.

One way to arrange a bay tour is to go to the **boat-owners' cooperative** in the red-and-yellow tin shack at the entrance to the marina. Prices are posted here, and you can buy tickets for sightseeing, snorkeling, or fishing. Besides La Entrega Beach, there are other beaches farther away that are noted for good offshore snorkeling, plus they also have palapa restaurants and other facilities. These include Maguey and San Agustín. Several of these beaches, however, are completely undeveloped and pristine, so you will need to bring your own provisions. Boatmen at the cooperative will arrange return pick-up at an appointed time. Prices run about $10 for 1 to 10 persons at La Entrega, and $30 for a trip to Maguey and Organo bays. The bay farthest out is San Agustinillo, and that all-day trip will run $60 in a private panga.

Another option is to join one of the organized day-long bay cruises, such as aboard the *Tequila,* complete with guide, drinks, and on-board entertainment. These can be easily arranged

Huatulco's Coffee Plantations

This region of Mexico is known for its rich Pluma coffee, grown in the mountainous areas surrounding Huatulco. Plantations that date back centuries continue to grow and harvest coffee beans, most of which continue to use traditional, more primitive methods. The majority of the plantations are located around the mouth of the Copalita River, in small towns including Pluma Hidalgo, Santa María Huatulco, and Xanica, located roughly an hour to an hour and a half from Tangolunga Bay. Both day tours and overnight stays to select coffee plantations are available from Huatulco.

Café Huatulco (☎ 9/587-0339) is a unique project of the area coffee producers' association, to raise awareness about the region's coffee and offer an unusual excursion for tourist. They have two modules that sell whole bean regional coffee, and serve coffee and espresso beverages. One is located in the kiosk in the central plaza of Santa Cruz, another is in the Plaza Esmerelda shopping center in Tangolunda Bay. The manager, Salvador López, can also arrange coffee tastings for groups of six or more, or provide details about overnight stays at the coffee plantations.

through any travel agency and cost about $25 per person, with an extra charge of $4 for snorkeling-equipment rental and lunch. Another, more romantic option is the *Luna Azul,* a 44-foot sailboat that also offers bay tours and sunset sails. Call ☎ **9/587-0945** for reservations.

In Crucecita, **Shuatur Tours** (Plaza Oaxaca, Local no. 20, ☎/fax **9/587-0734**) offers bay tours; tours to Puerto Ángel, Puerto Escondido, and associated beaches; an ecotour on the Río Copalita (7 hr.); or an all-day tour to the coffee plantations located in the mountains above Huatulco.

Ecotours are growing in both popularity and options throughout the Bays of Huatulco. **Eco Aventuras** (☎ **9/587-0669**) offers mountain biking, kayaking, birdwatching, river rafting, and rappelling excursions, tailored to the skill levels of the participants. **Huatulco Outfitters** (☎ **9/581-0315**) specializes in river rafting expeditions down the Copalita River. The mountain areas surrounding the Copalita River are also the site of other natural treasures worth exploring, including the **Copalitilla**

Cascades. Found 30 kilometers (18.5 miles) north of Tangolunda at 400 meters (1,300 ft.) above sea level, a grouping of waterfalls—averaging heights of 20 to 25 meters (65–80 ft.)—form natural whirlpools and clear pools for swimming. The area is also popular for horseback riding and rappelling.

An especially popular option is the day-long trip to **Oaxaca City** and **Monte Albán.** The trip includes round-trip airfare on AeroCaribe, lunch, entrance to the archaeological site of Monte Alban, and a tour of the architectural highlights of Oaxaca City, all for $100. It's available through any travel agency, or through the **AeroCaribe** office at ☎ **9/587-1220.**

SHOPPING

Shopping in the area is limited, and unmemorable, concentrated in both the **Santa Cruz Market** (by the marina in Santa Cruz, open from 10am to 8pm, no phone), and the **Crucecita Market,** on Guamuchil, half a block from the plaza in Crucecita. Among all of the prototypical souvenirs, you may want to search out regional specialties that include Oaxacan embroidered blouses and dresses, and *barro negro,* a pottery made from a dark clay, exclusively found in the Oaxaca region. Also in Crucecita is the Plaza Oaxaca, adjacent to the central plaza, with clothing shops including **Poco Loco Club/Coconut's Boutique** (☎ **9/587-0279**) for casual sportswear; **Mic Mac** (☎ **9/587-0565**), featuring beachwear and souvenirs; and **Sideout** (☎ **9/587-0254**) for active wear. **Coconuts** (☎ **9/587-0057**) has English-language magazines, books, and music. Several strip shopping centers in Tangolunda Bay offer a selection of crafts and Oaxacan goods, but are pricier than the markets.

WHERE TO STAY

Moderate- and budget-priced hotels are found in Santa Cruz and Crucecita, but are generally higher in price compared to similar hotels in other Mexican beach resorts. The luxury beach hotels have comparable rates, especially when part of a package that includes airfare. The trend here is toward all-inclusive resorts, which in Huatulco are an especially good option given the lack of memorable dining and nightlife options around town. Hotels that are not oceanfront generally have an arrangement with one of the beach clubs at Santa Cruz or Chahue Bays, with shuttle service. Low-season rates refer to the months of August through November only.

EXPENSIVE

Camino Real Zaashila. Bulevar Benito Juárez 5, Bahía de Tangolunda, 70989 Huatulco, Oax. ☎ **800/722-6466** in the U.S., or 9/581-0460. Fax 9/581-0461. www.caminoreal.com/zaashila/. E-mail: zaa@caminoreal.com. 120 rooms, 10 suites. A/C MINIBAR TV TEL. High season $210 double; $263 Camino Real Club. Low season $170 double; $252 Camino Real Club. AE, DC, MC, V.

One of the original hotels in Tangolunda Bay, the Camino Real Zaashila is located on a wide stretch of sandy beach secluded from other beaches by small rock outcroppings and with calm water, perfect for swimming and snorkeling, ideal for families. The white stucco building is Mediterranean in style and washed in colors on the ocean side, looking a little like a scene from the Greek isles. Each room on the lower levels—41 of them—has its own sizable dipping pool. All rooms are large and have an ocean-view balcony or terrace. Additional amenities include in-room safe, minibar, satellite TV, marble tub/shower combination bathrooms, wicker furnishings, and decors of bold colors. The main pool is a freeform design that spans 400 feet of beach, with chaises built into the shallow edges. Well-manicured, tropical gardens surround it and the guestrooms.

Dining/Diversions: Three restaurants and bars serve regional specialties. Chez Binni is their signature restaurant, and one of the most noted in Huatulco for its Oaxacan cuisine. The ocean-front Bel-La Grill specializes in seafood, while the Beach Club serves snacks and light meals by the pool or beach.

Amenities: In addition to the main pool, the Zaashila has a beachfront water sports center, outdoor whirlpool, lighted tennis court, plus complete tour and travel agency services.

✪ **Quinta Real.** Bulevar Benito Juárez Lt. no. 2, Bahía de Tangolunda, 70989 Huatulco, Oax. ☎ **888/561-2817** in the U.S., or 9/581-0428 and 9/581-0430. Fax 9/581-0429. 28 units. A/C MINIBAR TV TEL. High season $250 Master Suite; $290 Grand Class Suite; $350 with private pool. Low season $180 Master Suite; $220 Grand Class Suite; $250 with private pool. AE, DC, MC, V.

Double Moorish domes mark this romantic and relaxed hotel with a richly appointed cream-and-white decor and complete attention to detail. From the gentle reception at a sit-down desk to the luxurious beach club below, the staff emphasizes excellence in service. The small groupings of suites built into the gently sloping hill to Tangolunda Bay offer spectacular views of the ocean and golf course next door. Rooms on the eastern edge of the resort sit above the highway and have some traffic noise. Interiors are elegant and comfortable, with stylish Mexican furniture, wood-beamed ceilings and marble tub/shower-combination bathrooms with whirlpool tubs; original works of art and telescopes grace many of the suites. Balconies have overstuffed seating areas and floors have stone inlays. Eight Grand Class Suites and the Presidential Suite have ultra-private pools of their own. The Quinta Real is perfect for weddings, honeymoons, or small corporate retreats.

Dining/Diversions: The restaurant serves nouvelle international cuisine with signature dishes that include lobster medallion in a pink crab sauce, Oaxacan grilled beef tenderloin in a black-bean sauce, and shrimp marinated in cinnamon with pineapple. It's open for breakfast and dinner. The bar extends over a terrace with a stunning view and has comfy sofas and cowhide-covered chaises. Lunch is served in the Beach Club restaurant.

Amenities: The Beach Club has two pools (one for children) and a restaurant and bar, plus shade palapas on the beach and chair and towel service. All suites have bathrobes, hair dryers, in-room safe-deposit boxes. Laundry and room service, and in-room massage are available.

MODERATE

Gala Resort. Bulevar Benito Juárez s/n, Bahía de Tangolunda, 70989 Huatulco, Oax. ☎ **800/GO-MAEVA** in the U.S., or 9/581-0000. Fax 9/581-0220. 290 units. A/C MINIBAR TV TEL. $150 single; $250 double for 2 people; $100 per extra adult, $76 per child 12–15, $51 per child 7–11. Children under 7 stay free in parents' room. AE, MC, V.

With all meals, drinks, entertainment, tips, and a slew of activities included in the price, the Royal is a value-packed experience. It caters to adults of all ages (married and single) who enjoy both activity and relaxation. An excellent kids' activity program makes it probably the best option in the area for families. Rooms have tile floors and Oaxacan wood trim, large tub/shower-combination bathrooms, and ample balconies, all with views of Tangolunda Bay. Three restaurants serving a variety of meals are located at various points around the expansive property, with both buffet and à la carte options, as well as changing theme nights. Four bars serve drinks until 2am nightly. There's also a full gym, large free-form pool, four lighted tennis courts, and a complete beachfront water-sports center.

Hotel Meigas Binniguenda. Bulevar Santa Cruz 201, 70989 Santa Cruz de Huatulco, Oax. ☎ **9/587-0077** or 9/587-0078. Fax 9/587-0284. E-mail: binniguenda@huatulco.net.mx. 165 units. A/C TV TEL. High season $100 per person, all-inclusive; $90 double, room only. Low season $65 person, all-inclusive; $50 double, room only. AE, MC, V.

This was Huatulco's first hotel and retains the Mexican charm and comfort that originally made it memorable. A recent addition has more than doubled the hotel's size. Rooms have Mexican-tile floors, foot-loomed bedspreads, and colonial-style furniture; French doors open onto tiny wrought-iron balconies overlooking Juárez or the pool and gardens. The newer rooms have more modern furnishings of teak, and are generally much nicer— request this section, if available. There's a nice shady area around the hotel's small pool in back of the lobby. A large, palapa-topped restaurant with seating for 300 is adjacent to this pool. The hotel is away from the marina at the far end of Juárez, only a few blocks from the water. They offer free transportation every hour to the beach club at Santa Cruz Bay. They now have in-room safe-deposit boxes, plus complete travel-agency services.

INEXPENSIVE

Hotel Las Palmas. Av. Guamuchil 206, 70989 Bahías de Huatulco, Oax. ☎ **9/587-0060.** Fax 9/587-0057. 25 units. A/C TV. High season $35 double; Low season $24 double. AE, MC, V. Free parking.

The central location and accommodating staff are an added benefit to the clean, bright, but very basic rooms at Las Palmas. Located half a block from the main plaza, it's also connected to the popular El Sabor de Oaxaca restaurant (see "Where to Dine," below), which also offers room service to guests. Rooms have tile floors, cotton textured bedspreads, tile showers, and cable TV. Tobacco shop, money exchange, safe-deposit boxes, travel-agency services, and a public telephone are available.

✪ **Misión de los Arcos.** Gardenia 902, La Crucecita, Huatulco, 70989, Oaxaca. ☎ **9/587-0165.** Fax 9/587-1135. E-mail: losarcos@huatulco.net.mx. 13 rooms. High season $58.50 without A/C, $70 with A/C; $76 suite. Low season $30 without A/C, $35 with A/C; $40 suite. AE, MC, V.

This new hotel located just a block from the central plaza has a similar style to the elegant Quinta Real (see above)—at a fraction of the cost. The hotel is completely white, accented with an abundance of greenery (no flowering plants), giving it a very fresh, clean, and inviting feel. Rooms continue the same ambiance and are washed in white, with cream and beige bed coverings and upholstery. Built-in desks, French windows, and minimal but interesting decorative accents give this budget hotel a real sense of style. At the entrance level, there is a cafe with Internet access that is open from 7:30am to 11:30pm. A restaurant is scheduled to open sometime in 2000, when they also expect to add a swimming pool. At present, guests have the use of a beach club, to which the hotel provides a complimentary shuttle. The hotel is kitty-corner from La Crucecita's central plaza, close to all the shops and restaurants.

WHERE TO DINE

Outside of the hotels, the best choices are in Crucecita and on the beach in Santa Cruz.

✪ **El Sabor de Oaxaca.** Av. Guamuchil 206, Crucecita. ☎ **9/587-0060.** Fax 9/587-0057. Main dishes $1.50–$16. AE, MC, V. Daily 7am–midnight. OAXACAN.

This is the best place in the area to enjoy authentic and richly flavorful Oaxacan food, among the best of traditional Mexican cuisine. This restaurant is a local favorite that also meets the quality standards of tourists. Among the most popular items are their Mixed Grill for Two, with a Oaxacan beef fillet, tender pork tenderloin *chorizo* (a zesty Mexican sausage), and pork ribs; and the Oaxacan Special for Two, offering a generous sampling of the best of the menu with tamales, Oaxacan cheese, pork mole, and more. Generous breakfasts are just $2.22 and include eggs, bacon, ham, beans, toast, and fresh orange juice. There's a colorful decor and lively music, and special group events are happily arranged.

Noches Oaxaqueñas/Don Porfirio. Bulevar Benito Juárez s/n (across from Royal Maeva), Tangolunda Bay. ☎ **9/581-0001.** Main courses $15–$20. Show $15; dinner and drinks available à la carte. AE, MC, V. Fri–Sun 8:30pm–10pm. SEAFOOD/OAXACAN.

The colorful, traditional folkloric dances of Oaxaca are performed in an open-air courtyard reminiscent of an old hacienda despite being located in a modern strip mall. The dancers clearly enjoy performing this traditional ballet under the direction of owner Celicia Flores Ramirez (wife of Don Willo Porfirio). Dinner can be ordered from the menu—recommended is the plato Oaxaqueño, a generous, flavorful sampling of traditional Oaxacan fare, including a tamale, sope, Oaxacan cheese, grilled fillet, pork enchilada, and chile relleno for $10. Other house specialties include shrimps with mezcal, and spaghetti marinara with seafood. Meat lovers can enjoy American style cuts or a juicy arrachera. Groups are welcome.

Restaurant Avalos Doña Celia. Santa Cruz Bay. ☎ **9/587-0128.** Breakfast $2.50–$3.50; seafood $4–$25. No credit cards. Daily 8:30am–11pm. SEAFOOD.

Doña Celia, an original Huatulco resident, chose to stay in business in the same area where she started her little thatch-roofed restaurant years ago. Now she's in a new building at the end of Santa Cruz's beach, serving the same good eats. Among her specialties are *filete empapelado,* a foil-wrapped fish baked with tomato, onion, and cilantro; and *filete almendrado,* a fish fillet covered with hotcake batter, beer, and almonds. The ceviche is terrific (one order is plenty for two), as is the *Platillo a la Huatulqueño* (shrimp and young octopus fried in olive oil with chile and onion and served over white rice). The ambiance is basic, but the food is the reason for its popularity. If you dine here during the day, beach chairs and shade are available, so you can make your own "beach club" away from your hotel in this more traditional and accessible part of Huatulco.

HUATULCO AFTER DARK

There's a limited selection of dance clubs available—meaning that's where everyone goes. The newest addition is **Ven Aca** (☎ **9/587-1691**), a piano bar and restaurant on the main street, Juarez, in Santa Cruz. It's open every night from 8pm until midnight (or later!) and is a casual, more romantic option than the discos and dance clubs in town. The local branch of the popular Mexican club **Magic Circus** (☎ **9/587-0017**), in Santa Cruz, is the area's most popular disco. It's open from 9pm until the last dance is danced. **Poison** (☎ **9/587-0971**) is the top late-night spot, with open-air dancing on the Santa Cruz beachfront. Located next to the Marina Hotel on the beach, it's open until 5am, playing techno and rock. Across the channel, **Tipsy's** extends its daytime popularity and stays open until 5am on weekend nights, with dancing under the stars.

5

Inland to Old Mexico: Taxco & Cuernavaca

*I*nland from Acapulco, Taxco and Cuernavaca feature the artistry of Old Mexico. Taxco, with its famed silver factories and ornate buildings, is as picturesque a mountain village as you'll find in Mexico. It's worthy of at least a night's stay, and more if you can manage it. It's an hour's drive from Taxco to Cuernavaca, known as the "land of eternal spring" and a popular second home for Mexico City professionals and American expats. Cuernavaca, which seems to be perennially in bloom, features historic haciendas, interesting museums, good restaurants, and several full-service spas.

1 Taxco: Cobblestones & Silver

111 miles (178km) SW of Mexico City; 50 miles (81km) SW of Cuernavaca; 185 miles (298km) NE of Acapulco

In Mexico and around the world, the town of Taxco de Alarcón—most commonly known simply as Taxco (*tahs*-ko)—is synonymous with silver. Once here, you'll see that the town's geography is equally precious: Taxco sits at nearly 5,000 feet on a hill among hills, and almost any point in the city offers fantastic views.

Taxco was discovered by Hernán Cortez as he combed the area for treasure, but its rich caches of silver weren't fully exploited for another 2 centuries, by the French prospector Joseph de la Borda. In 1751 de la Borda commissioned the baroque Santa Prisca Church that dominates Taxco's *zócalo* (Plaza Borda) as a way of giving something back to the town.

That Taxco has become Mexico's most renowned center for silver design, although only a small amount of silver is still mined here, is due to an American, William Spratling. Spratling arrived in the late 1920s with the intention of writing a book; however, he soon noticed the skill of the local craftsmen and opened a workshop to produce handmade silver jewelry and tableware based on pre-Hispanic art. The workshops flourished, the goods

Taxco

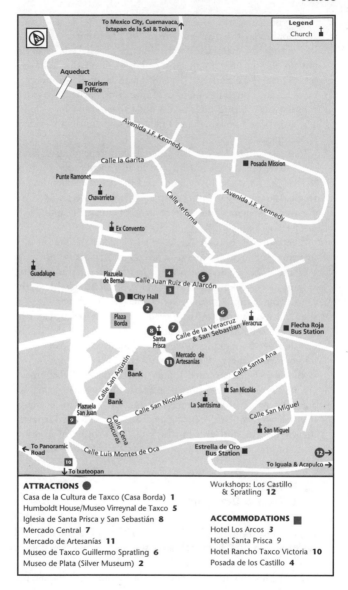

To Mexico City, Cuernavaca,
Ixtapan de la Sal & Toluca

Legend
Church ✝

Aqueduct

Tourism Office

Avenida J.F. Kennedy

Calle la Garita

Posada Mission

Punte Ramonet

Chavarrieta

Calle Reforma

Avenida J.F. Kennedy

Ex Convento

Guadalupe

Plazuela de Bernal

Calle Juan Ruiz de Alarcón

City Hall

Plaza Borda

Calle de la Veracruz & San Sebastián

Veracruz

Flecha Roja Bus Station

Santa Prisca

Mercado de Artesanías

Calle San Agustín

Bank

Calle Santa Ana

Bank

Calle San Nicolás

San Nicolás

Plazuela San Juan

La Santisima

Calle San Miguel

Calle Cena Obscuras

San Miguel

To Panoramic Road

Calle Luis Montes de Oca

Estrella de Oro Bus Station

To Iguala & Acapulco

To Ixateopan

ATTRACTIONS ●

Casa de la Cultura de Taxco (Casa Borda) **1**
Humboldt House/Museo Virreynal de Taxco **5**
Iglesia de Santa Prisca y San Sebastián **8**
Mercado Central **7**
Mercado de Artesanías **11**
Museo de Taxco Guillermo Spratling **6**
Museo de Plata (Silver Museum) **2**

Workshops: Los Castillo & Spratling **12**

ACCOMMODATIONS ■

Hotel Los Arcos **3**
Hotel Santa Prisca **9**
Hotel Rancho Taxco Victoria **10**
Posada de los Castillo **4**

were exported to the United States in bulk, Taxco's reputation grew, and today there are more than 200 silver shops.

The tiny one-man factories that line the cobbled streets all the way up into the hills supply most of Taxco's silverwork. Your success in finding bargains will depend somewhat on how much you know about the quality and price of silver, but nowhere else in the country will you find the quantity and variety available in Taxco. The artistry and imagination of the local silversmiths are evident in each piece.

You can get an idea of what Taxco is like by spending an afternoon here, but there's much more to this picturesque town of 87,000 than just the Plaza Borda and the shops surrounding it. Stay overnight to wander its steep cobblestone streets, and you'll discover little plazas, fine churches, and of course the abundance of silversmith shops.

The main part of town is relatively flat. It stretches up the hillside from the highway, and it's a steep but brief walk up. White VW minibuses, called *burritos,* make the circuit through and around town, picking up and dropping off passengers along the route, from about 7am until 9pm. The town's taxis are inexpensive, and you should use them even if you've arrived by car. The streets are so narrow and steep that most visitors find them difficult and nerve-wracking to navigate. Find a secured parking lot for your car, and forget about it until you leave.

Warning: Self-appointed guides will undoubtedly approach you in the zócalo (Plaza Borda) and offer their services—they get a cut (up to 25%) of the total amount you spend in the shops they take you to. Before hiring a guide, ask to see his **Departamento de Turismo** credentials. The Department of Tourism office on the highway at the north end of town can recommend a licensed guide.

ESSENTIALS
GETTING THERE & DEPARTING

BY CAR   From Acapulco you have two options. Highway 95D is the toll road through Iguala to Taxco. Or you can take the old two-lane road (95) that winds more slowly through villages; it's in good condition.

From Mexico City, take Paseo de la Reforma to Chapultepec Park and merge with the Periférico, which will take you to Highway 95D on the south end of town. From the Periférico, take the

Insurgentes exit and merge until you come to the sign for Cuernavaca/Tlalpan. Choose either CUERNAVACA CUOTA (toll) or CUERNAVACA LIBRE (free). Continue south around Cuernavaca to the Amacuzac interchange and proceed straight ahead for Taxco. The drive from Mexico City takes about $3^1/2$ hours.

BY BUS   From Mexico City, buses to Taxco depart from the **Central de Autobuses del Sur** station (Metro: Tasqueña) and take 2 to 3 hours, with frequent departures.

Taxco has two bus stations. Estrella de Oro buses arrive at their own station on the southern edge of town. Estrella Blanca, including their *Futura* executive class buses, and Flecha Roja buses arrive at the station on the northeastern edge of town on Avenida Kennedy, recently renamed *Avenida de los Plateros* (Avenue of the Silversmiths). Taxis to the zócalo cost around $1.

VISITOR INFORMATION

The **State of Guerrero Dirección de Turismo** (tourist office) (☎ 7/622-6616; fax 7/622-2274) has offices at the arches on the main highway at the north end of town (Ave. de los Plateros No. 1), useful if you're driving into town. The office is open daily from 8am to 8pm. To get there from the Plaza Borda, take a combi ("Zócalo-Arcos") and get off at the arch over the highway. As you face the arches, the tourism office is on your right.

CITY LAYOUT

The center of town is the tiny **Plaza Borda,** shaded by perfectly manicured Indian laurel trees. On one side is the imposing twin-towered, pink-stone **Santa Prisca Church,** and the other sides are lined with whitewashed, red tile buildings housing the famous silver shops and a restaurant or two. Beside the church, deep in a crevice of the mountain, is the **city market.** One of the beauties of Taxco is that its brick-paved and cobblestone streets are completely asymmetrical, zigzagging up and down the hillsides. The plaza buzzes with vendors of everything from hammocks and cotton candy to bark paintings and balloons.

FAST FACTS: Taxco

Area Code   The telephone area code is **7.**

Post Office   The post office (*correo*) is on the outskirts of Taxco on the highway heading toward Acapulco. It's in a row of shops with a black-and-white CORREO sign (☎ **7/622-0501**).

Spanish/Art Classes   The Universidad Nacional Autónoma de México (UNAM) is located on the grounds of the Hacienda del Chorrillo, formerly part of the Cortez land grant. Here, students can study silversmithing, Spanish, drawing, composition, and history under the supervision of UNAM instructors. Classes are small, and courses generally last for 3 months at a time. The school will provide a list of prospective town accommodations that consist primarily of hotels. More reasonable accommodations can be found for a lengthy stay, but that's best arranged once you're there. At many locations all over town you'll find notices of furnished apartments or rooms for rent at reasonable prices. For information about the school, contact either the **Dirección de Turismo** (tourist office) in Taxco (see "Visitor Information," above) or write the school directly: UNAM, Hacienda del Chorrillo, 40200 Taxco, Guerrero (☎ **7/622-3690**).

EXPLORING TAXCO

Since Taxco boasts more than 300 shops selling silver, shopping for jewelry and other items is the major pastime for tourists. Prices for silver jewelry here are about the best in the world, and everything is available, from $1 trinkets to artistic pieces costing hundreds of dollars.

In addition, Taxco is the home of some of Mexico's finest stone sculptors, and is also a good place to buy masks. However, beware of so-called "antiques"—there are virtually no real ones for sale.

Taxco also offers cultural attractions. Besides the opulent, world-renowned Santa Prisca y San Sebastián Church, you can visit the Spratling Archaeology Museum, the Silver Museum, and the Humboldt House/Museo Virreynal de Taxco.

Malasia Tours (☎/fax **7/622-7983** or 7/622-3808) offers daily tours to the Cacahuamilpa Caves and the ruins of Xochicalco for $59, including transportation, ticket, and the services of a guide. They also sell bus tickets to Acapulco, Chilpancingo, Iguala, and Cuernavaca. The agency is located on the Plazuela

Silver-Buying Tips

When entering a silver shop, first ask what the "price per gram" is, and then ask for the *precio de mayoreo,* or wholesale price. This tactic will usually help you get a better deal.

San Juan no. 5 to the left of La Hamburguesa. Another agency offering similar services is **Turismo Garlum** (☎ 7/622-3021 or 7/622-3037).

SPECIAL EVENTS & FESTIVALS   January 18 is the date that marks the annual celebration in honor of Santa Prisca, with public festivities and fireworks displays. **۞ Holy Week** in Taxco is one of the most poignant in the country, beginning the Friday a week before Easter with processions daily and nightly. The most riveting procession, on Thursday evening, lasts almost 4 hours and includes villagers from the surrounding area carrying statues of saints, followed by hooded members of a society of self-flagellating penitents chained at the ankles and carrying huge wooden crosses and bundles of penetrating thorny branches. On Saturday morning, the Plaza Borda fills for the **Procession of Three Falls,** reenacting the three times Christ stumbled and fell while carrying his cross. Taxco's **Silver Fair** starts the last week in November and continues through the end of the first week in December. It includes a competition for silver works and sculptures among the top silversmiths. Taking place at the same time is **Jornadas Alarconianas,** which features plays and literary events in honor of Juan Ruíz de Alarcón (1572–1639), a world-famous dramatist who was born in Taxco—and for whom Taxco de Alarcón is named. Both the silver fair and these readings were formerly held in the spring, but have been switched to the late fall. Art exhibits, street fairs, and other festivities are part of this dual celebration.

Sights in Town

Casa de la Cultura de Taxco (Casa Borda). Plaza Borda #1. ☎ **7/622-6617** or 7/622-6632. Fax 7/662-6634. Free admission. Tue–Sun 10am–9pm.

Kitty-corner from the Santa Prisca Church and facing Plaza Borda is the home José de la Borda built for his son around 1759. It is now the Guerrero State Cultural Center, housing classrooms and exhibit halls where period clothing, engravings, paintings, and crafts are displayed. Traveling exhibits are also on display.

Humboldt House/Museo Virreynal de Taxco. Calle Juan Ruíz de Alarcón 12. ☎ **7/622-5501.** Admission $1.75. Tues–Sat 9am–3pm.

Stroll along Ruíz de Alarcón (the street behind the Casa Borda) and look for the richly decorated façade of the Humboldt House, where the renowned German scientist/explorer Baron Alexander von Humboldt (1769–1859) stayed one night in 1803. The new museum houses 18th-century memorabilia pertinent to Taxco, most of which came from a secret room discovered during the recent restoration of the Santa Prisca Church. Signs with detailed information are in both Spanish and English. As you enter, to the right are two huge and very rare *tumelos* (three-tiered funerary paintings). The bottom two were painted in honor of the death of Charles III of Spain; the top one, with a carved phoenix on top, was supposedly painted for the funeral of José de la Borda.

The three stories of the museum are divided by eras, and by persons famous in Taxco's history. Another section is devoted to historical information about Don Miguel Cabrera, Mexico's foremost 18th-century artist. Fine examples of clerical garments decorated with gold and silver thread hang in glass cases. More excellently restored Cabrera paintings are hung throughout the museum; some were found in the displayed frames, others were haphazardly rolled up. And, of course, a small room is devoted to Humboldt and his sojourns through South America and Mexico.

Mercado Central. Plaza Borda. Restaurant open 7am–6pm; shops open 10am–8pm.

Located to the right of the Santa Prisca Church, behind and below Berta's (see below), Taxco's central market meanders deep inside the mountain. Take the stairs off the street. Among the curio stores, you'll find numerous food stands, always the best place for a cheap meal.

Museo de Taxco Guillermo Spratling. Calle Porfirio A. Delgado no. 1. ☎ 7/622-1660. Admission $1.50 adults, $1 children; free on Sun. Tues–Sun 10am–5pm.

A plaque in Spanish explains that most of the collection of pre-Columbian art displayed here, as well as the funds for the museum, came from William Spratling. You'd expect this to be a silver museum, but it's not—for Spratling silver, go to the Spratling Ranch Workshop (see "Nearby Attractions," below). The entrance floor of this museum and the floor above display a good collection of pre-Columbian statues and implements in clay, stone, and jade. The lower floor has changing exhibits. To find the museum, turn right out of the Santa Prisca Church and right again at the corner; continue down the street, veer right, then immediately left. It will be facing you.

✪ Santa Prisca y San Sebastián Church. Plaza Borda. ☎ 7/622-0184. Free admission. Daily 8am–11pm.

This is Taxco's centerpiece parish church; it faces the pleasant Plaza Borda. The church was built with funds provided by José de la Borda, a French miner who struck it rich in Taxco's silver mines. Completed in 1758 after 8 years of labor, it's one of Mexico's most impressive baroque churches. The ultracarved façade is eclipsed by the interior, where the intricacy of the gold-leafed saints and cherubic angels is positively breathtaking. The paintings by Miguel Cabrera, one of Mexico's most famous colonial-era artists, are the pride of Taxco. The sacristy (behind the high altar) contains even more Cabrera paintings.

Guides, both children and adults, will approach you outside the church offering to give a tour, and it's worth the few pesos to get a full rendition of what you're seeing. Make sure the guide's English is passable, however, and establish whether the price is per person or per tour.

Silver Museum. Plaza Borda. ☎ 726/2-0658. Admission $1.50 adults, $1 children. Daily 9:30am–5pm.

The Silver Museum, operated by a local silversmith, is a relatively recent addition to Taxco. After entering the building next to Santa Prisca (upstairs is Sr. Costilla's restaurant), look for a sign on the left; the museum is downstairs. It's not a traditional public-sponsored museum; nevertheless, it does a much-needed job of describing the history of silver in Mexico and Taxco, as well as displaying some historic and contemporary award-winning pieces. Time spent here seeing quality silver work will make you a more discerning shopper in Taxco's silver shops.

NEARBY ATTRACTIONS

The impressive **✪ Grutas de Cacahuamilpa (Cacahuamilpa Grottoes)** (☎ 5/150-5031) are 20 minutes north of Taxco. There are hourly guided tours daily at the grottoes, which are truly sensational and well worth the visit.

For a spectacular view of Taxco, ride the cable cars (*gondola*) to the Hotel Monte Taxco. Catch them across the street from the state tourism office, left of the arches, near the college campus. Take a taxi or the combi marked LOS ARCOS (exit just before the arches, turn left, and follow the signs to the cable cars). They operate daily from 8am to 6pm; the cost is $2.80 for a round-trip ride.

Spratling Ranch Workshop. 6 miles (10km) south of town on the Acapulco Hwy. No phone. Free admission. Mon–Sat 9am–5pm.

Spratling's hacienda-style home/workshop on the outskirts of Taxco still bustles with busy hands reproducing unique designs. A trip here will show you what distinctive Spratling work was all about, for the designs crafted today show the same fine work. Although the prices are higher than other silver here, the designs are unusual and considered collectibles. There's no retail store in Taxco, and unfortunately, most of the display cases at this workshop hold only samples. With the exception of a few jewelry pieces, most items are by order only. Ask about their U.S. outlets.

Los Castillo. 5 miles (8km) south of town on the Acapulco Hwy. and in Taxco on Plazuela Bernal. ☎ **7/622-1016** or 7/622-3471. Fax 7/622-1988. Free admission, but by appointment only. Workshop, Mon–Sat 9am–6pm; Sun 10am–3pm.

Don Antonio Castillo was one of hundreds of young men to whom William Spratling taught the silversmithing trade in the 1930s. He was also one of the first to branch out with his own shops and line of designs, which over the years have earned him a fine reputation. Castillo has shops in several Mexican cities. Now, his daughter Emilia creates her own noteworthy designs, including decorative pieces with silver fused onto porcelain. Emilia's work is for sale on the ground floor of the Posada de los Castillo, just below the Plazuela Bernal. Another store, featuring the designs of Don Antonio, is found in Mexico City's Zona Rosa, at Amberes 41. To visit the workshop, you must call first to make an appointment.

WHERE TO STAY

Taxco is an overnight visitor's dream: charming and picturesque, with a respectable selection of well-kept and delightful hotels. Hotel prices tend to "bulge" at holiday times (especially Easter week).

MODERATE

Hacienda del Solar. Paraje del Solar s/n (Apdo. Postal 96), 40200 Taxco, Gro. ☎/fax **7/622-0323.** 22 units. $100 double; $120–$135 junior and deluxe suite.

This hotel comprises several Mexican-style cottages, all located on a beautifully landscaped hilltop with magnificent views of the surrounding valleys and the town. The decor is slightly different in each one, but most include lots of beautiful handcrafts, red tile floors, and bathrooms with handmade tiles. Several rooms have vaulted tile ceilings and fine private terraces with panoramic views. Others come equipped with more modern amenities of televisions or a minibar. Standard rooms have no terraces and only showers in the bathrooms; deluxe rooms have sunken tubs (with showers) and terraces. Junior suites are the largest and most luxurious accommodations. The hotel is $2^1/_2$ miles (4km) south of the town center off Highway 95 to Acapulco; look for signs on the left and go straight down a narrow road until you see the hotel entrance.

Dining: La Ventana de Taxco restaurant, which has a spectacular view of the city, is the best place to dine in the area. The cuisine is Italian. Main courses run $10 to $20. It's open 8am to 10:30pm.

Amenities: Heated swimming pool, tennis court, laundry, and room service.

INEXPENSIVE

Hotel los Arcos. Juan Ruíz de Alarcón 4, 40200 Taxco, Gro. ☎ **7/622-1836.** Fax 7/622-7982. 21 units. $22 double. No credit cards.

Los Arcos occupies a converted 1620 monastery. The handsome inner patio is bedecked with Puebla pottery and a lively restaurant area to the left, all around a central fountain. The rooms are nicely but sparsely furnished, with natural tile floors and colonial-style furniture. You'll feel immersed in colonial charm and blissful quiet. To find the hotel from the Plaza Borda, follow the hill down (with Hotel Agua Escondida on your left) and make an immediate right at the Plazuela Bernal; the hotel is a block down on the left, opposite the Posada de los Castillo (see below).

☼ **Hotel Rancho Taxco Victoria.** Carlos J. Nibbi 5 and 7 (Apdo. Postal 83), 40200 Taxco, Gro. ☎ **7/622-0004.** Fax 7/622-0010. 63 units (some with TV). $45 double standard; $65 double deluxe; $70 junior suite. AE, MC, V. Free parking.

The Rancho Taxco Victoria clings to the hillside above town, with breathtaking views from its flower-covered verandas. It exudes all the charm of old-fashioned Mexico. The comfortable furnishings, though slightly run-down, whisper of the hotel's 1940s heyday. Each standard unit comes with a bedroom, and in front of each is a table and chairs set out on the tiled common walkway. Each deluxe unit has a bedroom and private terrace;

each junior suite has a bedroom, a nicely furnished large living room, and a spacious private terrace overlooking the city. There's also a lovely pool, plus a restaurant—both with a great view of Taxco. Even if you don't stay here, come for a drink at sunset, or any time, in the comfortable bar/living room, or sit on the terrace to take in the fabulous view. To get here from the Plazuela San Juan, go up a narrow, winding cobbled street named Carlos J. Nibbi. The hotel is at the top of the hill.

✪ **Hotel Santa Prisca.** Cenaobscuras 1, 40200 Taxco, Gro. ☎ **7/622-0080** or 7/622-0980. Fax 7/622-2938. 31 units. $36 double; $40 superior; $48 suite. AE, MC, V. Limited free parking.

The Santa Prisca, 1 block from the Plaza Borda on the Plazuela San Juan, is one of the older and nicer hotels in town. Rooms are small but comfortable, with recently remodeled bathrooms (showers only), tile floors, wood beams, and a colonial atmosphere. For longer stays, ask for a room in the adjacent "new addition," where the rooms are sunnier, quieter, and more spacious. There is a reading area in an upstairs salon overlooking Taxco, a lush patio with fountains, and a lovely dining room that's open from 7:30am to 10pm. Additional guest services include room service, laundry, money exchange, and safe-deposit boxes.

Posada de los Castillo. Juan Ruíz de Alarcón 7, 40200 Taxco. Gro. ☎/fax **7/622-1396.** 13 units. $25 double. MC, V.

Each room in this delightful small hotel is simply but beautifully furnished with handsome carved doors and furniture; bathrooms have either tubs or showers. The manager, Don Teodoro Contreras Galindo, is a true gentleman and a fountain of information about Taxco. To get here from the Plaza Borda, go downhill a short block to the Plazuela Bernal and make an immediate right; and the hotel is a block farther on the right, opposite the Hotel los Arcos (see above).

WHERE TO DINE

Taxco gets a lot of people on day-trips from the capital and Acapulco. There are not enough good restaurants to fill the demand, so prices are high for what you get. Besides those listed below, another top dining spot is La Ventana de Taxco at the Hacienda del Solar, mentioned above.

VERY EXPENSIVE

Toni's. In the Hotel Monte Taxco. ☎ 7/622-1300. Rese
mended. Only dinners. Main courses $10–$15. AE, MC, V. Tues–
STEAKS/SEAFOOD.

High on a mountaintop, Toni's is an intimate and classy
enclosed in a huge, cone-shaped palapa with a panoramic
the city below. Eleven candlelit tables sparkle with crystal and
linen. The menu, mainly shrimp or beef, is limited, but the
is superior. Try the tender, juicy prime roast beef, which com
with Yorkshire pudding, creamed spinach, and baked potato. Lob
ster is sometimes available. To reach Toni's, it's best to take a taxi.

MODERATE

Cielito Lindo. Plaza Borda 14. ☎ 7/622-0603. Breakfast $4.50–$7;
main courses $7.50–$10. No credit cards. Daily 10am–11pm. MEXICAN/
INTERNATIONAL.

Cielito Lindo is probably the most popular place on the plaza for
lunch, perhaps more for its visibility and colorful decor than for
its food, which is fine, but not overwhelming. The tables, covered
in white and blue and laid with blue-and-white local crockery, are
usually packed, and plates of food disappear as fast as the waiters
can bring them. You can get anything from soup to roast chicken,
enchiladas, tacos, steak, and dessert, as well as frosty margaritas.

Sotavento Restaurant Bar Galería. Juárez 8. No phone. Main courses
$3–$8. No credit cards. Tues–Sun 1pm–midnight. ITALIAN/INTERNATIONAL.

This restaurant's stylish decor has paintings decorating the walls
and a variety of linen colors on the table. The menu features
many Italian specialties—try the deliciously fresh spinach salad
and the large pepper steak for a hearty meal; or the Spaghetti
Barbara with poblano peppers and avocado for a vegetarian meal.
To find this place from the Plaza Borda, walk downhill beside the
Hotel Agua Escondida, then follow the street as it bears left (don't
go right on Juan Ruíz de Alarcón) about a block. The restaurant
is on the left just after the street bends left. (It was formerly called
La Taberna).

Sr. Costilla's. Plaza Borda 1 (next to Santa Prisca, above Patio de las Artesanías). ☎/fax 7/622-3215. Main courses $8–$17. MC, V. Daily 1pm–
midnight. MEXICAN/INTERNATIONAL.

The offbeat decor here at "Mr. Ribs" includes a ceiling decked
out with the usual assortment of cultural curios. Several tiny

)ld a few minuscule tables that afford a view of the
.church, and these fill up long before the large dining
.es. The menu is typical of Carlos Anderson restaurants
ay have encountered them in your Mexican travels), with
.lish sayings and a large selection of everything from soup,
.s, sandwiches, and spareribs to desserts and coffee. Wine,
.er, and drinks are served.

EXPENSIVE

.estaurante Ethel. Plazuela San Juan 14. ☎ **7/622-0788.** Breakfast
$2.50–$4.25; main courses $2–$6; comida corrida $4.30. No credit cards.
Daily 9am–10pm (comida corrida served 1–5pm). MEXICAN/INTERNATIONAL.

This family-run place is opposite the Hotel Santa Prisca on the
Plazuela San Juan, 1 block from the Plaza Borda. It's kept clean
and tidy, with colorful cloths on the tables and a homey atmosphere. The hearty daily *comida corrida* consists of soup or pasta,
meat (perhaps a small steak), dessert, and good coffee.

TAXCO AFTER DARK

Paco's is the most popular place overlooking the square for cocktails, conversation, and people watching, all of which continue
until midnight daily. Taxco's version of a disco, **Windows,** is
located high up the mountain in the **Hotel Monte Taxco**
(☎ **7/622-1300**). The whole city is on view from there, and
music runs the gamut from the hit parade to hard rock. For a
cover of $5, you can dance away Saturday night from 10pm
to 3am.

Completely different in tone is **Berta's,** next to the Santa Prisca
Church. Opened in 1930 by a lady named Berta, who made her
fame on a drink of the same name (tequila, soda, lime, and
honey), it's the traditional gathering place of the local gentry and
more than a few tourists. Spurs and old swords decorate the walls,
and a saddle is casually slung over the banister of the stairs leading to the second-floor room, where tin masks leer from the walls.
A Berta (the drink, of course) costs about $2; rum, the same.
Open daily from 11am to around 10pm.

National drinks (not beer) are two-for-one nightly between
6 and 8pm at the terrace bar of the **Hotel Rancho Taxco
Victoria,** where you can also drink in the fabulous view.

2   Cuernavaca: Land of Eternal Spring

64 miles (103km) S of Mexico City; 50 miles (81km) N of Taxco

Often called the "land of eternal spring," Cuernavaca is known these days as much for its rejuvenating spas and spiritual sites as it is for its perfect climate and flowering landscapes. If springtime is when the earth experiences her annual rebirth, then what better setting than here to undergo a personal renaissance? Spa services can easily be found in the area, but more than that, Cuernavaca exudes a sense of deep connection with its historical and spiritual heritage. Cuernavaca's palaces, walled villas, and elaborate haciendas today are home to museums, spas, and extraordinary guesthouses.

Wander the traditional markets and you'll see crystals, quartz, onyx, and tiger's eye for sale, in addition to tourist trinkets. These stones come from the Tepozteco Mountains—for centuries considered an energy source—which cradle Cuernavaca to the north and east. This area is where the country of Mexico begins to narrow, and several mountain ranges converge. To the east and southeast of Cuernavaca are two volcanoes, called Ixaccihuatl (the Sleeping Woman) and Popocatépetl (the Smoking Mountain), also potent symbols of earth energy. The geography and the wisdom of Cuernavaca's ancestral inhabitants passed down through the years have given a restorative energy to this privileged place.

Cuernavaca, capital of the state of Morelos, is also a cultural treasure, with a past that closely follows the history of Mexico— it was always considered a sanctuary for residents of the capital city. So divine is the landscape and climate that both the Aztec ruler Moctezuma and colonial Emperor Maximilian built private retreats here during their respective reigns over Mexico City. Today, the roads between Mexico City and Cuernavaca are jammed almost every weekend, as city residents seek the same respite. As a result, restaurants and hotels may be full as well. Cuernavaca even has a large American colony, plus many students attending the numerous language and cultural institutes in this large city.

Emperor Charles V gave Cuernavaca to Hernán Cortez as a fief, and the conquistador built a palace in 1532 (now the Museo de Cuauhnahuac), where he lived on and off for half a dozen years before returning to Spain. Cortez introduced sugarcane cultivation to the area, and African slaves were brought in to work in the cane fields, by way of Spain's Caribbean colonies. His sugar hacienda at the edge of town is now the luxurious Hotel de Cortez. The economics of large sugarcane growers failed to serve the interests of the indigenous farmers, and there were numerous uprisings in colonial times.

After Mexico gained independence from Spain, powerful landowners from Mexico City gradually dispossessed the remaining small landholders, converting them to virtual serfdom. It was this condition that led to the rise of Emiliano Zapata, the great champion of agrarian reform, who battled the forces of wealth and power, defending the small farmer with the cry of *"¡Tierra y Libertad!"* (Land and Liberty!) during the Mexican Revolution following 1910.

Today, Cuernavaca's popularity has brought with it an influx of wealthy foreigners and industrial capital. With this commercial growth, the city has also acquired the less desirable by-products of increased traffic, noise, and air pollution.

ESSENTIALS
GETTING THERE & DEPARTING

BY CAR   From Mexico City, take Paseo de la Reforma to Chapultepec Park and merge with the Periférico, which will take you to Highway 95D, the toll road on the far south of town that goes to Cuernavaca. From the Periférico, take the Insurgentes exit and continue until you come to signs for Cuernavaca/Tlalpan. Choose either the Cuernavaca Cuota (toll) or the old Cuernavaca Libre (free) road on the right. The free road is slower and very windy, but is more scenic.

BY BUS   *Important note:* Buses to Cuernavaca depart directly from the Mexico City airport. (See "Take a Bus Direct from the Mexico City Airport," below, for details.) The trip takes an hour. The Mexico City Central de Autobuses del Sur exists primarily to serve the route Mexico City–Cuernavaca–Taxco–Acapulco–Zihuatanejo, so you'll have little trouble getting a bus. Pullman has two stations in Cuernavaca; the downtown station is at the corner of Abasolo and Netzahualcoyotl (☎ **7/318-0907** or 7/312-6063), 4 blocks south of the center of town. The other station, Casino de la Selva (☎ **7/312-9473**), is less conveniently located near the railroad station.

Cuernavaca

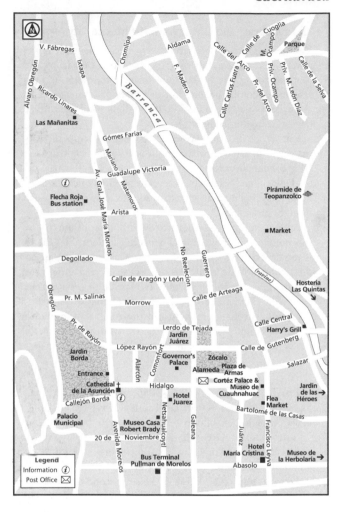

Líneas Unidas del Sur/Flecha Roja (☎ 7/312-2626), with 33 buses daily from Mexico City to Cuernavaca, has a new terminal in Cuernavaca at Morelos 329, between Arista and Victoria, 6 blocks north of the town center. Here, you'll find frequent buses to Toluca, Chalma, Ixtapan de la Sal, Taxco, Acapulco, the Cacahuamilpa Caves, Querétaro, and Nuevo Laredo.

Take a Luxury Bus Direct from the Mexico City Airport

This new airport-to-destination service takes the hassle out of travel to Cuernavaca. Buses serving these routes are deluxe, air-conditioned, and have video movies and a rest room. In most cases there's complimentary soft-drink service. (Passengers tend to stock up when they board, so if you think you'd like a drink, take one early on in the trip).

For service to **Cuernavaca,** Suburban takes up to seven passengers in a (guess what) Suburban, leaving approximately every 2 hours between 6am and 9pm daily. It's affiliated with the Pullman de Morelos bus line. The Suburban ticket kiosk is near Sala A. Pullman de Morelos also runs almost-hourly buses from the airport to Cuernavaca.

Buses for all of these lines are found in front of the covered concourse outside the terminal between exit doors for Gate D. If you have trouble locating any of these, ask for help at one of the information desks on the airport's main concourse. Most importantly, since this airport bus transportation service is new and could change, and/or if precise scheduling is essential to your trip, you might want to call the **Airport Information Office** (☎ 5/571-3600), in Mexico City, to verify names of buses, the place to find them, and current schedules.

Estrella de Oro (☎ 7/312-3055 or 7/312-8296), which is located on Morelos 900 in Las Palmas, serves Iguala, Chilpancingo, Acapulco, and Taxco.

Autransportes Oro (☎ 7/320-2748 or 7/320-2801), on Blvd. Cuauhnauac km 2.5 in Col. Buganvilias, serves Puebla and Izucar de Matamoros, among other destinations.

Estrella Roja (☎ 7/318-5934), a second-class station at Galeana and Cuauhtemotzin in Cuernavaca, about 8 blocks south of the town center, serves Cuautla, Yautepec, Oaxtepec, and Izúcar de Matamoros.

The **Autobuses Estrella Blanca** terminal in Cuernavaca is at Morelos Sur 503, serving Taxco.

VISITOR INFORMATION

Cuernavaca's **State Tourist Office** is at Av. Morelos Sur 187, between Jalisco and Tabasco (☎ 7/314-3872 or 7/314-3881;

☎/fax 7/314-3920), half a block north of the Estrella de Oro bus station and about a 15- to 20-minute walk south of the cathedral. It's open Monday to Friday from 8am to 5pm. There's also a **City Tourism kiosk** (☎ **7/329-4415**) in the wall of the cathedral grounds on Hidalgo close to Morelos. It's open daily from 8am to 8pm.

CITY LAYOUT

In the center of the city are two contiguous plazas. The smaller and more formal of the two, across from the post office, has a Victorian gazebo (designed by Gustave Eiffel of Eiffel Tower fame) at its center. This is the **Alameda.** The larger, rectangular plaza with trees, shrubs, and benches is the **Plaza de Armas.** These two plazas are known collectively as the **zócalo** and form the hub for strolling vendors selling balloons, baskets, bracelets, and other crafts from surrounding villages. It's all easy-going, and one of the great pleasures of the town is hanging out at a park bench or table in a nearby restaurant just to watch. On Sunday afternoons, orchestras play from the gazebo. At the eastern end of the Alameda is the **Cortez Palace,** the conquistador's residence that now serves as the Museo de Cuauhnahuac.

You should be aware that this city's street-numbering system is extremely confusing. It appears that the city fathers, during the past century or so, imposed a new numbering system every 10 or 20 years. Thus, you may find an address given as "no. 5" only to find that the building itself bears the number "506," or perhaps "Antes no. 5" (former no. 5). In descriptions of hotels, restaurants, and sights, the nearest cross-streets will be noted so you can find your way to your chosen destination.

FAST FACTS: Cuernavaca

American Express   The local representative is **Viajes Marín,** Edificio las Plazas, Loc. 13 (☎ **7/314-2266** or 7/318-9901; fax 7/312-9297; www.viajesmarin.com.mx; e-mail: vmarin@ mail.gia.com).

Area Code   The telephone area code is **7.**

Banks   Money can be changed from 9am to 3pm or 5pm, depending on the bank, through the bank tellers, or through automated tellers or casas de cambio at all other times. The closest bank to the zócalo is Bancomer at the corner of Matamoros and Lerdo de Tejada, kitty-corner to Jardín Juárez. Most banks are open until 6pm Monday to Friday, and half days on Saturday.

Elevation   Cuernavaca sits at 5,058 feet.

Hospital   Hospital Cuernavaca, Calle Cuauhtemoc 305, Col Lomas de la Selva, Cuernavaca, 62270 (☎ **7/311-2482** or 7/311-4539).

Internet   Café Internet, located in La Plazuela, Las Casas 8 (across from the Cortez Palace; ☎ **7/318-4330**), offers Internet access for $2.50 per hour, in addition to full computer services and monthly fee programs. It's open Monday to Saturday 9am to 9pm, Sunday 11am to 8pm.

Pharmacy   Farmacias del Ahorro, Av Teopanzolco (☎ **7/316-5563**).

Population   Cuernavaca has 400,000 residents.

Post Office   The post office (☎ **7/312-6105**) is on the Plaza de Armas, next door to Café los Arcos. It's open Monday to Friday from 8am to 7pm and Saturday from 9am to noon.

Spanish Lessons   Cuernavaca is known for its Spanish-language schools, aimed at the foreigner. Generally the schools will help students find lodging with a family or provide a list of potential places to stay. Rather than make a long-term commitment in a family living situation, try it for a week, then decide. Below are the names and addresses of some of the schools. The whole experience, from classes to lodging, can be quite expensive. The school may accept credit cards for the class portion. Contact the **Center for Bilingual Multicultural Studies,** San Jerónimo 304 (Apdo. Postal 1520), 62000 Cuernavaca, Morelos, ☎ **7/313-0011,** 7/317-1087, or 7/317-2488; **Instituto de Idioma y Cultura en Cuernavaca,** ☎ **7/317-0455,** fax 7/317-5710; or **Universal Centro de Lengua y Comunicación Social A.C.** (Universal Language School), J.H. Preciado 171 (Apdo. Postal 1-1826), 62000 Cuernavaca, Morelos, ☎ **7/318-2904** or 7/312-4902, www.universal-spanish.com.

EXPLORING CUERNAVACA

On weekends the whole city, including the roads, hotels, and restaurants, are filled with people from Mexico City. This makes weekends more hectic, but also more fun. You can spend 1 or 2 days sightseeing in Cuernavaca pleasantly enough. If you've come on a day-trip, you may not have time to make all the excursions listed below, but you'll have enough time to see the sights in town. Also notable is the traditional public market, or *mercado*, that is found adjacent to the Cortez Palace. It's open daily from 10am to 10pm, and the colorful rows of stands are a lively place for testing your bargaining skills to purchase pottery, silver jewelry, crystals, and other trinkets. Note that the museum, a key attraction, is closed on Monday.

If you're staying in Cuernavaca and want to rent a car to explore the surrounding areas on your own, try **Guizar Car Rental** (☎ 7/316-5658), Ave. Teopanzolco 3-A, which can offer delivery service to your hotel. Rates start at $40 per day (including tax and insurance) for a Tsuru without A/C and with limited mileage.

Museo de Cuauhnahuac. In the Cortez Palace, Leyva 100. ☎ **7/312-8171.** www.newton.net.mx/cuauhnahuac. E-mail: mrcinah@prodigy.net.mx. Admission $2; free Sun. Tues–Sun 10am–5pm.

The museum is housed in the Cortez Palace, the former home of the greatest of the conquistadors, Hernán Cortez. Construction started in 1530 on the site of a Tlahuica Indian ceremonial center, and was finished by the conquistador's son, Martín. The palace later served as the legislative headquarters for the state of Morelos. It's located in the town center at the eastern end of the Alameda/Plaza de Armas.

In the east portico on the upper floor, there's a large Diego Rivera mural commissioned by Dwight Morrow, U.S. ambassador to Mexico in the 1920s. It depicts the history of Cuernavaca from the coming of the Spaniards to the rise of Zapata (1910). On the lower level, there's an excellent bookstore with a selection of books on Mexican art, architecture, and literature (some English titles are available). It's open daily 10am to 8pm.

Tour guides are frequently found in front of the Palace, offering their services both in the museum as well as to other points of interest in Cuernavaca, for about $10 per hour. Make sure you see official credentials issued by SECTUR (the Tourism Secretariat) before securing the services of one of these guides.

Catedral de la Asunción de María. At the corner of Hidalgo and Morelos (3 blocks southwest of the Plaza de Armas). Free admission. Daily 8am–2pm and 4–10pm.

As you enter the church precincts and pass down the walk, try to imagine what life in Mexico was like in the old days.

Construction on the church began in 1529, a mere 8 years after Cortez conquered Tenochtitlán (Mexico City) from the Aztecs, and was completed in 1552. The churchmen could hardly trust their safety to the tenuous allegiance of their new converts, so they built a fortress as a church. The skull and crossbones above the main door is not a comment on their feelings about the future, however, but a symbol for the Franciscan order, which had its monastery here in the church precincts. The monastery is still here, in fact, and open to the public; it's located on the northwest corner of the church property. Also visible on the exterior walls of the main church are inlaid rocks, placed there in memory of the men who lost their lives during its construction.

An earthquake in 1999 caused significant damage to the belfry, so scaffolding may restrict entrance to certain areas. However, once inside, wander through the various sanctuaries and the courtyard, and pay special attention to the impressive frescos painted on the walls, in various states of restoration. The frescos date back to the 1500s, and have a distinct Asian style to them.

The main church sanctuary is stark, even severe, and with an incongruous modern feeling to it, having been refurbished in the 1960s. Additional frescos on the walls here, originally discovered during the refurbishing, depict the persecution and martyrdom of St. Felipe de Jesús and his companions in Japan. No one is certain who painted them. In the churchyard you'll see gravestones marking the tombs of the most devout—or wealthiest—of the parishioners. Being buried on the church grounds was believed to be the most direct route to heaven.

✪ **Museo Casa Robert Brady.** Calle Netzahualcóyotl 4 between Hidalgo and Abasolo. ☎ **7/318-8554.** Fax 7/314-3529. www.geocities.com/ thebradymuseum. E-mail: bradymus@mail.giga.com. Admission $2.50. Tues–Sun 10am–6pm.

This museum in a private home contains more than 1,300 works of art. Among them are pre-Hispanic and colonial pieces; oil paintings by Frida Kahlo and Rufino Tamayo; and handcrafts from America, Africa, Asia, and India. The collections were assembled by Robert Brady, born in Iowa with a degree in fine arts from the Art Institute of Chicago. He lived in Venice for 5 years before settling in Cuernavaca in 1960. Through his years and travels he assembled this rich mosaic of contrasting styles and epochs. The wildly colorful rooms are exactly as Brady left them.

Admission includes a guide in Spanish; English and French guides are available if requested in advance.

Jardín Borda. Morelos 271, at Hidalgo. ☎ **7/318-1038** or 7/318-1052. Fax 7/318-3706. Admission $1, free on Sundays. Tues–Sun 10am–5:30pm.

Across Morelos Street from the cathedral is the Jardín Borda (Borda Gardens). One of the many wealthy builders to choose Cuernavaca was José de la Borda, brother of the Taxco silver magnate, who ordered a sumptuous vacation house built here in the late 1700s. When he died in 1778, his son Manuel inherited the land and transformed it into a botanical garden. The large enclosed garden next to the house was actually a huge private park, laid out in Andalusian style with little kiosks and an artificial pond. Maximilian found it worthy of an emperor and took it over as his private summer house in 1865. He and Carlota entertained in lavish style amidst the gardens and held frequent concerts by the lake. After Maximilian, the Borda Gardens suffered decades of neglect.

The gardens were completely restored and reopened in October 1987 as the Jardín Borda Centro de Artes. In the gateway buildings are several galleries for changing exhibits and large paintings showing scenes from the life of Maximilian and from the history of the Borda Gardens. One portrays the initial meeting between Maximilian and La India Bonita, who was to become his lover.

On your stroll through the gardens you'll see the same little artificial lake on which Austrian, French, and Mexican nobility rowed in little boats beneath the moonlight. Ducks have taken the place of dukes, however. There are rowboats for rent. The lake is now artfully adapted as an outdoor theater, with seats for the audience on one side and the stage on the other. There's a cafe for refreshments and light meals.

✪ **Jardín Botánico y Museo de Medicina Tradicional y Herbolaría.** Matamoros 14, Acapantzingo. ☎ **7/312-5955,** 7/312-3108, or 7/314-4046. www.cib.uaem.mx. E-mail: cimor@mor.1telmex.net.mx. Free admission. Daily 10am–5pm.

This museum of traditional herbal medicine, in the south Cuernavaca suburb of Acapantzingo, was established in a former resort residence built by Maximilian, called the Casa del Olindo, or Casa del Olvido. It was here, during his brief reign, that the Austrian-born emperor would come for trysts with La India

Bonita, his Cuernavacan lover. The building was restored in 1960, and the house and gardens now preserve the local wisdom of folk medicine. The topic proved so popular that the museum was completely restructured and expanded in 1998. The shady gardens are lovely to wander through, and you shouldn't miss the 200 orchids growing near the rear of the property. However, the lovers' actual house, the little dark-pink building in the back, is closed. Take a taxi, or catch combi no. 6 at the mercado on Degollado. Ask to be dropped off at Matamoros near the museum. Turn right on Matamoros and walk 1 1/2 blocks; the museum will be on your right.

ACTIVITIES AND EXCURSIONS

GOLF   With its perpetual spring-like climate, Cuernavaca is an ideal place for golf. The Tabachines Golf Club and Restaurant, Km. 93.5 Carr. Mexico-Acapulco, ☎ 7/314-3999, is the city's most popular course, open for public play. Percy Clifford designed this 18-hole course, surrounded by beautifully mani-cured gardens blooming with bougainvillea, gardenias, and other flowers. The elegant restaurant is a popular place for breakfast, lunch, or the especially popular Sunday brunch. Greens fees are $50 during the week and $100 on weekends. American Express, Visa, and MasterCard are accepted. Open Tuesday to Sunday, 7am to 7pm.

Also in Cuernavaca is the Club de Golf Hacienda San Gaspar, Ave. Emiliano Zapata Col. Cliserio Alanis (☎ 7/319-4424 or 7/319-0002), an 18-hole golf course designed by Joe Finger. It's surrounded by more than 3,000 trees of different kinds (palms, laurels, and tabachines), and has two artificial lagoons, plus beau-tiful panoramic views of Cuernavaca, the Popocatepetl and Iztaci-huatl volcanoes, and the Tepozteco Mountains. Greens fees are $70 on weekends or $35 from Monday to Friday; carts cost an additional $25 for 18 holes, and a caddy is $100 plus tip. Amer-ican Express, Visa, and MasterCard are accepted. Additional facilities include a gym with Jacuzzi and sauna, pool, four tennis courts, and a restaurant and snack bar. Open daily from 7:30am to 6:30pm.

LAS ESTACAS   Either a side trip from Cuernavaca or a desti-nation on its own, Las Estacas, Km. 6.5 Carretera Tlaltizapán–Cuautla, Morelos (☎ 7/345-0077) is a natural waterpark, whose clear spring waters are reputed to have healing properties. In addition to the crystal-clear rivers, Las Estacas has two pools, wading pools for children, horseback riding, and a traditional-style spa (or *balneario*), open daily from 8am to 6pm. Several restaurants on site serve simple food, such as quesadillas, fruit with yogurt, sandwiches, and tortas. Admission is $8 for adults; $4 for children 4 to 10. There is also a trailer park and a small, basic hotel which charges $67 for a double room; this includes the entrance fee to the balneario and breakfast. MasterCard and Visa are accepted. On weekends the place is filled with families with children. Las Estacas is located 22.5 miles (36 km) east of Cuernavaca. To get there, take Highway 138 to Yautepec, then turn right on the first exit past Yautepec.

PYRAMIDS OF XOCHICALCO   This beautiful ceremonial center provides clues to the history of the whole region. Artifacts and inscriptions link this site to the mysterious cultures that built Teotihuacán and Tula, and some of the objects found here make it appear as though they were also in contact with the Mixtecs, the Aztecs, the Mayan, and the Zapotec cultures. The most impressive building in Xochicalco is the *pirámide de la serpiente emplumada* (pyramid of the plumed serpent), with its magnificent reliefs of plumed serpents twisting around seated priests. Underneath the pyramid is a series of tunnels and chambers with murals on the walls. There is also an observatory, where from April 30 to August 15 you can follow the trajectory of the sun as it shines through a hexagonal opening. It's located $22^1/_2$ miles (36 km) southwest of Cuernavaca.

WHERE TO STAY

Because so many residents of Mexico City come down for a day or two, tourist traffic at the hotels here may be heavy on weekends and holidays. Reservations during these times are recommended.

EXPENSIVE

✪ **Camino Real Sumiya.** Interior Fracc. Sumiya s/n, Col. José Parres, 62550 Jiutepec, Mor. ☎ **800/7-CAMINO** in the U.S., or 7/320-9199. Fax 7/320-9142. www.caminoreal.com/sumiya/. E-mail: sya@caminoreal.com. 163 units. A/C MINIBAR TV TEL. $160 double or single; $260–$380 suite. Low-season packages and discounts available. AE, DC, MC, V.

Sumiya's charm is in its relaxing atmosphere, which is best midweek since escapees from Mexico City tend to fill it on weekends. About 7 miles (11km) south of Cuernavaca, this unusual resort, whose name means "the place of peace, tranquility, and longevity," was once the exclusive home of Woolworth heiress Barbara Hutton. Using materials and craftsmen from Japan, she constructed the estate in 1959 for $3.2 million on 30 beautifully wooded acres. The main house, a series of large interconnected rooms and decks, overlooks the grounds and contains restaurants and the lobby. The house is an exact replica of one in Kyoto, Japan. The guest rooms, which are clustered in three-storied buildings bordering manicured lawns, are simple in comparison to the striking Japanese architecture of the main house. Rooms, however, have subtle Japanese accents, with austere but comfortable furnishings and scrolled wood doors. Each room has direct-dial, dual-line phones, three-prong electrical outlets, ceiling fans, and wall safes.

Hutton built a kabuki-style theater and exquisite Zen meditation garden on the grounds, which are now used only for special events. The theater is adorned with vividly colored silk curtains and gold-plated Temple paintings protected by folding cedar and mahogany screens. The garden, which was originally used by kabuki actors for meditation prior to a performance, has strategically placed rocks representing the *chakras*, or energetic points of the human body.

Cuernavaca is an inexpensive taxi ride away. Taxis to the Mexico City airport cost $58 one way. From the freeway, take the Atlacomulco exit and follow Sumiya signs. Ask directions in Cuernavaca if you're coming from there since the route to the resort is complicated.

Dining: La Arboleda, an outdoor restaurant shaded by enormous Indian laurel trees, is open 7am to midnight; Sumiya, with both terrace and indoor dining, is open Wednesday to Sunday from 1pm to 11pm; and there's a snack bar by the pool.

Amenities: Sculpted swimming pool, 10 tennis courts, golf privileges nearby, convention facilities with simultaneous translation capabilities, room service, business center.

Las Mañanitas. Ricardo Linares 107 (5 1/2 long blocks north of the Jardín Borda), 62000 Cuernavaca, Mor. ☎ **7/314-1466** or 7/312-4646. Fax 7/318-3672. www.lasmananitas.com.mx. E-mail: mananita@intersur.com. 22 units. $120–$300 double; $348 suite. AE. Valet parking.

This has been Cuernavaca's most renowned luxury lodging for years. But although it is impeccably maintained, Las Mañanitas has an overly formal feeling to it, which takes away from the comfort level of some guests. The rooms are formal in a style that was popular 15 years ago, with gleaming polished molding and brass accents, large bathrooms, and rich fabrics. There are several sections. Rooms in the original mansion, called terrace suites, overlook the restaurant and inner lawn; the large rooms in the patio section each have a secluded patio; and those in the luxurious and expensive garden section each have a patio overlooking the pool and emerald lawns, where peacocks and other exotic birds strut and fountains murmur. Thirteen rooms have fireplaces, and the hotel also has a heated pool in the private garden. The room above the restaurant (the least expensive) is the hotel's only standard room—but it's very nice and has an excellent view of the public garden. The hotel is one of only two in Mexico associated with the prestigious Relais & Château hotels.

Dining: The restaurant, which overlooks the gardens, is one of the premier dining places in Mexico (see "Where to Dine," below). It's open to nonguests for lunch and dinner only.

Amenities: Swimming pool, laundry and room service, concierge. Transportation to and from the Mexico City airport can be arranged through the hotel for $200 round-trip.

Hostería Las Quintas. Blvd. Díaz Ordaz No. 9, Col. Cantarranas, C.P. 62240 Cuernavaca, Mor. ☎ **877/784-6827;** fax 888/SPAS-MEX, toll-free from the U.S. and Canada; 800/990-1888 toll-free from Mexico, or 7/318-3889; fax 7/318-3895. www.hlasquintas.com. E-mail: lasquintas@hlasquintas.com. 60 units. MINIBAR TV TEL. $184–$241 double; $274 suite. Call for details on a changing variety of spa packages. AE, V, MC. Free parking.

Although this hotel bills itself as a spa resort, it is actually a traditional hotel that has sublet a portion of its land for a separate spa operation. The spa itself, although admirably managed, falls far short of the true spa experience. Although the spa technicians are very professional and welcoming, their training and skill level is basic at best. An extensive list of European spa services is offered in what I consider makeshift rooms. The spa program is clearly oriented toward a younger guest without much spa-going experience. A plus is the sensory deprivation flotation tank (the first in Latin America), next to a roof-top massage area.

As is the style in Cuernavaca, this hotel is set behind an imposing stone wall that provides the place with a sense of seclusion. However, it's very close to the center of town, and traffic noise permeates most of the rooms, especially those in the newer sections in the back. All rooms are large, and each is unique, though most have dated furnishings of heavy wood; all have tile floors.

Variable features include terraces, Jacuzzis, and (nonworking) fireplaces. Both rooms and facilities are housed in two-story Spanish colonial-style buildings, centered around a garden of flowering plants and trees. The meticulously maintained gardens are in constant bloom, and medicinal plants and herbs are all identified. As this is considered a popular family weekend getaway for Mexico City residents, children tend to populate the pools on weekends.

One reason to consider the Hostería is for its variety of packages that combine spa services with other natural, cultural, and historic attractions. Some packages include Spanish-language studies. The popular Eco-Fitness program offers guests the opportunity to get fit while exploring the area—think pyramid climbing, as opposed to a Stairmaster.

Dining: The restaurant, Jade, overlooks the Bonsai garden, and serves all meals with international, Mexican, and spa cuisine options. It's open from 7am to 11pm daily, and offers outside, terrace dining during the days.

Amenities: In addition to the complete spa services program, there are two heated swimming pools, one with a Jacuzzi; plus guest services that include a small boutique, baby-sitting, laundry, room service, tour desk, and concierge. Transportation to and from the Mexico City airport can be arranged through the hotel.

○ **Misión Del Sol Resort & Spa.** Av. General Diego Díaz Gonzalez 31. Col. Parres. 62550, Cuernavaca, Mor. ☎ **800/448-8355,** from the U.S. and Canada; 800/999-9100 toll-free inside Mexico, or 7/321-0999. Fax 7/321-1195. www.misiondelsol.com.mx; E-mail: inform@misiondelsol.com.mx, reserv@misiondelsol.com.mx. 40 units and 12 villas. A/C. $215 double deluxe room; $403.50 villa (up to 4 persons); $497 Villa Magnolia (up to 4 persons). Special spa and meal packages available as add-ons to room price. AE, MC, V. Free parking.

This adults-only hotel and spa offers a veritable, high-quality spa experience that rivals any in North America or Europe—and for an exceptional value. Tranquility and a sense of pure peace welcome you from the moment you enter this resort, which was created with loving detail, drawing from the mystical wisdom of the ancient cultures of Mexico, Tibet, Egypt, and Asia. Guests and visitors are encouraged to wear light-hued clothes to contribute to the harmonious flow of energy. Only children over 14 are welcome.

The guest rooms, villas, and common areas are grouped in architecturally stunning adobe buildings that meld with the carefully preserved natural environment. Garden areas are extensive, bordered by gently flowing streams. Group activities such as reading discussions, chess club, and painting workshops take place in the Salon; films are shown here on weekend evenings. The bedrooms are large and peaceful; each looks onto its own garden or stream. Bathrooms are very large, with sunken tubs, and dual-headed showers have river rocks set into the floor, as a type of reflexology treatment. Beds have magnets inlaid in them, for restoring proper energy flow; all linens are 100% cotton. A recessed sitting area with sofa offers a comfortable place for reading or relaxing. Villas have two separate bedrooms, plus a living/dining area, and a meditation room.

The spa has a menu of 32 services, with an emphasis on water-based treatments. Elegant relaxation areas are interspersed among the treatment rooms and Jacuzzi. The Oratorium is a special structure—built with all rounded corners and a domed ceiling with skylight—used for meditation; a flowing stream, bamboo, and verdant plants surround it.

Dining/Diversions: The restaurant serves exceptionally creative vegetarian and international cuisine. All meals are prepared with fresh, primarily organic ingredients. Most of the packages include meals.

Amenities: Rooms have three channels of ambient music, and no TVs. Spa services include a variety of massages, body wraps, scrubs, facial treatments, Temazcal (pre-Hispanic sweat lodge purification), Janzu, and, phototherapy. Classes and sessions in meditation, yoga, and tai-chi are offered daily, as well as more traditional activities such as tennis, paddle tennis, nature walks, and tours to the outskirts of town. There is also a very well-equipped gym. Airport transfers from Mexico City are available for $120 each way.

MODERATE

Hotel Posada María Cristina. Leyva 20 (Apdo. Postal 203), 62000 Cuernavaca, Mor. ☎ **7/318-6984** or 7/318-5767. Fax 7/312-9126. www. maria-cristina.com. 19 units. AC TV TEL. $76 double; $137–$197 suite and cabana. AE, MC, V. Free parking.

This hotel is on the southwest corner of Leyva and Abasolo, half a block from the Palacio de Cortez. The María Cristina's high walls conceal many delights: a small swimming pool, lush gardens with fountains, colonial-style furnishings, a good restaurant, patios, and large and small guest rooms. All rooms are exceptionally clean and comfortable, with firm beds. Bathrooms have inlaid Talavera tiles and skylights. There are ceiling fans and hair dryers in each room. Suites are only slightly larger than normal rooms. A pool is on the lower level of the grounds, and the bar/restaurant there is open on weekends. La Casona, the handsome little restaurant on the first floor, overlooks the gardens and serves excellent meals based on Mexican and international recipes. Even if you don't stay here, consider having a meal. The Sunday brunch is especially popular, and just $8 per person.

INEXPENSIVE

Hotel Juárez. Netzahualcoyotl 19, 62000 Cuernavaca, Mor. ☎ **7/314-0219.** 12 units. FAN. $18 double. TV. No credit cards. Limited street parking.

Its rates and location in downtown Cuernavaca, 1 block from the Casa Borda, makes the Juárez a good choice for those intent on exploring the cultural charms of Cuernavaca. Each of the clean, simple rooms of this two-story hotel is furnished with old-fashioned but well-kept details. There is a small pool and garden area. To get here from the Cathedral, go east on Hidalgo, then turn right on Netzahualcoyotl. The hotel is about a block down on the left.

WHERE TO DINE
EXPENSIVE

Restaurant Las Mañanitas. Ricardo Linares 107. ☎ **7/314-1466** or 7/312-4646. www.lasmananitas.com.mx. Reservations recommended. Main courses $12–$20. AE. Daily 1–5pm and 7–11pm. MEXICAN/INTERNATIONAL.

Las Mañanitas has set the standard for sumptuous, leisurely dining in Cuernavaca, but it has reached the point where its reputation surpasses the reality. Though the setting is exquisite and the service superb, the meal itself is not as noteworthy as one would expect. Tables are set on a shaded terrace with a view of gardens, strolling peacocks, and softly playing violinists or a romantic trio. The ambiance is lovely, and the service extremely attentive. When you arrive, you can enjoy cocktails in the cozy sala or on lounge chairs on the lawn; when you're ready to dine, a waiter will present you with a large blackboard menu listing a dozen or more daily specials. The cuisine is Mexican with an international flair, drawing on whatever fruits and vegetables are in season and offering a full selection of fresh seafood, beef, pork, veal, and fowl, but in standard preparations. Try the cream of watercress soup, the fillet of red snapper in cilantro sauce, and top it off with black-bottom pie, the house specialty. Las Mañanitas is 5½ long blocks north of the Jardín Borda.

MODERATE

Restaurant La India Bonita. Morrow 20 Col. Centro. ☎ **7/318-6967** or 7/312-5021. Breakfast $2.50–$5.50; main courses $8.50–$10. AE, MC, V. Tues–Sat 8am–11pm; Sun 9am–6pm. MEXICAN.

Housed among the interior patios and portals of the restored home of former U.S. Ambassador Dwight Morrow (1920s), La India Bonita is a gracious haven where you can enjoy the setting as well as the food. Specialties include *mole poblano* (chicken with a sauce of bitter chocolate and fiery chiles) and *fillet à la parrilla* (charcoal-grilled steak). There are also several daily specials. A breakfast mainstay is the *desayuno Maximiliano:* a gigantic platter featuring enchiladas. The restaurant is 2 blocks north of the Jardín Juárez between Matamoros and Morelos.

Restaurant Vienés. Lerdo de Tejada 12. ☎ **7/318-4044** or 7/314-3404. Breakfast $3–$5; main courses $6–$9. Daily 8am–10pm. AE, MC, V. VIENNESE.

This tidy and somewhat Viennese-looking place, located a block from the Jardín Juárez (between Morelos and Morrow), is a legacy of this city's Viennese immigrant heritage. The menu has old-world specialties such as grilled trout with vegetables and German potato salad. For dessert there's apple strudel followed by Viennese coffee. A daily "executive menu" offers a fixed-priced complete meal for $8.50. Next door, the restaurant runs a pastry/coffee shop called **Los Pasteles del Vienés.** Although the menu is identical, the atmosphere in the coffee shop is much more leisurely, and there the tempting pastries are on display in glass cases.

INEXPENSIVE

✪ **La Universal.** Guerrero 2. ☎ **7/318-6732** or 7/318-5970. Breakfast $3–$8; main courses $4–$9; comida corrida $4.50. AE, MC, V. Daily 7am–midnight. MEXICAN/PASTRIES.

This place does a teeming business, partly because of its great location (overlooking both the Alameda and Plaza de Armas), partly because of its traditional Mexican specialties, and partly because it has very reasonable prices for Cuernavaca. It's open to the street and has many outdoor cafe tables, usually filled with older men discussing the day's events or playing a game of chess.

These tables are perfect for watching the changing parade of street vendors and park life. The specialty here is a Mexican grilled sampler plate, including carne asada, enchilada, pork cutlet, and grilled green onions, beans and tortillas, for $6.50. A full breakfast special for $3 is served Monday to Friday from 9:30am to noon. There's also a popular Happy Hour each Monday through Friday from 2pm to 10pm.

CUERNAVACA AFTER DARK

Cuernavaca has a number of cafes right off the Jardín Juárez where people gather to sip coffee or drinks till the wee hours of the morning. The best are La Parroquia and La Universal (see "Where to Dine," above). There are band concerts in the Jardín Juárez on Thursday and Sunday evenings.

A recent—and welcome—addition to nightlife in Cuernavaca is **La Plazuelo,** a short stretch of a bricked street, closed off for pedestrian traffic only, located just across from the Cortez Palace. Here, coffee shops alternate with tattoo parlors and live-music bars—something is always going on. It's geared toward a 20-something, university crowd.

Harry's Grill, Gutenberg 5 (at Salazar, just off the main square; ☎ 7/312-7639) is another addition to the Carlos Anderson chain. It offers the chain's usual good food and craziness, with Mexican revolutionary posters and flirtatious waiters. Although it serves full dinners, I'd recommend you go for drinks. The restaurant is open daily 1:30pm to 11:30pm; the bar, Tuesday to Saturday, 9pm to 4am. Visa, MasterCard, and American Express are accepted.

Appendix:
Useful Terms & Phrases

1 Telephones & Mail

USING THE TELEPHONES

In 1999, an important change in local telephone service took place. Where previously you would dial a five- or six-digit number within a city for local calls, these now all conform to international standards of seven-digit numbers. In order to access any local number in this book, dial the last seven digits listed (most numbers listed in this book are a total of eight digits—the number plus the area code within Mexico). For local numbers within Mexico City only, eight digits are required: dial 5, and the remaining seven digits of the number.

To call long distance within Mexico, you'll need to dial the national long distance code **01** prior to dialing the two- or three-digit area code, and then the number. In total, Mexico's telephone numbers are eight digits in length. Mexico's area codes (*claves*) are usually listed in the front of telephone directories. Area codes are listed before all phone numbers in this book. For long-distance dialing you will often see the term "LADA," which is the automatic long distance service offered by Telmex, Mexico's former telephone monopoly and the largest phone service company in Mexico. To make a person-to-person or collect call inside Mexico, dial ☎ **020.**

International long distance calls to the United States or Canada are accessed by dialing ☎ **001,** then the area code and seven-digit number. To make a person-to-person or collect call to outside of Mexico, dial ☎ **090.** For other international dialing codes, dial the operator at ☎ **040.**

For additional details on making calls in Mexico and to Mexico, see chapter 1, "Planning a Trip to Southern Pacific Mexico."

POSTAL GLOSSARY

Airmail   **Correo Aéreo**
Customs   **Aduana**
General Delivery   **Lista de Correos**
Insurance (insured mail)   **Seguro (correo asegurado)**
Mailbox   **Buzón**
Money Order   **Giro Postal**
Parcel   **Paquete**
Post Office   **Oficina de Correos**
Post Office Box (abbreviation)   **Apartado Postal**
Postal Service   **Correos**
Registered Mail   **Registrado**
Rubber Stamp   **Sello**
Special Delivery, Express   **Entrega Inmediata**
Stamp   **Estampilla** or **Timbre**

2   Basic Vocabulary

Most Mexicans are very patient with foreigners who try to speak their language; it helps a lot to know a few basic phrases.

I've included a list of certain simple phrases for expressing basic needs, followed by some common menu items.

ENGLISH-SPANISH PHRASES

English	Spanish	Pronunciation
Good day	**Buenos días**	*bway*-nohss *dee*-ahss
How are you?	**¿Cómo está?**	*koh*-moh ess-*tah*?
Very well	**Muy bien**	mwee byen
Thank you	**Gracias**	*grah*-see-ahss
You're welcome	**De nada**	day *nah*-dah
Good-bye	**Adiós**	ah-*dyohss*
Please	**Por favor**	pohr fah-*vohr*
Yes	**Sí**	see
No	**No**	noh
Excuse me	**Perdóneme**	pehr-*doh*-ney-may
Give me	**Déme**	*day*-may
Where is . . . ?	**¿Dónde está . . . ?**	*dohn*-day ess-*tah*?
the station	**la estación**	lah ess-tah-*seown*
a hotel	**un hotel**	oon oh-*tel*
a gas station	**una gasolinera**	*oon*-uh gah-so-lee-*nay*-rah

a restaurant	**un restaurante**	oon res-tow-*rahn*-tay
the toilet	**el ban–o**	el *bahn*-yoh
a good doctor	**un buen médico**	oon bwayn
		may-thee-co
the road to . . .	**el camino a/hacia**	el cah-*mee*-noh
		ah/*ah*-see-ah
To the right	**A la derecha**	ah lah day-*reh*-chuh
To the left	**A la izquierda**	ah lah ees-ky-*ehr*-thah
Straight ahead	**Derecho**	day-*reh*-cho
I would like	**Quisiera**	key-see-*ehr*-ah
I want	**Quiero**	*kyehr*-oh
to eat	**comer**	ko-*mayr*
a room	**una habitación**	*oon*-nuh
		ha-bee-tah-*seown*
Do you have . . . ?	**¿Tiene usted?**	tyah-nay oos-*ted*?
a book	**un libro**	oon *lee*-bro
a dictionary	**un diccionario**	oon deek-seown-
		ar-eo
How much is it?	**¿Cuánto cuesta?**	*kwahn*-to *kwess*-tah?
When?	**¿Cuándo?**	*kwahn*-doh?
What?	**¿Qué?**	kay?
There is	**(¿)Hay (. . . ?)**	eye?
(Is there . . . ?)		
What is there?	**¿Qué hay?**	kay eye?
Yesterday	**Ayer**	ah-*yer*
Today	**Hoy**	oy
Tomorrow	**Mañana**	mahn-*yahn*-ah
Good	**Bueno**	*bway*-no
Bad	**Malo**	*mah*-lo
Better (best)	**(Lo) Mejor**	(loh) meh-*hor*
More	**Más**	mahs
Less	**Menos**	*may*-noss
No smoking	**Se prohíbe fumar**	say pro-*hee*-bay
		foo-*mahr*
Postcard	**Tarjeta postal**	tar-*hay*-ta pohs-*tahl*
Insect repellent	**Rapelente contra**	rah-pey-*yahn*-te
	insectos	*cohn*-trah een-*sehk*-tos

MORE USEFUL PHRASES

English	Spanish	Pronunciation
Do you speak English?	¿Habla usted inglés?	*ah*-blah oo-*sted* een-*glays*?
Is there anyone here?	¿Hay alguien aquí?	eye *ahl*-ghee-en kay
Who speaks English?	¿qué hable inglés?	*ah*-blay een-*glays*?
I speak a little Spanish.	Hablo un poco de español.	*ah*-blow oon poh-koh day ess-pah-*nyol*
I don't understand Spanish very well.	No (lo) entiendo muy bien el español.	noh (loh) ehn-tee-*ehn*-do moo-ee bee-ayn el ess-pah-*nyol*
The meal is good.	Me gusta la comida.	may *goo*-sta lah koh-*mee*-dah
What time is it?	¿Qué hora es?	kay *oar*-ah ess?
May I see your menu?	¿Puedo ver el menú (la carta)?	*puay*-tho veyr el may-*noo* (lah *car*-tah)?
The check please.	La cuenta por favor.	lah *quayn*-tah pohr fa-*vorh*
What do I owe you?	¿Cuánto lo debo?	*Kwahn*-toh loh *day*-boh?
What did you say?	¿Mande? (colloquial expression for American "Eh?")	*Mahn*-day?
More formal:	¿Cómo?	*Koh*-moh?
I want (to see)	Quiero (ver)	Key-*yehr*-oh vehr
a room	un cuarto or una habitacióno	on *kwar*-toh, *oon*-nuh ha-bee-tah-*seown*
for two persons	para dos personas	*pahr*-ah doss pehr-*sohn*-as
with (without) bathroom	con (sin) baño.	kohn (seen) *bah*-nyoh
We are staying here only	Nos quedamos aquí solamente	nohs kay-*dahm*-ohss ah-*key* sohl-ah-*mayn*-tay
one night	una noche	oon-ah *noh*-chay

one week	**una semana**	oon-ah say-*mahn*-ah
We are leaving	**Partimos (Salimos)**	Pahr-*tee*-mohss; sah-*lee*-mohss
tomorrow	**mañana**	mahn-*nyan*-ah
Do you accept?	**¿Acepta usted?**	Ah-*sayp*-tah oo-*sted*
traveler's checks?	**cheques de viajero?**	*chay* kays day bee-ah-*hehr*-oh?
Is there a Laundromat?	**¿Hay una lavandería?**	Eye *oon*-ah lah-*vahn*-day-*ree*-ah
near here?	**cerca de aquí?**	*sehr*-ka day ah-*key*
Please send these clothes to the laundry	**Hágame el favor de mandar esta ropa a la lavandería.**	*Ah*-ga-may el fah-*vhor* day mahn-*dahr* ays- tah *rho*-pah a lah lah-*vahn*-day-*ree*-ah

NUMBERS

1	**uno**	(*ooh*-noh)
2	**dos**	(dohs)
3	**tres**	(trayss)
4	**cuatro**	(*kwah*-troh)
5	**cinco**	(*seen*-koh)
6	**seis**	(sayss)
7	**siete**	(*syeh*-tay)
8	**ocho**	(*oh*-choh)
9	**nueve**	(*nway*-bay)
10	**diez**	(dee-ess)
11	**once**	(*ohn*-say)
12	**doce**	(*doh*-say)
13	**trece**	(*tray*-say)
14	**catorce**	(kah-*tor*-say)
15	**quince**	(*keen*-say)
16	**dieciseis**	(de-*ess*-ee-sayss)
17	**diecisiete**	(de-*ess*-ee-*syeh*-tay)
18	**dieciocho**	(dee-*ess*-ee-*oh*-choh)
19	**diecinueve**	(dee-*ess*-ee-*nway*-bay)

20	**veinte** (*bayn*-tay)
30	**treinta** (*trayn*-tah)
40	**cuarenta** (kwah-*ren*-tah)
50	**cincuenta** (seen-*kwen*-tah)
60	**sesenta** (say-*sen*-tah)
70	**setenta** (say-*ten*-tah)
80	**ochenta** (oh-*chen*-tah)
90	**noventa** (noh-*ben*-tah)
100	**cien** (see-*en*)
200	**doscientos** (*dos*-se-en-tos)
500	**quinientos** (keen-ee-*ehn*-tos)
1,000	**mil** (meal)

TRANSPORTATION TERMS

English	Spanish	Pronunciation
Airport	**Aeropuerto**	Ah-ay-row-*por*-tow
Flight	**Vuelo**	Boo-*ay*-low
Rental car	**Arrendadora de Autos**	Ah-rain-da-dow-rah day autos
Bus	**Autobús**	ow-toh-*boos*
Bus or truck	**Camión**	ka-mee-*ohn*
Lane	**Carril**	kah-*rreal*
Nonstop	**Directo**	dee-*reck*-toh
Baggage (claim area)	**Equipajes**	eh-key-*pah*-hays
Intercity	**Foraneo**	fohr-ah-*nay*-oh
Luggage storage area	**Guarda equipaje**	gwar-dah eh-key-*pah*-hay
Arrival gates	**Llegadas**	yay-*gah*-dahs
Originates at this station	**Local**	loh-*kahl*
Originates elsewhere	**De paso**	day *pah*-soh
stops if seats available	**Para si hay lugares**	*pah-rah see aye loo-gahr-ays*
First class	**Primera**	pree-*mehr*-oh
Second class	**Segunda**	say-*goon*-dah
Nonstop	**Sin escala**	seen ess-*kah*-lah
Baggage claim area	**Recibo de equipajes**	ray-see-boh day eh-key-*pah*-hay
Waiting room	**Sala de espera**	*Saw*-lah day ess-*pehr*-ah
Toilets	**Sanitarios**	Sahn-ee-tahr-*ee*-oss
Ticket window	**Taquilla**	tah-*key*-lah

See also Accommodations and Restaurant Indexes.

GENERAL INDEX

Acapulco, 4, 38–40, 42–51,
53–59, 61–71
  accommodations, 46–49,
    51–55
  activities and attractions,
    61–66
  beaches, 61, 63
  layout of, 42
  nightlife, 68, 70–71
  restaurants, 55, 57–58, 60
  shopping, 67
  transportation, 43
  traveling to/from, 39
  visitor information, 42
Airlines, 25, 27, 29
Año Nuevo (New Year's Day),
  12
Ash Wednesday, 12
Assumption of the Virgin
  Mary, 14
ATMs (automated teller
  machines), 10

Bahías de Huatulco, 4, 102,
  124–125, 127–134,
  136–137
  accommodations, 132,
    134–135
  bay cruises & ecotours, 130,
    131
  beaches, 129
  coffee plantations, 131
  nightlife, 137
  shopping, 132
Banks, 9

Barra de la Cruz Beach (near
  Puerto Ángel), 109
Barra de Potosí Lagoon, 97
Beaches
  Acapulco, 61, 63
  Bahías de Huatulco, 129
  Puerto Ángel, 122
  Puerto Escondido, 108
  safety, 64
Bird watching, Ixtapa/
  Zihuatanejo, 95, 97
Boat rentals
  Acapulco, 65
  Ixtapa/Zihuatanejo, 96
Boat trips and cruises
  Acapulco, 63
  Bahías de Huatulco, 130
  Ixtapa/Zihuatanejo, 95
Bribes and scams, 20
Bullfights, 66
Bus travel, 26
  Acapulco, 42–43
  Bahías de Huatulco, 126
  Cuernavaca, 152, 154
  Ixtapa/Zihuatanejo, 76
  in Mexico, 31
  Puerto Ángel, 121
  Puerto Escondido, 105
Business hours, 32

Caleta Beach (Acapulco), 61
Caletilla Beach (Acapulco), 61
Candlemass, 12
Carnaval, 12
Cars and driving
  Acapulco, 39, 44
  Bahías de Huatulco, 126

Cars and driving (*cont.*)
   in Mexico, 30
   Ixtapa/Zihuatanejo, 74
   Puerto Ángel, 121
   Puerto Escondido, 105
   rentals, 30
   safety, 42, 74
   to Mexico, 25
Catedral de la Asunción de
   María (Cuernavaca), 157
Centro Internacional de
   Convivencia Infantil (CICI),
   66
Chacahua Lagoon National
   Park, 111
Chahué Bay, 128, 130
Children, families with, 21
Christmas, 15
Christmas Posadas, 15
Cinco de Mayo, 13
Climate, 11, 44
Coffee plantations, Huatulco,
   131
Condesa Beach (Acapulco),
   62
Consular agents, 44
Corpus Christi, 13
Costera Miguel Alemán, 43
Coyuca Lagoon, 63, 64
Credit cards, 10
Crime, 19, 20
Crucecita, 125, 127–128,
   131–132, 135–136
Cruise lines, 26
Cuernavaca, 4, 138, 151–162,
   164–165, 167–168
   accommodations, 161–162,
      164–166
   activities and excursions,
      160–161
   bus travel, 152
   layout of, 155

   nightlife, 168
   restaurants, 166–167
   sights and attractions, 156,
      158, 160
   traveling to/from, 154
   visitor information, 154
Currency and exchange, 8, 45
Customs allowances, 7

Day of the Dead, 14
Día de la Candelaria, 12
Día de Reyes, 12
Diarrhea, travelers' *(turista)*,
   18
Disabilities, travelers with, 22
Divers, in Acapulco, 67
Doctors/dentists, 33
Dolphin shows, Acapulco, 66
Drug laws, 33
Drugs, over-the-counter, 17

Electricity, 33
Embassies/consulates, 33
Emergencies, 34
Entry requirements, 6
Escobilla Beach (near Puerto
   Escondido), 109

Feast of the Virgin of
   Guadalupe, 15
Fishing
   Acapulco, 65
   Ixtapa/Zihuatanejo, 96
Fuerte de San Diego
   (Acapulco), 66

Gay men and lesbians, 22
Golf
   Acapulco, 65
   Cuernavaca, 160
   Huatulco, 129
   Ixtapa, 77, 97

Gran Noche Mexicana
(Acapulco), 68
Guelaguetza Dance Festival, 13

Health concerns, 17–18
Highway, 200 42, 74, 121
Holy Week, 12
Hornitos Beach, 62
Hornos Beach, 62
Horseback riding
Acapulco, 65
near Ixtapa, 97
Hospitals, 45
Huatulco. See Bahías de
Huatulco
Hurricane season, 11

Icacos Beach (Acapulco), 62
Iglesía de Guadalupe
(Huatulco), 129
Independence Day, 14
Information sources, 5
Insurance, 21
automobile, 31
Internet access, 35, 45
Acapulco, 45
Ixtapa, 78
Puerto Escondido, 107
Isla Ixtapa, 95
Ixtapa, 4, 73, 75, 77–78
accommodations, 78, 80
beaches, 93–94
nightlife, 100
restaurants, 88
shopping, 99
traveling to, 74
visitor information, 76

Jamiltepec, 110
Jardín Borda (Cuernavaca), 159
Jardín Botánico y Museo de
Medicina Tradicional y Her-
bolaría (Cuernavaca), 159

Juárez, Benito, Birthday, 12

Kayaking, Ixtapa/Zihuatanejo,
96

La Entrega Beach (Bahías de
Huatulco), 130
Las Estacas (near Cuernavaca),
161
Las Gatas, 94
Liquor laws, 35
Lost documents, 7

Madera Beach, 93
accommodations, 83
Massage, Puerto Escondido,
109
Mazunte Beach, 110
Mercado Parazal (Acapulco),
67
Mexican Tourist Permit (FMT),
6
Money, 8–10
Monte Albán, 132
Mountain climbing, 16
Museo Casa Robert Brady
(Cuernavaca), 158
Museo de Arqueología de la
Costa Grande (Zihuatanejo),
93
Museo de Cuauhnahuac
(Cuernavaca), 157
Museo Histórico de Acapulco
(Acapulco), 66

New Year's Day (Año Nuevo),
12
New Year's Eve, 15
Newspapers, 35
Nopala, 110
Nuestra Señora de la Soledad
(Acapulco), 61

Oaxaca City, 132
Olmedo, Dolores, home of
    (Acapulco), 62

Package tours, 26, 28
Parasailing
    Acapulco, 65
    Ixtapa/Zihuatanejo, 96
Parks, 16
Pepe's Piano Bar (Acapulco), 71
Pharmacies, 35
Pie de la Cuesta, 63
Playa Bacocho (Puerto
    Escondido), 109
Playa La Ropa, 93
    accommodations, 84–86
    restaurants, 92
Playa Larga (Zihuatanejo), 94
Playa las Cuatas (Ixtapa), 95
Playa Linda (Ixtapa), 95
Playa Madera, 93
    accommodations, 83
Playa Majahua (Ixtapa), 95
Playa Manzanillo (Acapulco),
    62
Playa Manzanillo (Puerto
    Escondido), 109
Playa Marinero (Puerto
    Escondido), 108
Playa Marqués (Acapulco), 63
Playa Municipal (Zihuatanejo),
    93
Playa Palmar (Ixtapa), 94
Playa Panteón (Puerto Ángel),
    122
Playa Principal (Puerto
    Escondido), 108
Playa Puerto Marqués
    (Acapulco), 63
Playa Quieta (Ixtapa), 94
Playa San Augustinillo (Puerto
    Ángel), 123

Playa Vista Hermosa (Ixtapa),
    95
Playa Zipolite (Puerto Ángel),
    122
Police, 36
Post offices
    Acapulco, 45
    Bahías de Huatulco, 128
    Cuernavaca, 156
    glossary, 170
    Ixtapa, 78
    Puerto Escondido, 108
    Taxco, 141
Puerto Ángel, 4, 102, 120–121,
    123–124
Puerto Angelito, 109
Puerto Escondido, 4, 102–112,
    114–120
    accommodations, 112–116
    beaches, 108–110
    layout of, 106
    nightlife, 119–120
    shopping, 111
    transportation, 107
    traveling to, 104
    visitor information, 106
Pyramids of Xochicalco, 161

Rainy season, 11
Resorts, 28
Revolcadero Beach (Acapulco),
    63
Ridley turtles, 109
Roqueta Island, 61, 64

Safety, 19, 42, 45, 108
Santa Cruz Huatulco, 13,
    125–127, 132, 135
Scuba diving, 16
    Acapulco, 64
    Ixtapa/Zihuatanejo, 96
    Puerto Escondido, 111

Seasons, 11
Seniors, 23
Singles, 23
Spanish classes
    Cuernavaca, 156
    Taxco, 142
Spanish vocabulary, 170–171,
    173–174
    numbers, 173
    phrases, 170–172
    transportation terms,
    174
Special events and festivals,
    12–15
Stolen luggage, 21
Stolen wallets or purses, 11
Students, 24
Surfing
    Ixtapa/Zihuatanejo, 96
    Zicatela Beach (Puerto
    Escondido), 109

Tangolunda Bay, 125–127,
    129–134, 136
Taxco, 4, 138, 140–143,
    145–146, 148–150
Taxes, 36
Taxis, 20, 31
    Acapulco, 39, 43
    Bahías de Huatulco, 128
    Ixtapa/Zihuatanejo, 77
    Puerto Ángel, 121
Telephone, 36, 45, 169
Tennis
    Acapulco, 65
    Huatulco, 129
    Zihuatanejo, 97
Three Kings Day, 12
Time zone, 36
Tourist information, 5
Tourist Permit, Mexican
    (FMT), 6

Tours
    Acapulco, 61
    eco- and adventure, 16,
    110, 130
    Ixtapa/Zihuatanejo, 97
    package, 28
Traveler's checks, 10–11
Traveling to Mexico, 24–25,
    27, 29
Travelocity, 25
Turista, 18
Turtle Museum (Puerto
    Escondido), 109
Turtles, Ridley, 109

Virgin of Guadalupe, Feast of
    the, 15
Visitor information, 5
Vocabulary, Spanish, 170–171,
    173–174
    numbers, 173
    phrases, 170–172
    transportation terms, 174

Water parks
    Acapulco, 66
    near Cuernavaca, 160
Water sports
    Acapulco, 64
    Ixtapa/Zihuatanejo, 95
Water, drinking, 37
Waterskiing, Acapulco, 64
Web sites
    package tours, 26, 28
    travel-planning and
    booking, 25
Women traveling alone, 24

Xochicalco, Pyramids of, 161

Zicatela Beach (Puerto
    Escondido), 108

Zihuatanejo, 4, 73, 75, 77–78
    accommodations, 80, 83,
        85–87
    beaches, 93–94
    layout of, 76
    nightlife, 100
    restaurants, 89
    shopping, 98
    traveling to, 74
    visitor information, 76

ACCOMMODATIONS

Apartamentos Amueblados
    Valle (Zihuatanejo), 82
Barceló Ixtapa, 79
Best Western Posada Real
    (Puerto Escondido), 112
Bungalows & Cabañas Acuario
    (Puerto Escondido), 114
Bungalows Ley (Playa Madera),
    83
Calinda Beach Acapulco
    (Acapulco), 52
Camino Real Acapulco
    Diamante (Acapulco), 46
Camino Real Sumiya
    (Cuernavaca), 161
Camino Real Zaashila
    (Tangolunda Bay), 133
Casa Cuitlateca (Playa La
    Ropa), 84
Fiesta Americana Condesa
    Acapulco (Acapulco), 48
Gala Resort (Tangolunda Bay),
    134
Grand Meigas Acapulco Resort
    (Acapulco), 53
Hostería Las Quintas
    (Cuernavaca), 163
Hotel Arco Iris (Puerto
    Escondido), 114
Hotel Casa Blanca (Puerto
    Escondido), 115

Hotel Castillo de Reyes (Puerto
    Escondido), 115
Hotel Costa Linda (Acapulco),
    54
Hotel Elcano (Acapulco), 49
Hotel Flor de María (Puerto
    Escondido), 116
Hotel Juárez (Cuernavaca), 166
Hotel Las Palmas (Bahías de
    Huatulco), 135
Hotel Los Flamingos
    (Acapulco), 54
Hotel Meigas Binniguenda
    (Santa Cruz), 135
Hotel Misión (Acapulco), 55
Hotel Posada María Cristina
    (Cuernavaca), 165
Hotel Raul 3 Marias
    (Zihuatanejo), 82
Hotel Sands (Acapulco), 52
Hotel Santa Fe (Puerto
    Escondido), 113
Hotel Susy (Zihuatanejo), 82
Hotel Villa Romana
    (Acapulco), 55
Hyatt Regency Acapulco
    (Acapulco), 50
Krystal (Ixtapa), 80
La Casa Que Canta (Playa La
    Ropa), 84
Las Mañanitas (Cuernavaca),
    162
Misión de los Arcos
    (Crucecita), 135
Misión Del Sol Resort & Spa,
    164
Paraíso Escondido (Puerto
    Escondido), 114
Plaza Las Glorias/El Mirador
    (Acapulco), 53
Posada Cañon Devata (Puerto
    Ángel), 123

Posada Citlali (Zihuatanejo), 83

Puerto Mio (Zihuatenejo Beach), 87

Quinta Real (Tangolunda Bay), 133

Sotavento and Catalina Beach Resorts (Playa La Ropa), 85

Villa del Sol (Playa La Ropa), 86

Villa Vera Hotel & Racquet Club (Acapulco), 51

Villas Miramar (Playa Madera), 83

Villas San Sebastián (Playa La Ropa), 87

Westin Brisas Resort (Ixtapa), 79

Westin Las Brisas (Acapulco), 47

RESTAURANTS

Art & Harry's (Puerto Escondido), 116

Arte la Galería (Puerto Escondido), 117

Beccofino (Ixtapa), 88

Cabo Blanco, 117

Carmen's La Patisserie (Puerto Escondido), 118

Casa Nova (Acapulco), 56

Casa Puntarenas (Zihuatanejo), 91

Coconuts (Zihuatanejo), 89

El Amigo Miguel (Acapulco), 59

El Cabrito (Acapulco), 59

El Cafecito (Puerto Escondido), 118

El Gota de Vida (Puerto Escondido), 118

El Olvido (Acapulco), 57

El Patio (Zihuatanejo), 90

El Sabor de Oaxaca (Crucecita), 136

Golden Cookie Shop (Ixtapa), 89

Herman's Best (Puerto Escondido), 118

Ika Tako (Acapulco), 59

Kau-Kan (Zihuatanejo), 90

La Perla (Playa La Ropa), 92

La Petite Belgique (Acapulco), 58

La Sirena Gorda (Zihuatanejo), 91

La Universal (Cuernavaca), 167

Mariscos Pipo (Acapulco), 60

María's Restaurant, 119

Mezzanotte Acapulco (Acapulco), 56

Mi Parri Pollo (Acapulco), 60

Noches Oaxaqueñas/Don Porfirio (Tangolunda Bay), 136

Nueva Zelanda (Zihuatanejo), 91

Posada Cañon Devata (Puerto Ángel), 123

Restaurant Avalos Doña Celia (Bahías de Huatulco), 137

Restaurant La India Bonita (Cuernavaca), 167

Restaurant Las Mañanitas (Cuernavaca), 166

Restaurant Paul's (Zihuatanejo), 90

Restaurant Santa Fe (Puerto Escondido), 117

Restaurant Vienés (Cuernavaca), 167

Ruben's (Zihuatanejo), 92

Spicey (Acapulco), 57
Su Casa/La Margarita
   (Acapulco), 58
Tipsy's (Huatulco), 129

Un Tigre Azul (Puerto
   Escondido), 119
Villa de la Selva (Ixtapa), 88
Ziwok (Playa La Ropa), 92

FROMMER'S® COMPLETE TRAVEL GUIDES

Alaska
Amsterdam
Arizona
Atlanta
Australia
Austria
Bahamas
Barcelona, Madrid &
  Seville
Beijing
Belgium, Holland &
  Luxembourg
Bermuda
Boston
British Columbia & the
  Canadian Rockies
Budapest & the Best of
  Hungary
California
Canada
Cancún, Cozumel &
  the Yucatán
Cape Cod, Nantucket &
  Martha's Vineyard
Caribbean
Caribbean Cruises & Ports
  of Call
Caribbean Ports of Call
Carolinas & Georgia
Chicago
China
Colorado
Costa Rica
Denmark
Denver, Boulder & Colorado
  Springs
England
Europe

European Cruises & Ports
  of Call
Florida
France
Germany
Greece
Greek Islands
Hawaii
Hong Kong
Honolulu, Waikiki &
  Oahu
Ireland
Israel
Italy
Jamaica
Japan
Las Vegas
London
Los Angeles
Maryland & Delaware
Maui
Mexico
Miami & the Keys
Montana & Wyoming
Montréal & Québec City
Munich & the Bavarian
  Alps
Nashville & Memphis
Nepal
New England
New Mexico
New Orleans
New York City
New Zealand
Nova Scotia, New Brunswick
  & Prince Edward Island
Oregon
Paris

Philadelphia & the
  Amish Country
Portugal
Prague & the Best of the
  Czech Republic
Provence & the Riviera
Puerto Rico
Rome
San Antonio & Austin
San Diego
San Francisco
Santa Fe, Taos & Albuquerque
Scandinavia
Scotland
Seattle & Portland
Singapore & Malaysia
South Africa
Southeast Asia
South Pacific
Spain
Sweden
Switzerland
Thailand
Tokyo
Toronto
Tuscany & Umbria
USA
Utah
Vancouver & Victoria
Vermont, New Hampshire
  & Maine
Vienna & the Danube Valley
Virgin Islands
Virginia
Walt Disney World &
  Orlando
Washington, D.C.
Washington State

FROMMER'S® DOLLAR-A-DAY GUIDES

Australia from $50 a Day
California from $60 a Day
Caribbean from $70 a Day
England from $70 a Day
Europe from $60 a Day

Florida from $60 a Day
Hawaii from $70 a Day
Ireland from $60 a Day
Italy from $70 a Day
London from $85 a Day

New York from $80 a Day
Paris from $85 a Day
San Francisco from $60 a Day
Washington, D.C.,
  from $60 a Day

FROMMER'S® PORTABLE GUIDES

Acapulco, Ixtapa &
  Zihuatanejo
Alaska Cruises & Ports of Call
Bahamas
Baja & Los Cabos
Berlin
California Wine Country
Charleston & Savannah
Chicago

Dublin
Hawaii: The Big Island
Las Vegas
London
Maine Coast
Maui
New Orleans
New York City
Paris

Puerto Vallarta, Manzanillo
  & Guadalajara
San Diego
San Francisco
Sydney
Tampa & St. Petersburg
Venice
Washington, D.C.

FROMMER'S® NATIONAL PARK GUIDES

Family Vacations in the
  National Parks
Grand Canyon

National Parks of the
  American West
Rocky Mountain

Yellowstone & Grand Teton
Yosemite & Sequoia/
  Kings Canyon
Zion & Bryce Canyon

FROMMER'S® MEMORABLE WALKS

Chicago
London

New York
Paris

San Francisco
Washington, D.C.

FROMMER'S® GREAT OUTDOOR GUIDES

New England
Northern California

Southern California & Baja
Southern New England

Washington & Oregon

FROMMER'S® BORN TO SHOP GUIDES

Born to Shop: China
Born to Shop: France

Born to Shop: Italy
Born to Shop: London

Born to Shop: New York
Born to Shop: Paris

FROMMER'S® IRREVERENT GUIDES

Amsterdam
Boston
Chicago
Las Vegas

London
Los Angeles
Manhattan
New Orleans

Paris
San Francisco
Seattle & Portland
Vancouver

Walt Disney World
Washington, D.C.

FROMMER'S® BEST-LOVED DRIVING TOURS

America
Britain
California

Florida
France
Germany

Ireland
Italy
New England

Scotland
Spain
Western Europe

THE UNOFFICIAL GUIDES®

Bed & Breakfasts in
  California
Bed & Breakfasts in
  New England
Bed & Breakfasts in
  the Northwest
Beyond Disney
Branson, Missouri
California with Kids
Chicago

Cruises
Disneyland
Florida with Kids
Golf Vacations in the
  Eastern U.S.
The Great Smoky &
  Blue Ridge
  Mountains
Inside Disney

Hawaii
Las Vegas
London
Miami & the Keys
Mini Las Vegas
Mini-Mickey
New Orleans
New York City
Paris

Safaris
San Francisco
Skiing in the West
Walt Disney World
Walt Disney World
  for Grown-ups
Walt Disney World
  for Kids
Washington, D.C.

SPECIAL-INTEREST TITLES

Frommer's Britain's Best Bed & Breakfasts and
  Country Inns
Frommer's Britain's Best Bike Rides
The Civil War Trust's Official Guide
  to the Civil War Discovery Trail
Frommer's Caribbean Hideaways
Frommer's Food Lover's Companion to France
Frommer's Food Lover's Companion to Italy
Frommer's Gay & Lesbian Europe
Frommer's Exploring America by RV
Hanging Out in Europe
Israel Past & Present

Mad Monks' Guide to California
Mad Monks' Guide to New York City
Frommer's The Moon
Frommer's New York City with Kids
The New York Times' Unforgettable
  Weekends
Places Rated Almanac
Retirement Places Rated
Frommer's Road Atlas Britain
Frommer's Road Atlas Europe
Frommer's Washington, D.C., with Kids
Frommer's What the Airlines Never Tell You